Parenting Our Children in a Changing World

Adlerian child psychology concepts and ideas, compiled, summarized, edited, updated, and supplemented for the twenty-first century.

William L. Camp, PhD, FACAPP

ISBN 978-1-0980-7652-8 (paperback)
ISBN 978-1-0980-7653-5 (digital)

Christian Faith Publishing, Inc.
832 Park Avenue
Meadville, PA 16335
www.christianfaithpublishing.com

Printed in the United States of America

Dedicated to the memory of Rudolph Dreikurs, MD,
my teacher whose ideas appear frequently throughout
this volume along with those of Dr. Alfred Alder.
During the summer of 1970, Dr. Dreikurs and several psychologists
met in Dr. Don Verger's home in Platteville, Wisconsin. At that
time, Dr. Dreikurs stated that if he had our youth, he would write
another book or books, the outlines of which he briefly discussed.
This is part of my attempt to create three of those books
of which this is one—my best effort to comply with the
details of his long-remembered suggestions/request.

William L. Camp, PhD

Dedicated to my mother and father, Julia and William Camp, my
wife and best friend, Mildred, our children, Christine Lick and
Jonathan Camp, and their spouses, Benjamin and Iwona, and our
grandchildren, Katherine, Julia, Carolyn, Olivia, and Austin. I have
learned a great deal from observing and interacting with each one.
Upon reading some of this manuscript, Julia Camp
(WLC's mother) said, "Yes, but above all, be kind."

Many thanks to Nancy Basile for the countless hours she has spent
typing and helping to edit the manuscript for this book and others.

Contents

Preface

Richard E. O'Conner, M.D.
Child and Adolescent Psychiatrist

In the years after World War II innovations and changes in the field of psychology, particularly in areas of treatment, came almost too fast and in too great a number to follow. In psychoanalysis such workers as Karen Horney, Melanie Klein and Frieda Fromm-Reichman brought new insights into both theory and therapy. Such people as Carl Rogers and B.F. Skinner opened new approaches to therapy and new ways of dealing with human behavior. In many ways they have brought changes to the field of therapy which have produced a "new look," which for people schooled in analytic approaches, make the field at times almost unrecognizable.

Then there were those who went back to earlier theorists in the area of psychoanalysis and brought the insights of some of these earlier analysts to an American scene which was changing and which required new approaches. Again, although the list is not exhaustive, one thinks of Frederick Allen applying the ideas of Otto Rank to the field of child guidance and child therapy, and of Rudolph Dreikurs applying Adlerian therapy to the area of child therapy and also to the entire field of parenting.

What Dreikurs saw in post-war America were children growing up in a society without traditions. Not only were the old world traditions, which often shaped identity and sometimes shaped lives completely not a feature of American society, but in addition, the mobility which, prior to the war, had really been restricted to a small portion of American society now involved everybody. This mobility insisted that each person must somehow become his own creation and that parents, with their own childhood experiences contributing very little, would have to somehow help their children to "create themselves" in this way.

In addition to the lack of traditions, there was general weakening of extensive family ties so that families tended to become very much nuclear families and identification of children was with a very small group of family people, and a larger group of community people, including teachers, peers, and public heroes such as athletes and television stars. Here again, the parents, whose own childhood had perhaps prefigured some of this change, were often at a loss to have methods to deal with the demands of society on them and on their children.

Into this state of confusion Dreikurs introduced the work Children: the Challenge in 1964. He offered principles, and in addition, suggestions, for helping children to achieve their own sense of identity and the sense of respect, of being loved, and of optimism about themselves and their own futures which is so necessary to healthy growth. However, Dreikurs was well aware that principles are not prescriptions. Although he was sometimes quite specific in his suggestions, he knew that the love, the respect, and the optimism had to be within the parents before it could be sincerely expressed and transmitted to the child. Dreikurs did not offer a new way to write on the "tabula rasa" but rather offered ways in which firm, positive parental identity and parental feeling could be consistently made manifest to the child. At no point did he mean the book to be a cookbook, nor a guarantee that actions A, B, and C would always result in desirable situation D.

If Dr. Dreikurs wrote an excellent book for parents in 1964, is there reason for Dr. Camp to write this book and its two companion books, *Understanding and Managing the Difficult Child and Understanding the Adult-Child Relationship*, which in a sense do cover some of the same ground? To answer this question, one has only to consider the changes which have occurred in American society from 1964 until the present day. The year 1964 represented, perhaps, a culmination of some sixty years of change which had not been slow, but had had something in it of gradual change, with the war bringing a somewhat faster pace. The changes since 1964 have been anything but gradual and they have been monumental. The role of the child in our society has changed. There is now an emphasis on children's rights which often seem to put parents and their children, supported by social forces, in adversarial positions. The protest movements of the late sixties and since that time not only created suspicion in youth regarding their parents' values, but left many parents unsure of their own beliefs and values. The intrusion of the world outside the family, especially through the mediums of television and computer/information technology, has become almost total. As has been recently pointed out by a recent President, the great historical events of the era have left Americans feeling unsure, pessimistic about their future, and not in control of their own destinies. How then can parents be helped to help a child "create himself?"

Adlerian and related principles continue to have meaning and they need to be stated in the vernacular of today, and within the perspective of American society of today. This Dr. Camp has undertaken to do and I think in large measure with success. However, we must again return to the point that there are principles. The methods and the behaviors which are sometimes quite specifically drawn in Dr. Camp's work are still not infallible formulae for the successful raising of children. They can help to deal with a parent's sense of unsureness. They can bring to the parent a skill in expressing to the child what is positive and important in the relationship. However, we must all remenber that much of parenting is intuitive. Much of children's security comes from a feeling that the parents are in control and do know best. Much of their growth comes with parents who can limit, restrict and discipline when children need that type of help in dealing with their impulses; who can support when the child is unsure and feels a need to be supported; and who can give freedom when freedom is what the child wants and really needs. Dr. Camp's contribution is important. It will not simply help to make us "good parents." It will offer a means to convey to children our hope and our love in a way which will promote their own self-respect, their own growth and their ability to "create themselves."

Introduction

During the last several generations, developments in the field of education and child guidance have begun to corroborate the set of ideas and observations presented here, which were first presented in Europe during the first third of the last century, and refined during the last third. Many of these concepts, which were controversial when first suggested, are now being further refined and are becoming generally accepted by modern psychologists and educators. Those who study childhood development and behavior are now less inclined to regard certain restrictions imposed on the child as repressive and therefore damaging. The tendency in recent decades for parents to be over-permissive is now being recognized as detrimental.

The focal point for corrective procedures has shifted toward changing the interaction between parent and child as the fact that parents often need specific instruction in child-raising has found wider acceptance. This shift in attitude has evolved as more has been learned during the last few decades about the effects of cultural and other changes as they influence human behavior. Today we need—and are developing—new traditions for raising children, which will better conform to the democratic principles for family living that now define and give meaning to the location we all now occupy in the process of democratic evolution in our society.

Modern parents need to learn to become a match for their children and to become both wise in their ways and capable of guiding each individual without either letting them run wild or stifling their development. But age-old child-rearing problems continue to arise and continue to exist. In fact, the problems which our children present are increasing in frequency and intensity, and many parents simply do not know how to cope with them.

Although many parents may realize that children cannot be treated as they were in the past, they do not know what else to do when children misbehave. And although a variety of new methods for dealing with children do exist and have been tested, the variety of conflicting suggestions available to parents seem to negate claims of validity made for any specific approach. Much of the flood of information which has been presented concerning this issue during the last few decades seems only to have produced additional confusion rather than the direction which now seems so badly needed. Why, then, should anyone trust the approach advocated in this volume?

Following the specific suggestions that are summarized in the pages that follow, many parents have discovered for themselves that these ways to reach children and win their cooperation do indeed work well. As this information—which includes specific methods— has been used and tested by parents for the solution of family problems, it has become evident that the system and procedures are effective. But why do children act as they do? And why do these methods enable parents to succeed?

The chapters included in this volume were designed to answer these and related questions as well as to present a set of principles in a form readily useable by parents in the home, teachers in the classroom, and other adults in other circumstances and situations. This book presents concepts, which are further developed and applied in a companion books entitled *Understanding and Managing the Difficult Child* and *Understanding the Adult-Child Relationship*.

1

Guiding Childhood Development

All human behavior, including childhood behavior, is purposeful, even if the child, adolescent, or adult is not consciously aware of that purpose. This means that we can only understand an individual's actions by recognizing the goal which that person pursues. Unless we are aware of what motive or motives direct an instance of behavior, we have little chance to change it. Conversely, we can induce an individual to behave differently by discovering and altering that person's motivation. This is especially true during childhood.

Through his or her actions, whatever they may be, the child expresses feelings or emotions that reflect motivation. Perhaps the actions say, "Look at me. Say something to me instead of doing whatever you are doing." Each child first seeks to find a place by means of getting attention, which may be negative attention as well as positive. Since the child is a social being, his or her strongest motivation is a desire to belong. The child's security or lack of it depends on a feeling of belonging within some group or groups. This is basic, and as such, it forms the root of the incentive system which underlies childhood behavior. Everything a child does is aimed at finding a place in the group.

In other words, we may say childhood behavior is goal-directed. However, a child is never consciously aware of the motive that directs his behavior. The child does not plan his behavior but rather acts from and in response to his inner motivation. Through experimentation and observation of reactions of others to his behavior, essentially through trial and error, he repeats those behaviors which provide a sense of having a place and abandons those which cause him to feel left out. Here we have the basic premise necessary for use in the effective guidance of childhood behavior.

As this spontaneous yet purpose-directed activity occurs, it forms a distinct and individual pattern, which is different from that of each other child. The form of this pattern or plan of action most often involves attempts to attract attention to make one's self the center of interest. This is especially true in the case of a youngest child or the oldest child. The plan, most often seen as a desire to be first or best—as a method of gaining attention—can appear in a thousand different variations. For this reason, as we examine the child's calculated desire to be first in every endeavor, we must bear in mind that this is only a general theme of which each specific case will be a subtle but unique variation.

Although children are very astute observers, they make errors in the interpretation of what they perceive. These mistakes lead to errors in the methods they use to obtain the all-important feeling of belonging. We call these errors *the mistaken goals of childhood.* Specifically, they are the goal of attention-seeking, plus the additional goals of power-seeking, revenge, and to be left alone (giving up). Each will be discussed later in detail in chapters 2 and 3.

Until about the sixth year of life, it is relatively easy for a parent to change the child's latent and sometimes obscure plan of behavior, i.e., his plan to reach his goal or goals. During these early years of life, the child will promptly set out on a new course and try to find other more effective methods to achieve his goal(s) when experience teaches him that a specific method will not get him what he wants or that his present course of conduct seems impractical or unproductive. By age six or soon after, however, the child's mental powers have developed sufficiently to permit him to preserve his schemes by employing a series of ruses or tricks for their maintenance.

As the child grows, he chooses to rely only on those of his experiences and impressions which coincide with his plan. This scheme—the elements of which the individual will try and test to his satisfaction in the specific situations of his childhood—will later become his *life plan*. This permanent plan of conduct is a basic scheme which remains essentially unconscious throughout the remainder of that person's life.

Throughout his or her life, the person will then try to evade any and all issues in which the logic of life makes it impossible for that person to act according to this plan. Where this process fails, the individual may begin to distort his perceptions to fit his life plan. He will seek out reasons and arguments for justifying his conduct without ever realizing that a definite plan controls all his activities. It is this life plan which gives each person his or her individuality, resulting in a distinctive *lifestyle*. It further determines the character and disposition of the individual and, to a significant extent, may mold one's destiny since it constitutes the motivation for all further actions and behaviors. For this reason, if one does not understand a child's motivation and fails to discover that child's hidden plan of conduct, that person may be inclined to mistakenly regard many extraordinary personal qualities such as faults or peculiarities to be the outcomes of biologically inherited predispositions. They are not; they are learned.

Nature Plus Nurture

Although human beings are subject to the same laws of heredity that control all other living things, the operation of these laws is restricted to basically unchangeable characteristics such as blood type, stature, eye color, and certain other physical features which are beyond the reach of individual education and training. The same is not true, however, with regard to the child's environment within which there are two other general factors that directly affect the development of personality. The first is the general atmosphere of the family in which the child is raised, which includes the social, economic, racial, and religious influences of his environment. Here he absorbs the values, attitudes, mores, and conventions of his family as he adjusts his behavior in terms of the pattern of standards set by the family. As he does so, he carefully observes how his parents treat each other. This relationship between parents sets the pattern for all other relationships within the family. Cooperation can become a family standard, but if parents are hostile and compete for dominance with each other, *this* pattern is just as likely to develop among the children.

In other words, relationships between parents provide children with a model from which they may easily choose to develop their own individual roles. Keen competition between parents can make competition the family standard. In fact, traits seen in common among all children of a family are usually a direct expression of the family atmosphere established by the parents. However, all children of a particular family are not alike. In fact, they are usually very different in many respects. The reason for this constitutes the second major factor in the child's environment, which influences his personality development.

This second factor is the *family constellation*, which is the characteristic relationship of each family member to each other member. In the mutual interchange of influences and responses within the family unit, different personalities emerge. The position of each member within the family constellation determines the roles he or she will play. More generally, it influences the patterns of interaction within the family and the personality development of each family member.

Within each family unit, a definite pattern of interaction develops. In families with one child, one of the parents may side with the child against the other parent. Such alliances are, in most cases, provoked by the child and imposed upon the parents by the child's behavior. With the arrival of a second baby, however, the positions of the original three family members will change. The first born—"king baby"—is suddenly dethroned. He must now take a stand concerning the change in his position, both in regard to this new usurper and in regard to his parents who permitted the change of circumstances to occur. Simultaneously, the new baby is discovering his or her position as "baby" of the family. This position will have a different meaning to the new second child than it did to the first, however because of the presence of an older sibling.

With each succeeding birth, the family constellation takes on a new configuration with new meanings leading to new interactions from each individual's point of view. As the second child is dethroned in his turn, he finds himself in the middle, between the oldest child and the baby. This is why we find that children in the same family are not at all alike, in spite of areas of similar experience. In fact, it is much more common to observe similarities between the oldest children in two different families than between the first and second in the same family.

In this way, the family constellation evolves with each child finding his or her place in his or her own way. Often, however, one child will come to envy the position of another sibling. Initially, for example, the second child presents a threat to the first. As he adjusts to his perceived environment, the first child will in certain areas either give up or compensate by trying to stay ahead. The same is true for the second child in relationship to the first. The second child will usually resent the advancement of the first child and will either seek to surpass him or will give up in that area of competition. The significance of each child's numerical position in the family will depend entirely on how that child interprets his or her position. And, of course, all firstborn children do not automatically race to stay ahead as we shall see.

Most children are highly competitive, with the competition between the first and second child usually the most intense, stimulating each to move in an opposite direction until they differ significantly in their personalities, interests, and abilities. This is further accentuated when parents pit one child against the other in the mistaken idea that competition will stimulate each to greater effort. Such competition in reality achieves the opposite effect as each child yields specific fields of behavior to the more successful sibling and in discouragement takes an opposite path. In areas of life where the first child has found success, the second child will consider that field as conquered and for this reason will seek a different approach to finding success for himself.

In a family of three children, the second child—who once had the distinction of being the baby—has been dethroned and is now the middle child. This is an extremely difficult position because the first and third child are often in alliance against the second as their common enemy. Squeezed between the two, this child soon discovers that she does not have the advantages and rights of being older nor does she any longer have the privileges of being the baby. She tends, as a result, to feel abused and slighted. She develops the impression that people and life are unfair. For this reason, the middle child may become provocative and in so doing may feel increasingly convinced that her impressions or assumptions about people and life are correct.

All three children will keep their parents busy with them, but each in a different way. Further, each will act according to her interpretation of her position and will cooperate with the others to maintain this equilibrium. In a family of four children, the second and fourth frequently form a similar alliance. In this way, each family constellation will become unique according to the interpretations made by its members. Each child tries to find his or her own place, role, or lifestyle, as it is sometimes called, through the transactions which occur between and among all children and their parents. As these interpretations are made, they lead to impressions which are carried throughout life.

A child may become cross and flighty, for example, to get even with her parents for paying too much attention to another sister who seems—or seemed—mature for her age. If the family includes four, five, six, or more children, we also look for groupings, by age, with two or three children closest in age usually forming each group. These groups can develop the same relationships as those we see for individuals. But the youngest child will try to overrun them all. He or she remains the baby throughout life.

But what about the only child? The only child usually functions as a second child. What do we mean by this? Simply stated, if it is a boy, he competes with his father for his mother's attention. This is what Freud called the Oedipus Complex, which actually has nothing to do directly with sexual behavior as some people mistakenly believe. The little boy soon finds that if he can provoke his father, his mother will come to his aide. But this "complex" will disappear within a week if the mother stays out of the fight between her two men. An analogous situation may occur as the daughter competes with her mother for attention from her father.

An only child also encounters another particularly difficult situation. Such a child either develops adult viewpoints and is precocious, hoping to reach the adult level, or he becomes the eternal baby who continually feels and acts inferior to others. Since there are no siblings close to his own age, his goal will most often become one of both pleasing and manipulating adults. Further, he will not develop a feeling of belonging among children unless he is exposed to early group experiences with them. Often, since he fails to understand children, his relationship with them will become somewhat strained and uncertain.

The baby of the family also has a unique place. She soon discovers that because she starts out as a relatively helpless being, she has many servants to do things for her. It becomes very easy for the baby to maintain her privileged position and to keep other members of the family busy waiting on her, unless her parents very carefully prevent or otherwise avoid this occurrence. Unless her parents remain alert, such a child will find that the role of helpless baby will become more appealing than doing for herself. Similarly, the child who is born after the death of a first child now assumes the position of the first child. His mother, in most cases, will become overprotective. The child may choose to succumb to this overprotection or may rebel and strive for independence.

But suppose the children are twins. Is this going to change anything? No. It changes nothing because of the significance of their age difference. Ask a mother which is the older twin. She knows often almost exactly in terms of minutes or even seconds. It has been widely noted that when discussing or summoning their twin children, many parents almost invariably name the oldest first. And when we ask the children who is older, the reply is often immediate: "I am by ten minutes." This conflict will usually appear, as outlined above, unless the twins are truly identical in appearance, in which case they may learn to enjoy deceiving the whole of society around them as they respond to others who cannot tell them apart.

Within the family constellation, then, each person behaves according to the way that child sees his or her position within the family. Each child sees his position in ways which depend upon the interpretation which he gives to his situation and to his chances for success or failure. In one family, Sarah—age nine-and-a-half—may be a bright, efficient, clever child who holds the conviction that she has significance only if she is first in what she does. Her brother, Bobby—age eight-and-a-half—may appear ineffective, discouraged, and weak, convinced that he has significance only when he is success-ful in making others feel sorry for him. Each person has a distinct place, a distinct role, and well-defined feelings about how he or she can make his or her way in life.

Competition between children is expressed through these fun-damental differences in their interests and, more generally, their per-sonalities. For example, an only boy among girls, regardless of his position, will find his sex to be either an advantage or a disadvantage, depending on the value placed by his family on the male role and on his own estimate of his ability to live up to it. The same would be true of an only girl among boys. Similarly, a weak or sickly child among healthy active children might discover the role of invalid to be advantageous if the family pities or babies him. However, in a family where robust health is given high-value and weakness scorned, he would be faced with an obstacle. Such a child would have a choice of giving up and living in self-pity through compensation or of striving to overcome the weakness or illness.

There is no ideal-sized family, and no matter how many chil-dren are born, there will always be specific problems. These problems will vary with the numbers within the family and with the interpre-tation each makes of his or her place within the family. The actions of each child will always present problems for each child and adult within the family. When a child's interpretation of his place is faulty, it is easy to see how mistaken orientations may develop. When par-ents are aware of these mistaken concepts, they can better guide the child into more correct evaluations and choices. However, parents and potential parents need to remember that there are no perfect relationships among human beings.

In the development of personality, the child's inherited endowment is less significant than what he does with what he has. The extent to which this is true is clearly illustrated by the fundamental differences in character, interests, and inclinations among children of a particular family, which would be impossible if their development were determined solely by hereditary predisposition.

Still, the influence of beliefs about heredity and inherited aptitude continues to exert a detrimental influence on the minds of parents as well as other adults, which leads to a fatalistic pessimism characterized by statements such as, "Oh, he's just like his old man!" This, of course, is in large part incorrect, but it nevertheless produces results. Instead of learning and applying better methods of training, the discouraged parent or other child caretaker may use the argument of poor natural endowment to rationalize and justify his or her own poor performance. Adults whose relationship with children is based on this mistaken assumption only hinder their own development of further understanding of the real forces, which motivate and direct the behavior of the child.

Development of Social Interest

Parents whose fundamental concept of the nature of man has led them to believe that they must tame the natural "badness" of children will adopt measures quite different from those adopted by parents who feel their primary duty is not to impede but to encourage in every way the development of healthy energies and natural impulses. However, the issue of what man is by nature seems really to be irrelevant to our consideration here since the essential fact is that everyone can become good or at least can improve. In everyday usage, the concept of good is relative, but for our purposes, we define it as "that which is desirable when the consequences are known." The concept of child development and training being outlined in this volume includes methods designed to assist each child as well as each parent to become his or her best possible self by utilizing what is now known about the development of human personality and behavior. When doing so, parents must strive to encourage and promote human development toward known and dependable ends or outcomes.

From the first day of his life, the child begins to adapt himself to the regulations he encounters. In terms of general everyday usage, the concept of "good" refers to rules and precepts laid down by communities of persons with everyone who follows the rules of the community regarded as "good." Understanding and observance of the social rules utilized by such groups requires development of a certain quality of personality, which we call *social interest*. This quality of humanness first evolved with the realization during the early history of man that collective life makes certain levels of cooperation necessary among individuals as they find need to adapt themselves to the requirements of the groups in which they live.

From the individual viewpoint, the amount of social interest which any child acquires will determine the extent to which he or she will find success or happiness in later life. Because social interest is the expression of human solidarity, it is revealed in the interest one takes in the problems of others and in the common welfare. It determines the extent to which one can and will cooperate with other human beings. For example, it will determine whether the individual will arouse antipathy or meet with approval, whether she can correctly interpret each key life situation as it arises and act accordingly; and even more basically, whether she can or cannot win and hold friends.

Because one experiences social interest as an urge to make useful contributions to the lives of other persons and to live and work in partnership with others, an individual's social interest can be roughly measured in terms of willingness and performance in cooperating and respecting the rules of human society, even though such observance may involve personal sacrifice. The person with social interest will indeed feel that he or she does have a responsibility for the welfare and fate of his or her fellow man or woman.

While the complexity of life often prevents an accurate appraisal of social interest in adults, it is much easier to evaluate in children whose correct or incorrect behavior is more obvious. As the child grows, he continually faces new interpersonal problems, which he will be unable to solve satisfactorily unless his social interest is allowed to develop freely and fully. It is the child's social interest that will determine whether or not she behaves correctly, which means in proper keeping with conditions at home or in school, regardless of whether she is alone or in the company of others. As adults learn to recognize, promote, and encourage those factors which advance the growth of social interest, they will also learn to avoid those conditions that impede its development. With this knowledge in hand, they will be much better able to evaluate the methods of child training they now use or plan to use.

Development of Social Discomfort, Uncertainty, and Insecurity

Parents may be overly severe with their child or too indulgent; they may pay too much attention to him or none at all. But whether they are unnecessarily harsh or over affectionate, whether they idolize or humiliate him, the results are almost identical. Instead of conformity, they foster rebellion, antagonism, and hostility which, although it may be mingled with other emotions such as affection, will be directed primarily against the perpetrator. Because the adult from the child's viewpoint appears to be the representative of society as a whole—since adults act as agents for societies rules or laws—the rebellion first directed against parents or teachers expands uniformly and continually to the various other aspects of social life. The struggle against parent or teacher over periods of time invariably develops into a struggle or revolt against all order and regulation, which means society in general. Within this context, the child's feeling of solidarity with others is possible only so long as he or she is assured of being accepted and of not being slighted or neglected. It is the quality of personal contacts which chiefly control the development of feelings of well-being.

The greatest pain or suffering of childhood does not grow out of bodily discomfort or physical illness but rather from the far more oppressive sense of being excluded from the group as the young boy or girl attempts to interrelate with others. The most painful experiences in the life of every child involve feelings of neglect, disregard, not belonging and indifference. As the child suffers, he does so without clearly realizing the cause of his frustration and unhappiness, which is the feeling that he has, in some way or another, been made inferior. Although this sense of inferiority may be quite evident in a child's behavior, it does not enter that child's consciousness. The effects of this condition must be counteracted using the same method with the child as with the adult, which involves raising that individual's self-esteem.

The young child is especially sensitive to being slighted since his position in the family alone provides sufficient reason for an assumption that he is inferior or inadequate. Such a child will receive his status through others who are bigger and seemingly more important than he who is smaller, more awkward, and more dependent than others in his family and neighborhood group. Because such a child may often feel completely ignored and because his rights must often give way to those of others, he or she may attempt to compensate for these feelings of social insecurity. This usually leads directly to a striving for power, which is the characteristic effect of a sense of inferiority since very human being wishes to be significant.

The revolt of the child, which stems from an exaggerated feeling of inferiority, constitutes the primary obstacle to his or her development of social interest. Since human beings who feel socially inferior seek to rise in social status, they become increasingly interested in their own elevation at the expense of remaining interested in social participation. Earlier efforts toward social integration become diverted to a drive for superiority, and it is from this tendency that bad habits, defensiveness, failings, and weaknesses develop. It is our belief that the difficulties of nearly all, if not all, children can be traced to their sense of inferiority and to their drive to compensate or make up for real or imagined social differences or weaknesses.

Feelings of Inferiority and the Struggle for Adequacy

It has been argued that the two principle reactions to feelings of inferiority and its related discouragement are surrender and over-compensation. For this reason, all heredity and organic inferiorities as well as psychological feelings of inferiority permit one of two possible courses of action: (1) They may lead to the evasion and neglect of the impaired function; or (2) they may give impetus to a special development of this same function, which may result in exceptional achievement. Bob Mathias, for example, overcame poor muscle coordination due to a severe case of childhood polio through persistent self-training and went on to acquire the unusual degree of physical development necessary to become an Olympic decathlon champion. Teddy Roosevelt overcame eye defects which led to poor vision by developing the keen observation and visual sensitivity necessary to pursue his interest in nature study. These well-known examples are cited only to illustrate the wide variety of circumstances in which natural deficiencies—which may cause some children to develop asocial or inadequate behavior—can in other cases provide the impulse for outstanding accomplishments. Because the same compensatory possibilities are inherent in literally hundreds of interpersonal as well as physical difficulties which arise in the lives of all children, each child will have many choices which involve either giving up or learning to overcome.

The single factor which determines the choice to be made in each case is the courage with which each child approaches the problems that he or she will encounter during the process of growth and development. Observation has revealed that children can accomplish a great deal, which may seem almost impossible from the viewpoint of an adult. Although this striking ability of children is generally attributed to their brisk new energies and great mental rigor, it is in most cases probably directly due to the greater courage which they possess during childhood as compared to adult life. As long as the child believes in his or her own powers and is not discouraged by faulty training, that child will struggle almost unceasingly to master a difficulty. Because the innate courage of the healthy child is remarkably great, defects which challenge the child and arouse his energies at the very outset of life—such as the organ inferiority of the eyes used in our earlier example—are much more likely to result in over-compensation than in evasion and failure. As the child grows older, however, physical handicaps become increasingly likely to lead to lasting defects since with age and experience comes discouragement.

As children grow older, most gradually lose courage due in large part to the effects of improper training methods which progressively work to diminish the child's self-assurance. Because most adults seem unaware of the crucial importance of courage or because they feel they can in no way influence its development, they often disregard this fundamental need of children in their interaction with them. Some parents discourage their children by carefully removing every obstacle from their path so that they are denied the opportunity to experience their own strength and the development of their capac-ities. Others place too many obstacles in the child's way so that his powers prove insufficient. In both types of situation, the child will lose self-confidence.

Through indulgence and oppression, overprotection and neglect also result in a similar breakdown of the child's courage, self-reliance and self-confidence. Parents discourage their children in hundreds of small ways, often without knowing it, with the cumulative result of discouragement which nurtures a growing sense of inferiority in the child. Discouragement and the related sense of inferiority lead directly to maladjustment and failure. Parents must learn that each child's self-evaluation does not depend on that child's actual deficien-cies or abilities, but instead (1) on her (his) own subjective judgment of her (his) relative ability and strength; (2) on her (his) interpre-tation of her (his) comparative status in the group; (3) on her (his) own supposition of being adequate or inadequate in handling her (his) own social and personal problems; and (4) on her (his) inter-pretation and appraisal of her (his) own deeds and actions as failures or successes.

All human beings, including children, struggle for adequacy and, where possible, superiority. Within each human being is a deeply rooted desire to have a place in the community, and for this reason, no one is ever content to see himself or herself as inadequate or to be seen as inadequate by others. Individual human beings are conditioned to feelings of inferiority through the experience of biological inferiority in the struggle for life and health as well as through awareness of their cosmic insignificance as each visualizes his or her future and inevitable death. Within this context, the child experiences his personal inferiority still more directly through his smallness and relative weakness in a world of adults. These feelings of social inferiority affect each child as an individual, distinguishing him in his own eyes from the rest of the group. As he compares himself with his older and younger siblings as well as with his parents and other adults, the child is unable to feel secure in his position.

This constant fear of losing his position is accentuated by the atmosphere of competition, which is characteristic of our society and which penetrates into the family, thereby corrupting relationships between and among all members of the family group. As long as the child is courageous, he will try to prove his importance by social contributions and by useful accomplishments. A child's social interest becomes restricted only when that child becomes discouraged. Then, if and when the road to useful achievement becomes blocked, the child will seek other means of increasing his personal superiority but now on "the useless side of life."

As this occurs, the child's urge for superiority motivates him to lay down certain guides for his conduct. Since the child's rational powers are still limited, this will be done mainly in an intuitive way, which may involve modeling himself after a person who to the child seems influential and powerful. This striving for recognition is especially obvious in children who have developed a strong feeling of inferiority with the ideals of power, authority, and masculinity which are so overrated in our social system, often exerting an especially strong influence.

As the child uses every opportunity to increase his prestige, ideas of superiority come to reflect his concept of security. To the degree (1) that he feels unsure of being good enough or of being accepted, and (2) that he cannot solely rely on his own strength, he comes to believe he can be made secure only through outside support which he in turn learns to expect. His ideas of security now involve being loved, receiving service, having power or influence over others, and receiving admiration and attention from others. Some children do not consider themselves to be socially acceptable unless they can be the leader of the group, do something unique, or succeed in depressing other children to a lower level of social acceptance or esteem. In such cases, they do not act for the sake of contribution but rather to gain significance, recognition, and other self-elevation. This sort of contribution to the group, even though it may sometimes be socially useful, does not reflect social interest but rather selfish self-interest.

Within this context, the vast majority of misdeeds that occur during childhood are a sign of the fictitious superiority for which the discouraged child is striving by punishing others for his own feelings of rejection and being disliked by getting undue attention or by dominating with temper or violence. All such petty vices, frailties, and faults of children are miscalculated efforts to get ahead of others and are directed against both parents and the social order more generally. For this reason, parents and teachers are at a marked disadvantage in any contest with a child who can gain a kind of superiority over the parent by eluding definite tasks and demands which are required of him. Then, as the young person more frequently gets his own way, the adult finds that the child has acquired a permanent problem over which he or she can never gain more than a short-term victory.

For these reasons, stubbornness in the child is not only an expression of revolt but is also a tool for securing power, which may further break down the bounds of parental order and authority. Particularly between the ages of two and four, as the child reaches a more complete understanding of the system and general structure of the family group, he may, through ill-advised pressure, be forced into opposition as he gradually becomes more discouraged. It is for this reason that the child may frequently develop a stubborn pattern in his behavior during this period of his development.

Development of Conscience

During the first year of life, the child's actions are not based on conscious thought at the verbal level, although his acts *are* intentional in that they *do* have purpose. However, even though it may be quite obvious to a trained observer, the child may be entirely unaware of this purpose, especially when it is directed against the environment generally. Although the child may realize that he or she wants a glass of water, a toy, or to go to the toilet, he or she is not aware of wanting attention or showing his or her power. But these unconscious goals are just as definite as are conscious goals and must be recognized if one wishes to understand and deal adequately with the child.

As the child gradually comes to realize what is right to do and what is wrong, he or she acquires insight into the general rules of the social game of life. At this stage of development, the child will accommodate himself naturally and without objection to these rules or laws *if* his relations with his family are free of antagonism. Our society and typical family life being what it is, however, the child may soon find that it seems necessary to fight for his position. It is at this point—when his efforts to gain superiority as a compensation for his precarious social position is bound to be at odds with moral precepts—that he faces two specific channels for his subsequent development.

If the child does not accept moral standards and social conventions, the result will be open rebellion. This occurs when his opposition to his parents and other family members becomes so strong that he loses sight of common interests and drops every vestige of close interpersonal feelings. At this point, he accepts neither social conventions nor moral standards of behavior, willfully resisting all rules and precepts and refusing to acknowledge any order other than that which he will define situation by situation. His lack of conscience is similar to that also found in children who have grown and developed in families, which are themselves at odds with society—families which do not recognize generally accepted standards of behavior.

The second possibility for expression of antagonistic intentions occurs much more frequently. Here the child accepts law and order in a general way, remains attached to his parents, develops sufficient conscience, knows right from wrong, and tries to conform. But this does not prevent him from wanting to do things his own way. As he eventually does so, often against both the standards of society which he has accepted and against his better judgment, he acts according to what has been called his private logic or private sense. In this condition, he may pretend to accept the rules but break them whenever they interfere with his efforts to gain prestige and position. He follows the rules only when his prestige is not in any way endangered. He knows what he should do while deciding to the contrary in situations where he can gain something for himself. This conflict between "private sense" and "common sense" may be characteristic of adults as well as children and, in some cases, may become almost a compulsion.

Because those acts which emanate from this sense of private logic are often antisocial, the child cannot accept responsibility for them if she also desires to maintain her good intentions. This leads to development of excuses sought to help explain related emotions and perplexing impulses and actions. As the child discovers that whatever she does wrong will elicit less retaliation and criticism from her parents if she can find a plausible excuse, she very quickly learns by experience the value of the good excuse as a "justification" for her acts. As long as the child seeks an excuse, she at least demonstrates her good will. Further, most parents are receptive to good excuses because they themselves rely on them in attempts to justify some of their own conduct. It is defiance which most parents cannot tolerate since nothing upsets most adults more than an open admission of bad intentions on the part of the child.

When little Samuel breaks an object, it will make a great difference if he says, "I'm sorry it happened. It slipped out of my hands," instead of admitting that he was angry at mother and wanted to hurt her, even though there may be no real doubt of his intention. In fact, if the child himself is asked why he misbehaves, he will be unable to give a satisfactory answer since he is unaware of his real goal. His answer that he does not know why he did it, although it may infuriate the disciplining parent, is nevertheless correct. The excuses the child does give are merely rationalizations which may be intended for the benefit of his parents or, as he matures, to quiet his own conscience. In addition to inventing them to relieve his parents' scorn and his own feelings of guilt, however, it is possible that he may believe them. But conscience and conscious will, which develop simultaneously with the ability to talk and express thoughts verbally, are only part of the total personality.

Although the faculty which enables one to judge correctly on moral issues—which we call conscience—is necessary for the child's adequate development, adults often overrate its educational significance. Education which occurs on the verbal level is directed only toward the child's conscious perception, which includes the "conscience." However, since education at this level does little to influence all other aspects of the child's personality, his emotions, impulses, and certain habits are regarded as beyond the reach of knowledge and willpower. Because these elements of personality resist correction on the verbal level and because they are not well understood by most adults, they are often regarded as an incorrigible mass of deeply mystical emotional urges, inherited predispositions, and senseless instincts. However, these expressions of the child's personality are true indications of the child's intentions, which are not admitted to conscious perception because they are not in accord with his conscience.

This means that pointing out to the child that he is wrong may be necessary if he really does not know he is wrong, but in most cases he knows very well what he is doing. In such situations, an appeal to his conscience is not only superfluous but may often be harmful since it will intensify the child's inner conflict between his "common sense" and his "private sense," which already existed at the moment of his misbehavior. Here, moralizing and preaching lead only to the development of guilty feelings which are not an expression of remorse as is so commonly believed, but on the contrary are a preparation for continuous behavior of the same type. One does not develop guilty feelings if he or she is now willing to do the right things, regardless of how much that individual may regret what he or she has done. Guilty feelings are found only in people who pretend to be sorry for something they have done who in fact intend to (if possible) do it again.

Individuals who "feel guilty" may greatly regret having been found out or may fear being exposed, but such guilty feelings must be distinguished from active remorse, which always refers to what happened in the past instead of considering what should be done in the future. The child may clearly realize that he did wrong, but because he does not realize which intentions were responsible for his action, he maintains these same intentions that lead to a repetition of the same mistake. For this reason, parental responses to misbehavior—such as preaching—which increase the child's feeling of guilt succeed only in blocking the possibility of his improvement. Effective parental response must make the child aware of his real intentions.

While we as adults often manage to pacify our conscience by self-deception and rationalization, the child has not yet organized this complicated scheme of self-delusion. For this reason, the act of revealing to the child his immediate goal or purpose often results in rather abrupt change in that child's methods for obtaining his goal. For example, when a young child is informed that he is wiggling in his chair just to attract attention, he in most cases will stop this behavior almost immediately. This result would not occur, however, if his parent were to tell him that it is not nice to wiggle. The device used by a child to obtain his goal is no longer useful once he is helped to discover its real meaning. However, if he still wants to attract attention, he will seek another method to get it, again without recognizing its meaning until he is made aware of it.

If the child misbehaves in this way, his act of doing so reveals the erroneous concept that he has developed about himself. When this occurs, reproaches, appeals to his conscience, and moral preaching are futile because they in no way affect his emotions or impulses. These will change only when his intentions and concepts are in accord with social obligations and no longer in opposition to the patterns of his conscious thinking and conscience. In other words, antagonism between emotional impulse and conscience will disappear once the child's private goal falls in line with his common sense.

Only correct social attitudes permit integration of emotional desires with the conscious will. This suggests that while conscience development alone is not sufficient to mold the child's behavior, it is of real importance since without an adequate conscience, social living and social adjustment are impossible. Unless parents recognize, supervise, and when necessary, stimulate change in the child's private goals and lifestyle, that child may choose methods to obtain his place in society and develop outlooks on life which are not conducive either to his ability to live harmoniously with others or to his more general happiness in living.

2

Effective Methods and Procedures for Training the Child

Unless and until adults learn to recognize the psychological and environmental factors which influence the development of the child's personality, they will lack the necessary basis for appropriate education and training of children.

Maintain an Orderly Home

The atmosphere of any home environment is determined in large part by the parents' general outlook on life, by the quality of their marital relations, by their level of education, by their character development and refinement, by their intellectual and spiritual interests, and by various socioeconomic factors. While it is often not possible for parents to modify even small elements of their circumstances or background, it is possible for resourceful parents to use even those elements which are unfavorable and cannot be avoided—such as economic and social predicaments or disease—as tools for constructive stimulation of healthy motivations and attitudes.

Even before their child's birth, parents can begin to prepare the way for his or her satisfactory emotional development. Since kindness, forbearance, and mutual respect are necessary for successful cooperation and since the child will derive his first impressions of harmony from his parents, they must learn to keep close check on their own conduct and improve it to the best of their ability. Parents must realize that after the child's birth, it will be the concepts that they give him of the outside world which will focus the content of his developing social awareness.

Most prejudices—of all kinds—are implanted in children's minds by their parents. In general, (1) whether the parents are hypocritical and overly ready to believe the worst of others or try to be fair-minded, (2) whether they gossip about their neighbors and treat them condescendingly or discuss others with friendly interest and understanding, and (3) how they relate to and speak about other persons will have great influence on the child's emotional and social development. Because children first see the world and "reality" through the eyes of their parents, both the parental view and the ways in which it is imparted to the young are of great importance.

In providing the guidance children need, it is always a great advantage for parents to have some definite, well-established outlook on life. Whether the set of beliefs encompassed by this "philosophy" are securely based on scientific or ethical principles or whether they are religiously rooted in some particular denomination makes much less difference than whether specific concepts are or are not well defined. A well-defined philosophy or outlook on life is a constructive force since parental attitudes concerning the problems of life, and their solutions are often clearly revealed in adult conversation. Work with families has shown that the more consistently parents observe a moral order with which they both feel comfortable, the clearer and more adequate will be their view of the world and the easier it will be for their children to accept social adaptation to the tenets of that view.

Parents must always be careful of what they say in the presence of their children since what a child learns at home is of utmost importance to his development. Never underrate the child's powers of comprehension since regardless of his age, he understands a great deal more than most parents would guess. Even at a very early age, children are able to grasp the essential meaning or tone of conversations between adults, even though they may be unable to logically or rationally understand all of the words used.

Parents should present their conception of the world to each of their children in ways which will stimulate that child's mental and spiritual growth. We would argue that this exposure should show the child the beauty of the earth as well as the dignity of art and ideas. A child can be taught through experience to delight in aspects of nature as well as in the pleasures of thought and knowledge. Much arduous labor will be saved in the child's later training if her upbringing is calm and constructive from the beginning. It is the atmosphere of the home and family itself apart from any educational or training measures which may be employed, which serves to guide the child's intellectual, emotional, and spiritual development by exerting a lasting influence on her temperament, character, and mentality. Although the perfect domestic atmosphere may rarely be found in our era of intense competition, insecurity, and strife, parents must guard against the temptation to shift the blame for lack of harmony to teachers, neighbors, conditions in general or each other. Disturbances of domestic peace and order, such as illness, undesirable relatives, poor or crowded living quarters, character defects of or incompatibility with parents, or economic difficulties do, of course, require increased attention to the implementation of methods used to influence the child.

Those adults who carry a grudge or display discouragement or resentment, regardless of how justified and understandable their attitudes and feelings may seem, will only add new complications to an already difficult situation and may impair the child's development much more than did some original detrimental situation or circumstance. Parents who tend to find someone or something to blame succeed only in aggravating situations that are already strained, giving rise to further conflicts. Any parent will be most successful in changing and improving conditions of a child's home environment when that parent decides (1) to watch and manage his/her own conduct and (2) when he/she tries in every possible way to improve his/her own contributions to each child's growth, development, and welfare.

Win the Cooperation of the Child

Most parents would probably report agreement with the concept that family cooperation is important in the maintenance of an orderly home. But what is cooperation? In earlier times, when authority was vested in those who were in control, it simply meant doing as one was told. The "inferior" was required to cooperate with his "superior." The growth of democracy, however, has revised the meaning of the concept for which this word stands. Now it is no longer "you" but "we" who must work together to meet the demands of the situation.

Because modern parents have lost the power of superior status, they now need to utilize practical techniques to stimulate cooperation. And while parents may now experience some degree of greater equality and freedom in a democratic social atmosphere, all also have greater responsibilities within this more egalitarian context. Parents can simply no longer demand that children obey or cooperate only on adult terms. Instead, they must first recognize the need to win truly democratic cooperation and then must act intelligently on that realization.

This ideal, however, too rarely occurs in our society. Many parents arbitrarily decide what each child should do and then proceed to try to force their children to comply. But having been raised in an increasingly democratic atmosphere, our children are stimulated to rebellion against this oppressive approach while they are at the same time permitted to succeed in what may become rebellious defiance. Very often, the attitudes displayed by parents when assigning tasks clearly reveals their determination to be boss, which only prompts the children to respond with a "you just try to make me" attitude. This is not cooperation—it is a power contest. Parents too often attempt to impose their will upon "their" children, rather than acting as they should to win each child's cooperation in the business of living together in a cooperative productive manner.

The rebellion of youth is part of a general rebellion of the disenfranchised. Many women no longer allow themselves to be controlled by men, children no longer allow it by adults, labor no longer allows it by management, and minorities—especially Blacks—in our society no longer accept the supremacy of Whites. This struggle, on all of these fronts, is part of the same rebellion of the underdog. But what is this conflict really about? It is a fight for participation in decision-making. We are moving toward a time when virtually no one, out of a sense of equality, will voluntarily allow someone else to dictate his or her life. Within this context, what has been labeled "the generation gap" means that youth are no longer willing to give in to dictatorial authorities. This means that adults must learn to allow participation in decision-making. If they do not, they may experience a full-scale rebellion.

Some young people have rebelled against "law and order" more generally in our society because they have seen it as only a traditional label and excuse for influencing people through use of impersonal, external pressure. And those in authority who have called for untempered law and order have often succeeded only in creating increased rebellion. Why? Because under these sorts of circumstances, no one is willing to give in. Those who try to subdue such rebellion will in the long run only hurt themselves and their own cause, but most people fail to realize this. Parents try to control their children, teachers try to control their students, authorities try to control "the people," but no one succeeds in doing so. This failure highlights a need for entirely new methods of stimulation.

While it is true that parents, teachers, and other adults as well as children need to learn to accept order, this order must come through stimulation from within the individual and not through pressure and punishment from without. Traditional autocratic methods no longer function adequately; they no longer work. Many American families simply do not know how to establish the order necessary for cooperative living. There is evidence for this in the fact that many families actually seem to begin each new day with a fight.

But how can a parent stimulate a child to real cooperative effort? As a beginning, that parent can take time for a discussion/meeting with all members of the family. Mother, for example, may list the jobs which have to be done around the house. She can clearly state that which *she* is willing to do, and then ask what is to be done about the remainder of the jobs necessary to maintain the family. Father and the other family members may then select the work which they are willing to undertake. In this way, mother shows her respect for other family members by allowing an atmosphere of free choice where each may make his or her own decision. If some family member neglects his chosen chores, nothing need be said nor is the work done by mother. After a week of neglect, mother may request another conference if one has not already been scheduled. Here she may point out that, "Peter chose to keep the garage picked up this week. He has not done it. What are we going to do about it?" (See the section on establishing a family council at the end of this chapter.)

Mother's use of the pronoun "we" in the above example placed the responsibility on the group where it belongs. It also removes mother from the role of authority figure and puts her into a role of leadership where a group solution to the problem may be reached when all suggestions have been carefully considered. This is true because adult-imposed authority stimulates rebellion while group pressure is effective in motivating action and change. Probably the most significant value of this method, however, is that it focuses the attention of each member of the family on the needs of the group as a whole. When a family functions as a group, it stimulates each individual to cooperate with others for the benefit of all.

At times when the harmony of family living is disturbed, we can be sure that a disruption in cooperation has occurred. Further, when we speak of training the child to cooperate, we presuppose full parental cooperation. No one person should be expected to yield or "give in" to another. Rather, what is needed is a sense of the entire family unit moving together in harmony toward a desired and well-defined goal. To assure this harmonious progress, it is necessary that each member of the family learns to think in terms of what will be best for the group. It is not, "What do I want?" but rather, "What does the situation demand?" When we as adults (parents) impose our will on another (child), we violate respect for that individual. Our act of giving in to undue demands, on the other hand, violates our own self-respect.

The real meaning of cooperation implies the acceptance of common ground rules. For example, many parents have difficulty deciding at what age their children should begin to help around the house. When the child is a toddler, she wants to help, but her parents may say, "No, you are too little." Then perhaps by age seven, they may demand that she help. By this age, however, such a child has begun to learn to feel unnecessary or unimportant. He or she feels, "You have gotten along all right without me so far. Why should you need me now?" At this point, the child either feels forced to help, feels patronized or looked down on by his or her "teacher," or both.

As parents, we waste untold opportunities to allow our children to contribute. If a child is allowed but not forced to contribute from the very beginning, he will learn to enjoy helping and will develop a sense of pride in his accomplishment. Ideally, parents should start this nurturance very early. However, most fail to do so. For this reason, in order to win cooperation, it may become necessary to help the child regain feelings of respect and of being truly necessary and of value as that child seeks to find his or her place in the family group.

Tone of voice and manner of approach are other crucially important factors in winning the child's cooperation. Often a child may resist our requests, either because the nature of what must be done is distasteful to the child or perhaps only because it was badly timed. In such cases—in fact, in any case—politeness can go a long way toward winning the child's cooperation. There is simply no point in fighting or pressing a child into submission. In our work with families, it has been most enlightening to learn how many children believe their parents are stubborn or cruel, while at the same time, the parents report their own conviction that it is only their children who are. Both parents and children in such families are very likely to hold mistaken points of view which to them seem entirely real, correct, and fair.

Under some circumstances, however, children will capitulate and cooperate. Why? We have found that in many cases, the child will begin to review his position as soon as it becomes obvious that his reasoning, his rights, and his point of view are being fairly understood and appreciated. At this point, most children lose their feeling of being imposed upon and become more free to examine the needs of the total situation. The situation may then often be resolved in a cooperative manner with neither parents nor child feeling pushed or defeated as each becomes more easily able to recognize the rights of the other.

Perhaps it is now becoming clear that the parent is obligated to forego making arrangements for the child without advanced consultation with that child. This statement is made with a full realization that cooperation does exist at all times in all interpersonal relationships, although we seldom recognize it for what it is. For example, siblings often cooperate to keep mother busy, perhaps scolding John while praising Tony. But a shift or change anywhere in an established pattern of mutual interaction or cooperation will change the total situation. To tell John that he too can be good would be futile. Rather, we must quietly stimulate him to change his form of cooperation. But as John becomes less "bad" and more "good," his sibling—a brother in this case—will redouble his efforts to make John "bad."

The mother in such a situation, through her understanding, can move to alter the pattern of her son's interaction by changing her response to each boy's behavior. She can begin by refraining from making any evaluative comments regarding "good" or "bad." Because mother knows that John sees himself as the bad child, she can refuse to accept his evaluation. Each time Tony displays how good he is, she can quietly accept this behavior and simply say, "Fine Tony, I'm glad you enjoy doing it." When John misbehaves, she can hug him and simply say, "I understand." Although this procedure may at first seem strange or difficult, it *can* be done effectively by parents.

Teach Personal Order

All parents must induce, and all children must learn a respect for order. Once we have shown our respect for the child and have established respect for parental firmness, it will be much easier to guide the child further into learning respect for order. In every area of living where respect for order is needed, the child must learn through experience, not through our words. Just as we add training wheels to his bicycle and remove them as he develops balance skills, we must take advantage of other environmental and action situations to provide various other necessary training experiences. The child must learn to live within the limitations of his physical world. He must learn to use the laws of nature to the advantage of himself and others. No child will develop respect for order if he is shielded from experience and the results of disorder.

Children display their lack of respect for order when they use tools or play materials and simply abandon them when finished with their activity. Children, of course, know they should pick up after themselves since they have often been told to do so, but most do not. By their actions, they show that they neither have respect for other family members in this situation nor for the needs of the situation itself. The fact that a mother (or father) is still reminding her (or his) children to pick up after themselves after many years of training indicates that those years of talking and preaching have done little if any good. Often, in such situations, the moment mother begins to speak, her children will placate her with promises, which they have no intention of keeping. Statements such as, "Yes, mother," "All right, mother," "We will, mother" as well as the tone of voice used indicate their lack of intent to obey her demand for order as well as their feelings of resentment in response to her reminder.

Lack of respect for order is one of the most common complaints of modern parents. Children often utilize this form of rebellion, not only against their parents but against adults in general. To put things away is a demand resented by most children and made by all parents. And the more parents display their concern over orderliness and neatness, the more vulnerable they become to the resistance of their children. This, of course, involves a problem of mutual respect. For this reason, especially, children need to experience order as a part of freedom. Where disorder prevails, there is a loss of freedom for all.

What are parents to do in such a situation? Each can determine what action he or she will take when such circumstances present themselves. By making appropriate decisions and then acting accordingly, a parent can induce respect for order. For example, if mother finds things that belong to her children, which are out of place, she can pick them up and put them away, not for her children but for herself since they are in her way. It is mother alone, however, who now knows where they are since it was she who picked them up.

Since the child did not put his belongings away, how can he know where they are? Obviously, any child who did not do so cannot know. Mother should remain firm but friendly at this point with the knowledge that her action is not punishment. Gradually, as the child learns that her disorder bears consequences, she may decide that order is more convenient. When disorder results in the disappearance of items which belong to a child, that child may decide to be more careful to put her possessions away on future occasions.

An alternative method for dealing with toys and other belongings left out of place is to secure a large cardboard box into which everything can be put. Mother picks up what is in her way. Everything then goes into the box. The experience of finding and retrieving valued possessions from this box can also teach a valuable lesson.

The use of force is not effective in teaching children the need for order, however, since it merely creates feelings of hostility and rebellion. Quiet insistence usually proves to be much more effective. Father may bring Samuel's wagon in and put it where it will be difficult for a three-year-old to get at it without help. Later, when Samuel wants it again, his parent may say, "I'm sorry, Samuel. Since you did not feel like putting your wagon away the last time you used it, you may not have it out again at this time, but you may try again after you have lunch." The last part of this remark gives the child encouragement so that he may want to put it away himself the next time he uses it. An alternative would be for father to take his son by the hand so that both could put the wagon away together, but even this could be the beginning of a bad habit if done frequently.

In situations such as the wagon illustration cited above, several elements add to the success which one may expect to obtain. Probably most important is the fact that the parent involved felt the spirit of a teaching experience. This parent did not have a hidden intention of forcing or making the child put things away. Also, there was no sense of retaliation or punishment. Finally, the parent remained friendly and kept the situation pleasant. He refrained from preaching and said relatively little about the matter at issue.

Creative parents will be able to think of many other examples, which can be dealt with in this way. Gross disrespect for order, however, usually involves significant disturbance in the relationship between parents and children. In these more infrequent cases, the situation may be correctable by one of several means, such as the use of logical consequences (more on this later in the chapter). Here, the parent may require outside professional help and at the very least will need to develop a plan to improve or, if possible, correct the faulty family relationship.

Maintain Family Routine

No one feels comfortable in situations in which they do not know what to expect. Routine gives a feeling of security. Established routine provides a sense of order from which freedom can grow. When parents allow children to do whatever they want to do, they are not granting freedom but license. And children are simply in no position to develop wisdom from parental decisions, which deprive them of opportunity to experience the natural consequences of their own mistaken acts (the concept of natural consequences is developed later in this chapter).

As children grow and develop, they search for the comfort of limitations and boundaries. Children will push their parents and teachers to find out just what the limits or rules of a situation are. When limits are not clearly defined, they will test the reality of each situation to find its limits. When adults respond by telling or showing them, children feel much more secure. The ambiguity of not knowing what is safe or acceptable prompts anxiety, which can only be eliminated by defining limits and rules for each child. This, of course, is not to say that the child will not attempt to modify or transcend the rules once he knows what they are. Each child simply seeks to discover how far he or she can safely go.

When the sky is the limit, the child will predictably become bewildered, then demand the right to do as he pleases in an attempt to find a limitation. Then, inevitably, and usually suddenly, he will one day behave in such an outrageous manner that someone in his environment will respond with punishment, leaving him stunned, and wondering what has happened. For this reason, it is important that parents set up family routines within which each member can function comfortably. When parents have established and maintained this daily order for a period of time—usually a relatively short period—their children will begin to adapt to it. No child is ever too young to experience order and routine. Once it has been clearly established, children will sense it and know what to do almost as a matter of course.

Self-sufficiency and social integration are the goals of this type of parental guidance. Parents, of course, have a choice concerning the types of routine they wish to establish for their family, but some routine is always needed. It should not be so rigid that no room is left for flexibility since there will always be some occasions when a routine will have to be adjusted to fit some unexpected need or situation. Breaks in the routine should always be the exception rather than the rule, however, and they should not be created for the convenience of adults nor for the satisfaction of the whim of a child.

Many children demand almost constant attention and entertainment from their mother and/or father. Hence, parents should have an established routine for playtime. The establishment of such a routine gives parents a tool that they may use when they either wish to or need to resist their child's undue demands for family play. When a child is sure of a specific playtime with mother, for example, the child will be more ready to accept the demand for order implied in mother's refusal to give in to the child's constant requests. Because children do need to share activity with specific adults, there is often no better method of establishing happy, harmonious family relationships than through establishment of a definite unchangeable playtime. This specific period of the day for having fun together then belongs to both the child and the parent(s). The child needs to know that he can count on it and on his parents.

As a further example of this need for routine, we may consider the typical power contest which in many families occurs at bedtime. Here again, a routine should be established, and parents should be firm about it. Bedtime is bedtime—period. Only when routine is experienced casually and is a matter of course with quiet insistence and without verbal battles can parents hope to win compliance to a system of order within the family. As children experience the repeated firmness of a routine, they will seldom feel inspired to misbehave in an attempt to find boundaries. They know the boundaries; hence, they do not feel the anxiety so often associated with ambiguity. For this reason, not only is their pressure on the parent unnecessary, it is clearly futile.

Where common activities such as mealtime are involved, it is obviously best to establish one routine for the entire family. However, the various functions of family members may require development of different routines. For example, the two-year-old will have a much earlier bedtime than either his teenage brother and sister or his parents. Difference in routine must be clearly within the range of these different functions, however, and must never occur in those areas where all family members function in the same way.

It is usually up to mother or father or both together to set the boundaries and to establish the routine within which the family will grow and develop. Then, whenever a child transgresses that order, mother (or father) must be prepared to quietly insist that it be maintained. Almost without exception, serious disruption of family routine will result only when parents permit frequent transgressions.

Ordered patterns for living involve many seemingly simple elements, such as time and mode of appearance at the table for meals or the making of beds before involvement in other daily tasks, which may be taken for granted, unless they are not done in a systematic fashion. These and numerous other family activities make up an important part of the family routine, which will in turn allow a more enriched and pleasant family life if handled correctly.

Teach Respect for the Rights of Others

In a situation which involves equals, it must be recognized that each individual does possess the same rights as the others. Many parents, however, too often behave either as if they have all the rights or as if their children possess them all. When this occurs, there exists a very subtle line between being a dictator and demanding one's own rights when dealing with a child. The difference lies in the intent of the parents. For example, if five-year-old Bobby continually plays with his mother's computer, it must be recognized that he has no right to do so. In responding to him, his mother must be firm. Not only will pleading or explaining be futile, it will also miss the point. Bobby's behavior is infringing upon the rights of another person.

The same error is true of a mother's behavior when she continually obtains unkept promises from her child to refrain from an activity. All mother needs to say is, "Bobby, this is my work computer. I am the only one who will use it. You have your own computer." Then, each time her son attempts to play with it, mother needs only to ask if he wishes to leave the room himself or be taken out. This way of dealing with the issue displays respect for Bobby's rights to make the decision that he must leave. Mother does not demand that Bobby play with his own child computer, although he may choose to do so. Rather, she shows him her intention to demand respect for her rights. In doing this, she is helping to induce in him a more general respect for the rights of others.

This same procedure should be used, regardless of the infraction. Families do not usually codify their rules and regulations, but their validity is firmly established in most family units by tacit custom or agreement. Although some define the respective rights of individual members while others apply uniformity to all members of the group, social living at our time in history does necessitate certain rules of conduct.

When rules are established, parents must themselves abide by these regulations if they hope to have their children recognize them as obligations, which apply to everyone and accept them as a matter of course. The essential element in the use of rules is that they be subject to no exceptions since they would then appear to the child to be schemes of unfair impositions rather than necessary forms of social order. Although each member of a family will have different functions, which imply different rights and different duties, children of all ages are sensitive to equality and will be suspicious of anyone who enjoys more privileges than the rest.

When a child attempts to vindicate his resentment against his own role by referring to a sense of injustice, that child's parents should realize that he is motivated only by a sense of rivalry and by a feeling of rebellion against the existing order as a whole. By his rebellion, the child reveals that he has not recognized and accepted the fact that both his older and his younger sisters and brothers as well as his parents have logically and unavoidably different functions, and hence, different responsibilities with their accompanying rights and privileges.

Since no social group exists in which all members have identical functions and privileges at all times, the most important point for the child to understand is that difference in function does not mean social inequality. It is the social right of each family member to be recognized, appreciated, and respected for what he or she contributes, regardless of what others are, do, or contribute. It is in the individual's own particular function that each family member can and must receive full and appropriate recognition as he or she is given or conceded full importance as a significant and appreciated member of the group.

Because any one family member may be easily tempted to disregard this necessary right of every other member to be respected in and for his or her own personal family functions, it is important that all recognize that any infringement on another's social status will lead to an impairment in the functioning of that individual. The truth is that the less recognition and respect granted to the function of any specific family member, the less adequately that individual will perform his or her function. But what are the rights of the child? Our answer to this question within the context of the points made in the paragraph above is that each child is a full member of the family from the first day of his postnatal life. He has definite rights and definite obligations, even during the early period of complete physical helplessness.

It is when the child is deprived of his natural privileges or when he gets too many that he is likely to try to assume a great variety of others to which he has no just claim. His rights, originally to rest, sleep, and regular feeding periods during infancy, multiply as the sphere of his activity expands. As he grows and develops, he is entitled to enjoy an increasing degree of freedom and independence to experience his strength, to develop his own initiative, and to have suitable opportunities for play with companions of his own age. And all children, even when they are very young, need opportunities to help around the house to make useful contributions and, in general, to be of service to others.

Coupled with these opportunities, the child needs a certain amount of recognition, even though much of what he or she does may be labeled as "play." It is always a mistake to either belittle such play activity or to think that all play is entertainment as is the play of most adults since everything that the child does is a serious preparation for life. It is important for parents to realize that the play of children is as serious and important as is the work of adults. In a very real sense, the child's play *is* his work. It is through his play that the child acquires the skills, capacities, and competencies which he will need for success in his later life.

As the parent displays his or her recognition of the child's first attempts at independent action, such as working to dress himself or keeping his clothes, toys, and other possessions in order, it is especially important that the activity of any one child of the family—regardless of sex or age—not be treated as either more or less significant than the activity of any other. As the child grows, he may need some guidance to realize that his responsibilities will develop in direct relation to his rights and privileges. The child must learn that he must fit himself into family patterns, that neither he nor anyone else can be allowed to disturb the order of the household, and that he must respect the rights of others just as they must respect his own. Since reciprocity is the basis of all cooperation, it requires a dynamic equilibrium of the rights and interests of all individual members of the family. Anything less is simply not enough.

Stay Out of Fights

Children do not have to fight, although fighting is so common among siblings that it has become accepted by some as a normal form of childhood behavior. Still, it is *not* normal, simply because it occurs so regularly. Although many children seem to eventually "out-grow" fighting, many continue their hostility into adulthood and may never make peace with their brothers or sisters. Most parents have probably tried every procedure they could think of to stop the fighting but without success. At the very least, such parents should have learned from experience that no amount of preaching or anger will ease the friction which periodically reoccurs between siblings. But relatively few act as if this lesson has really been learned.

Because home environments where children do not fight are possible, parents must realize that where fights do occur, there is something wrong with the interpersonal relationship within that family unit. Since no one can honestly feel good while fighting, the gain in satisfaction must come not so much from the fight itself as from its results. Study of young people has revealed that this is exactly the case; behavior is purposive. Within this context, the usual explanation that fighting is caused by an aggressive nature or by a drive or by heredity is not satisfactory. Because we now know that childhood behavior is goal-directed, we need to learn to understand the child's behavior in terms of both the field or context in which it occurs as well as the purpose which it serves.

Consider the following situation: Murray, age four, pushes close to his eight-year-old sister, Barbara, as she watches television. She rebuffs him. He persists by poking her and later by twisting her ear. Barbara responds by biting his wrist, and the shouting and fighting begins, punctuated by a scream from Murray. Why? What was the purpose of the fight? And what were its results? As we examine the details of the situation, we see that Barbara retaliated with anger after having been annoyed. Then mother rushed into the room to scold

Barbara for fighting with her "little" brother. As Murray displayed Barbara's tooth marks, Barbara protested that, "He kept bothering me." "I don't care what he was doing," replied mother. "You had no right to do that to your brother or anyone else." In this case, quite obviously, Murray who is the baby of the family wants both his mother's attention and protection and knows how to get it. He simply behaves in such a manner as to precipitate a situation in which he will get what he wants.

Knowing this, what could mother have done? She should have controlled her first impulse to run at the first scream to intervene. She should have stayed out of it. For a mother to be able to take this action—or rather, inaction—requires that she discipline herself.

When children fight, parents become annoyed. When children annoy, they are utilizing an effective means of obtaining and keeping parental attention. As parents move in to arbitrate, they provide undue attention and service. Regardless of what provokes the fighting among children, parents only make matters worse when they interfere, separate the children, or try to solve or "settle" the quarrel.

In most cases involving disputes among children, parents simply have no business butting in. In place of their usual reactions, parents can stop being annoyed over behavior as soon as they realize that they do not *have* to do anything about it. They should merely go on about their business, letting their children settle their own problems. The parent—usually the mother—will then be placing the responsibility with her children where it belongs. She will do so by refusing to get involved in what is their business and not her business. Such parental action will be effective because it deprives the children of those expected results, which would have made the bickering or fighting useful in eliciting mother's undue concern and involvement.

When quarreling leads to the abuse of a very young or the youngest child, we can be quite sure that the older children are creating a commotion rather than actually doing harm. Older children who threaten violence in a parent's presence do so to involve the parents. Except for rare instances of true impulsive behavior, they will not hurt their younger brothers and sisters. Johnny, age five, who holds a truck over his eleven-month-old sister's head as mother passes the open door will gently lower it when she has gone on to return to her own work. Children often cooperate in such behavior to involve mother. Even prior to her first birthday, a child knows that if she screams, mother will come, and things will happen to her older brother. And older brother Johnny knows that if he makes her scream, mother will come running. Children often work as a team to manage their parents' behavior toward them.

When the child's desire is for attention, he will not hurt his sibling; instead, he will create a situation to gain the attention he craves. In the example above, it was not Johnny's intention to hurt his sister with the toy truck but rather to provoke his mother into giving him attention and then perhaps her love after having been "bad." This scheme often works beautifully and is predictable as long as attention is the child's goal. If the child's goal is revenge against a sibling, however, the desire to hurt may be real. Revenge as a goal of childhood behavior is discussed later in this chapter. When a parent is directly confronted by one child threatening another with a dangerous object, he or she should simply come near and quietly remove it. The key point, of course, is to do it quietly without the words, excitement, or fuss which our children so often produce for our benefit.

Whenever a parent interferes in a fight or quarrel, he or she deprives the children involved of an opportunity for learning how to solve their own conflicts. Since all human beings have experienced and will again experience situations involving conflict of interests, we all have to learn the give and take of life as well as the skills necessary for dealing with life's conflict situations. Whenever a parent sets himself up as an arbitrator or authority, however, that parent's children learn nothing about adjustment, fair play, and cooperation. As long as we as parents do things for our children, they will not and cannot learn to manage for themselves. This applies to fighting as well as to the development of independence.

The child who has all his problems and conflicts—including fights—settled for him may never learn how to adequately resolve life's major difficulties. Further, he may learn to feel a need to resort to pressure or violence in cases where he finds he cannot have things his own way. Particularly, if a mother overprotects her younger child, she will reinforce that child's concept of self as a "baby" who can demand special consideration. In such a case, she will reinforce the child's feeling of inferiority while simultaneously teaching him—"the victim"—to use deficiency and weakness to gain special consideration. In doing so, the parent augments the very predicament she desires to eliminate.

It is important that parents teach their children not to fight to solve problems, but the point is to succeed in doing so. Interference and arbitration, unfortunately, do not bring about this result, although they may stop the fighting momentarily. Interference and arbitration are bound to fail because they in no way teach the child either how to settle his conflicts by other means or how to avoid the next fight. To become effective in training our children in this area of life, we must help each to develop a sense of responsibility for his or her siblings. This means that although mother may assist in taking care of a bloody nose, she should do so without taking sides and without comment as to who was right or wrong.

Parents who take sides in fights between their children succeed only in keeping the teeter-totter in motion. The child who is defeated in turn attempts to get even with his previously successful sibling. Whenever parents take sides, one child becomes the victor while the other becomes the vanquished. For this reason, no sooner does one fight seem settled than another is brewing. Sibling rivalry clearly lies at the root of such fighting. One can be quite sure that the victor—the one who has managed to convince the parent of his innocence—is usually the child who started the fight either by subtle or overt provocation of his rival. Since sibling children who deliberately provoke fights do so to get another child into trouble, parental interference in their quarrels usually succeeds only in reinforcing each child's self-concept and his mistaken opinion of his own value. Rather than teaching the children to stop fighting, such action only suggests to them how profitable fighting may be.

Parents who learn to ignore conflict situations through their emotional control express their confidence in each child's ability to take care of himself. When a mother is able to restrain her reactions to simple statements such as, "I'm sorry you were hurt in your fight" and "I think you can solve your problem yourself," her response is sufficient. Even young children can manage their affairs and take care of themselves much better than most parents might believe. When children are left to work out their own differences, fighting may soon lose its interest, value, and glamor. As we have seen before, the child's piercing scream is usually not the result of a blow but rather is simply a learned attention-getting technique. When parents show that they will no longer be impressed each time a child screams, their children may decide to abandon that behavior as a useless technique.

Each time a fight does occur, however, parents must realize that a power contest is also involved. When one child's feelings of status are threatened by the behavior of another, a conflict becomes a contest. As hostility is aroused to justify disregard for politeness or consideration, one child seeks to restore his supposed loss of status at the expense of his opponent. And, of course, if mother and daddy fight, their children may imitate them. As children see fighting used by adults as a technique for settling differences, it is likely that they will easily adapt it for their own use. In such cases, fighting as a means for problem solving may become a family value, although the rebellious child may move in a different or opposite direction to develop other values contrary to those of his parents.

Ideally, parents can and should conduct friendly discussion about fighting at times when it is not the focus of family attention. This should be done without accusation or moralization, using an approach designed to work *with* the children to identify ways and means for peaceful settlement of differences or difficulties. However, this can never be done successfully when the fight is taking place. At these moments, words neither teach nor help; they merely become additional weapons to further the fight already in progress. When "fights" are arguments in progress, children should always be left to their own devices. Parents who have carefully observed the behavior of their offspring know that children can establish far more just and equal relationships among themselves than those which we as adults are likely to provide for them. And they learn by the impact of reality to develop justice, consideration, diplomacy, equality, fair play, and respect for each other. This, of course, is what we want our children to learn. We can help them most by stepping out of the non-dangerous situation to give them the opportunity they need to learn to work together.

Be Consistent and Follow Through

Children learn only by the recurrence of similar experiences. For this reason, they can comprehend definite rules and requirements only if these rules apply uniformly at all times and under all circumstances. Children must, of course, be clearly aware of what is expected of them before they can adjust themselves properly. For example, if parents are to establish the habit of washing hands before meals, they must establish a pattern of this behavior at the earliest possible time and then hold firmly to it with no exceptions.

Because children will accept and follow a rule automatically once they realize it is permanently binding and invariable, it is neither practical nor wise to be indulgent—even at the beginning of training—in the mistaken belief that the child will learn to meet the necessary requirement as time goes on, even without consistency. It is particularly important that parents be careful when the child encounters a new responsibility since such first impressions of new situations will strongly influence the course of the child's subsequent conduct. Only through the consistency of established rules will a child acquire habits of orderliness in their lives.

A child will have every reason to think that bathing is unimportant, for example, if occasionally, when time runs short, he is allowed to go to school only half washed. Or if he is not always obliged to straighten his books and papers after studying, he will feel that he does not need to comply to sporadic parental commands to do so. The same is true for all sorts of other behaviors he must learn as part of the process of his training and socialization. Parents should not expect their child to keep order or to follow orders if they themselves cannot learn to be consistent in their demands.

Parents should know exactly what they want before they ask anything of a child. More specifically, they should be decisive when making specific requests of the child. It is important that parents consult directly with the child if they are not certain of what should be done, especially when dealing with their older children. The following are simple examples of questions designed to initiate such consultation.

"What do you think about you and me inviting Mrs. Jones and Tommy for coffee tomorrow morning?"

"Do you feel well enough to go to the play tonight?"

"Will Bill be with you on Saturday?"

Parents must then decide whether the situation requires or even permits a definite request or order. On those occasions where the parent has reached a specific decision to ask something of the child, decisiveness should be indicated by firm insistence on execution of the instruction. The tone of the parent's voice will clearly indicate to the child whether or not he can expect determination; the powers of observation of children are extremely sharp. Parents betray their thoughts and feelings to a far greater extent than most may realize through facial expressions as well as voice modulations.

Some parents attempt to communicate firmness through loudness, but this is an error. Not only does shouting fail to produce a proper response; in most cases, it indicates an inner insecurity which the child is quick to recognize and use to his or her own advantage. An order to a child will be much more effective if delivered in a low tone of voice since it is the modulation of the voice which brings out firmness of intention.

It is, of course, best to avoid direct commands whenever possible, or at the very least, they should be used sparingly to maintain their effect. When used, they should be reserved for real emergencies when danger is present and the child must respond immediately. In environments where children learn to feel that they need not comply immediately with parental commands, adults lose use of this tool as an important aid which may be of crucial importance in future crisis situations. Since many if not most commands can be replaced by friendly suggestions, such as "I wish you would" or "I would like to see," it is best to use these kinds of replacements whenever possible. Emergencies, of course, are the exception.

Throughout their lives, our children will be faced with choices which will require that they make decisions. If we hope to teach them to choose wisely and courageously, we must give them opportunities to choose, take responsibility, and when necessary, make mistakes. Study of children reveals that they learn well from experience but very poorly from parental lectures and/or sermons and that they resent unnecessary commands or orders.

Consider the example of Mrs. Jones* who takes her nine-year-old daughter, Cindy, to the shoe store to buy a new pair of shoes. The Jones family has never been very close, but mother is willing to try to display trust in her child's judgment as the result of an article she has recently read. On the way to the store, mother tells Cindy that she may make her own shoe selection. After trying on shoes for a short time, the child decides on a red pair, but her mother soon expresses preference for a navy-blue pair. Mrs. Jones coaxes and argues. Cindy whines and pouts. As they leave the store, Mrs. Jones attempts to distract her daughter to another subject. Cindy, having grudgingly accepted her mother's decision, continues to pout.

In this example, Mrs. Jones first told her daughter she could choose, then made the choice herself and forced Cindy into acceptance of that forced choice. This mother is not consistent in dealing with Cindy nor did she keep her word. Cindy, on the other hand, sees mother as arbitrary but strong enough to enforce her choice. Since she cannot have what she wants, Cindy feels resentment. With this attitude, she neither cares nor does she understand whether or not her own choice was practical. She has learned nothing but further distrust from this situation.

Suppose mother had allowed Cindy to select her own shoes as she had originally promised. Cindy might have discovered for herself that the color of the shoes she had chosen did not match well with much of her clothing. However, more shoes could not be purchased until the red shoes were worn out or outgrown. If this reality had been stated by Cindy's parents before the trip to the shoe store,

---

* This example and the one which follows were frequently used as examples by Dr. Rudolph Dreikurs' in lectures and writing as well as by his students. They are paraphrased here much as Dreikurs used them.

Cindy would then have had to live with her decision. Under such circumstances, she might have become much more willing to give greater consideration to a similar problem the next time it occurred. If Cindy's mother had prepared her daughter in this way and then had allowed Cindy to make the final decision, she would have taken the position of educator rather than that of authority figure or "boss."

Some children are actually, if unintentionally, trained for disobedience. The mother who makes a request of her child but does not follow through does exactly that. Children of such mothers soon learn that they can disregard what their mothers say to them. Mothers in such cases invariably "tell" too much while failing to act appropriately. Consider the example of Mrs. Smith who is working in her flower garden. Periodically, she calls to her five-year-old daughter, Ann, who is playing in the sandbox with a request that she put on her sun hat. Mother's hands are dirty, and she really does not want to get up to put it on the child herself. Finally, mother gives up, stops calling, and continues to hurry to complete her work before dinnertime.

This mother's procedure shows disrespect for herself, for her daughter, and for the rays of the sun. To Ann who knows nothing about the danger of sunburn, mother's demand is arbitrary and tyrannical. Made in the form of a command, it prompts rebellion instead of cooperation within the context of an unnecessary power contest. If mother had really felt that Ann needed protection from the sun after her child had ignored her request, she should have followed through and personally put the hat on the child's head. If Ann then resisted further, mother's decision that her daughter be protected from the sun would have required that she move Ann indoors. Mrs. Smith must learn to think before demanding compliance. Then she must follow through with firmness of action. The counterpart of demanding compliance is firmness when refusing a child's demand.

Some children quickly learn that their parents will eventually and predictably succumb to pestering, wheedling, crying, or pleading. Through experience, they discover that mother will first say "no" but will then give in if they persist. Such parents lack the necessary courage to refuse a request and to remain firm. This is often the case either because (1) they have learned to pity their child when he displays unhappiness as a result of not having what he wants, or because (2) they feel embarrassed at his public display in response to their refusal.

Martha is six years old. She will beg, plead, and ignore her mother's refusal to give her a coin for the shopping center gum ball machine until eventually, in desperation, mother agrees to "just one piece." Through her inconsistent behavior, Martha's mother is training the child to disrespect her word and to feel that through persistent harassment, Martha can get what she wants. If this does not work, the child may resort to "water power," since tears, too, will usually defeat a mother. Regardless of what a child wants, if he or she has found a technique which works, that child will use the method again and again with increasing persistence.

The simple solution to this problem is that any child who is old enough to want to buy things should have an allowance. Then, when the child asks for money, mother need only suggest that she use her allowance money. If she has none left, that is the end of the matter. Mother neither answers, reasons, argues, responds with pity, gives in, nor allows borrowing against next week's allowance. If her child does not have the money necessary to purchase the gum or a candy bar or a mechanical ride or whatever else it might be, that is the child's affair. Mother must remain consistent in her "no" response and follow through when necessary by withdrawing from the child's provocation.

Children can feel secure and learn to feel confidence in their family environment only if we as their parents are consistent and follow through in an orderly fashion with our training programs. When we do so, our children learn respect for order and feel the confidence, which comes from knowing exactly where they stand with their parents. Since consistency is a part of order, its use helps to establish limitations and boundaries which are necessary to provide developing children with a sense of security.

Learn the Mistaken Goals of Childhood

Children both want and need to belong. A child will do what each situation requires and in doing so will acquire a sense of belonging through participation and feeling useful. If this process goes well, the child will maintain courage and present few problems. As a child becomes discouraged, however, his sense of belonging becomes progressively more restricted. As this occurs, his interest will turn from participation in the group to increasingly desperate attempts to achieve self-realization through and at the expense of others. The entire pattern of his behavior may be turned toward this end. Whether through pleasant or disturbing behavior, the child feels he has to find a place.

As this process occurs, the child's behavior may be directed to any one of four mistaken goals. If parents are to guide a child toward constructive behavior and social integration, it is essential that they understand the dynamics of these goals. The *first* goal, the desire for undue *attention,* is used by discouraged children as a means for feeling that they belong. And they feel they belong only when they are being noticed or served. A child whose behavior is directed toward this goal may be delightfully charming, witty, or coy. Regardless how pleasant he may be, however, his goal is to win attention rather than to participate. Such children are influenced by the mistaken assumption that they have status, value, and significance only when they are the center of attention. Based on this mistaken assumption, such children develop great skill in the use of attention-getting behaviors.

When delightful or charming means of getting attention fail, however, the child will switch to disturbing methods to achieve the same goal. She may spill her cereal or milk, mark on the walls with pencils or crayons, whine, tease, or try any number of other attention-getting devices. Such a child has a damaged or mistaken self-concept. As her parents yield to her undue demands for attention, they simply reinforce this flawed self-concept and increase her conviction that this mistaken method will serve the sense of belonging which she craves. From the viewpoint of such a child, when her parents are angry or upset with her, she is at least sure they know she is there.

We may diagnose the child's unconscious intentions by observing our own response to her behavior. If by watching our own reactions, we observe that we are merely prompted by the child's efforts to gain constant and undue attention, i.e., we feel annoyed, we can then be quite sure (1) that this is what the child wants us to do and (2) that this is his mistaken way of attempting to find his place. If adult action and response seem out of keeping with demands of the situation, i.e., we develop a tendency to remind and coax, the child is most likely demanding undue attention.

Effective participation and cooperation require that each individual within a family be situation-centered rather than self-centered. The attention-seeking child is a self-centered child. Since the interaction being described here takes place on an unconscious level for parents as well as children, parents, mothers, and fathers may very easily and naturally respond to the child's designs. As parents become aware of the dynamics of this situation, however, they can acquire skill in its interpretation. In doing so, they bring it to the conscious level and thereby have the means to promote redirection, i.e., to offer constructive guidance to the child.

A *second* major mistaken goal is the struggle for power. It usually occurs after the parent has tried for a period of time to stop the child's demands for attention. At this point, the child is gaining increasing satisfaction from refusing to do what his parents want him to do. He is becoming increasingly determined to use his power to defeat his parents. A child caught up in this power struggle feels that if he was to comply with his parents' requests, he would be submitting to a stronger power and, in so doing, would lose his sense of personal value. As this fear of being overwhelmed by greater power becomes an increasing reality, it leads children to extreme efforts to demonstrate their own power. They feel they belong only if they are in control or are "the boss" or that "no one can boss me." To such children, the pain and insult of punishment is a price worth paying for victory. The victory they achieve is keeping mother (or father) completely exasperated and frustrated, causing her (or him) to "declare emotional bankruptcy," which is what parents do when they feel utterly defeated and lose their temper.

When parents' behavior reveals that they have "nothing left," even though they possess superior strength and size, children clearly recognize and utilize this weakness. Parents feel provoked or angry as if their authority is threatened. Under these conditions, it is a serious mistake to try to overpower a power-drunk child. Parents develop a tendency to fight or give in. In the chronic battle that ensues, the child merely develops increasing skill in using his power. As he does so, however, he also finds increasing reason to feel worthless unless he can demonstrate his power. This process leads many children to the point where they find satisfaction only when they assume the role of bully or tyrant. This problem is becoming increasingly prevalent in today's society because of the changes which have occurred and are occurring in our concept of equality.

Parents can easily recognize that a struggle for power exists when child and parent each attempt to show the other who is boss. An important distinction between a demand for attention and a demonstration of power is the child's behavior—at least upon correction. If the child wants only to get attention, he will stop his disturbing behavior—at least for the moment—when he is reprimanded and later resumes the same behavior or disturbs in another way. However, if this intention is to demonstrate power, attempts to stop him will only intensify. If his goal is power, his passive or active behavior is intensified or he will temporarily submit with defiant compliance.

A *third* mistaken goal arises from intensification of the power contest. As parents and child become increasingly involved in a power struggle, and as each attempts to subdue the other, a transaction of increasingly intense retaliation may develop. These children feel unloved and feel a need to hurt others as they feel hurt. Parents also feel hurt with a tendency to retaliate or get even. The child, in his discouragement, may proceed to seek *revenge* as his only means of feeling important and significant. At this stage, he is convinced that he counts only if he can hurt others as he feels he has been hurt by them. The child feels deeply discouraged and powerless in his attempt to find a place. Because he feels that he cannot be liked by others, his mistaken goal now becomes one of revenge and retaliation, perhaps choosing another weapon.

Such a child needs encouragement most but often gets it least because his behavior is so disagreeable. At this point, genuine acceptance and understanding of the child in his present condition is required to help him rediscover his worth. When parents punish this child, they succeed only in offering further proof that he is "bad." Such experience will provide the child with further incentive to provoke, which will lead directly to further mutual retaliation. Hence, parents need to build a trusting relationship and convince the child that he or she is loved.

The *fourth* goal is displayed by the completely discouraged child as he tries to demonstrate his *complete inadequacy*. Completely discouraged children *give up* entirely. They feel they have no real chance to succeed in any way either by useful or useless means. The seemingly stupid child, for example, is frequently a discouraged child who uses stupidity as a means of avoiding any effort whatsoever. Such children no longer try to put others into their service; they simply give up. They become helpless and use helplessness to exaggerate both real and imagined weakness and deficiency. This is done to avoid all tasks or activities where the child feels failure is to be expected. Such children usually *desire to be left alone* since they believe any effort on their part will only reveal their worthlessness, hopelessness, and totally inadequate condition to others.

Whenever a mother finds herself at the point of saying, "I give up," she can be quite sure that this is exactly what the child wants her to feel. But of course, no mother or child is ever worthless. The child's view of himself is a mistaken concept resulting from a series of experiences which he has seen as presenting impossible obstacles. It is through this series of experiences that he has become discouraged. He fails to respond or passively responds to whatever is done. He shows no improvement.

When parents are aware of the four mistaken goals which influence children's behavior, they have a solid basis for action. If the desired result of a child's misbehavior is removed, that particular behavior becomes useless. When the child fails to achieve her goal, she will reconsider her direction and choose an alternative course of action.

In some cases, it is helpful to tell the child directly what we believe her mistaken goal may be. Although some adults may fear that revelation could be damaging to the child, such is not the case. However, this information should be used only as a basis for corrective action and never as a weapon against the child. Once we are aware of the child's mistaken goal, we are in a position to understand the purpose of his behavior. All behavior is caused. What may have seemed senseless now begins to make good sense as we see it from the viewpoint of the child. It is on this basis that effective action may be taken.

As parents realize that a child is demanding excessive attention, they can avoid yielding to his undue demands, i.e., ignore misbehavior when possible. There is simply no point in demanding the attention of a mother who removes herself from the scene. However, she should give attention for positive behavior when the child is *not* making a bid for it. Avoid giving undue service, and realize that reminding, coaxing, punishing and rewarding as well as service are undue attention. Parents who find themselves involved in a power contest may suddenly withdraw from the field of battle and not allow themselves to become involved in the fight. For the child, there is no point in attempting to win without an opponent who will lose. Parents now have the opportunity to help the child learn how to use power constructively by requesting the child's help and engaging her cooperation.

Realize that both fighting and giving in serve only to increase the child's desire for power. When a child seeks to hurt us, we can be aware of his deep discouragement. We should avoid feeling hurt ourselves and refrain from retaliation through undue restraint and punishment. Instead, work to build a trusting relationship and convince the child that he or she is loved. Finally, parents can refuse to be discouraged by the seemingly helpless child and instead arrange success experiences for him where he can discover and nurture his own potentialities and abilities. It does the child no good to give up if his parents simply will not believe that he is helpless. To do this, stop all criticism. Focus on assets. Encourage any and all positive attempts, no matter how small. But perhaps most important, don't be caught up in pity and *don't give up*.

These four goals or life approaches to find one's place in the family are obvious only in the young child. By the age of eleven or twelve, the child's relationships with his peers have become sufficiently important so that he will pursue a wide variety of behaviors as he now attempts to find his place in his peer group. At this age, disturbing behavior, which continues to represent a mistaken effort to find one's place, can no longer be entirely explained by one of the mistaken goals of childhood. As persons reach adolescence and later adulthood, provocative actions can sometimes be explained in terms of these four goals, but other forms of mistaken approaches to finding one's place such as attainment of material possessions, thrill-seeking, and excessive concerns with masculine or feminine physical attributes become increasingly evident.

Parents can only attempt to stimulate their children toward appropriate changes in behavior. However, even though they may seem to do exactly the right things, success will not always be guaranteed. Influences from outside the home, especially those of the child's peers, impress the young person increasingly as he or she grows toward adolescence. When parental efforts to guide children in other directions seem unsuccessful, we must recognize that each child is an individual, and as such, in a democratic society, will make his or her own choices. The child must then learn to take responsibility for his or her choices and decisions. Parents cannot and should not usurp this responsibility which belongs to the child and which in a democracy is part of the meaning of equality.

Solutions to family problems can rarely, if ever, be found in a moment. The moment of problem is only one of a series which includes events that may move either toward or away from solutions. Each moment contributes either to training for improvement of relationships or to the opposite development of both detrimental attitudes and poor social integration. If parents can learn to do the right thing at the right moment, they can successfully guide their offspring toward improvement. If, however, they do not fulfill the requirements of given situations because they do not know how to respond to them, the chances of improvement are poor.

In most cases, with most parents, it seems sufficient to know what to do or what not to do in specific situations. At earlier times in our history, this knowledge was commonly held by parents because it consisted of a set of traditions for raising children that were passed from generation to generation. However, a relatively rapid evolution to our present state of democratic society has created a need for clarification of new approaches, which are effective within this new evolving tradition of child-raising.

When the child's mistaken goals and erroneous learning are so deeply ingrained that more than simply "correct" responses to acts of provocation are required, individualized professional counseling or psychotherapy may be required. Professionals work with the child within the context of his family environment, toward a reconstruction of his personality pattern, or more specifically, his basic assumptions concerning himself and his surroundings. In such cases, a more comprehensive insight into the dynamics of patterns of the child's behavior and environment may be required to bring about necessary changes in behaviors and interpersonal relationships. In some cases, full controlled "behavior modification" programs may be required.

Eliminate Reward and Punishment (While Keeping Requests Reasonable)

The concepts of human relationships common to our culture have undergone a fundamental change during the past century. As the individual man or woman has become more "the equal" of other adults in social and political relationships, a similar change has taken place in the relationship between parents and children. Still, although much has changed, much also remains the same. For example, many procedures used by parents to train and educate their children continue to be based on the mistaken assumption that adults should respond to the actions of children with either punishment or reward. These methods—which have been employed generation after generation—are so deeply embedded in the social conditions that have characterized human relationships of the past that many adults have difficulty conceiving the possibility of training a child without the application of punishment and reward. In our work with parents, however, we have frequently heard their reports that repeated spankings usually do not modify the behavior of children in desired directions. In fact, although may parents use spanking and a wide variety of other physical punishments, most find that they rarely work well, if at all. Why is this the case?

The preface to this book includes a brief outline of the changing social climate in our society. There it was pointed out that an increasing realization of democracy has become part of our way of life, leading to a situation in which parents can no longer assume the role of authority. There can be no such dominance among equals, no authority that implies one individual having "power" over another.

Under the old autocratic social system, children watched and waited for the time when they too would be privileged adults. At the present time in history, however, our children have acquired some measure of belief in and acceptance of their own equal social status with adults. Consequently, adults no longer enjoy a truly superior position in relation to children. Children no longer recognize adults as superior in power or intellect, or in many cases, even in the information they possess. For this reason, we as parents must realize the ultimate futility of trying to impose our will upon our children.

Because today's children are willing to take vast amounts of punishment in order to assert what they see as their rights, no amount of punishment will bring about lasting submission. At best, parents can expect to gain only temporary results from punishment. However, without realizing that they are actually getting nowhere with their methods, many bewildered and confused parents mistakenly hope that punishment, if increased or continued, will eventually yield results. But in reality, continued use of punishment succeeds only in prompting the child to develop even greater assertive powers of defiance and resistance.

During many periods of history when one man was the servant or slave of another, behavior could be controlled, and services could be attained or guaranteed only through force or bribery. Under such conditions, the individual or group in control was free to impose its will using various methods of subjugation with punishment and other retaliation being useful tools to bring this about. This pattern was also clearly predominant as part of the patterns of family interactions characteristic of these periods of history. In our present society, however, parents no longer enjoy the favorable position of powerful superiority that was part of a process of mutual retaliation, which was common within family units of earlier times.

Although the adult may try to maintain this superior position, he or she is now influenced—perhaps without being entirely aware of it—by new, changed, and more democratic concepts. As the parent shifts toward attempts to treat the child more as an equal, these attempts at change may—and often do—make the child master of the parent. Precisely because the currently accepted standards of human behavior deprive parents of the right to treat their children as they please, the power of children to retaliate may begin to exceed that of parents. For this reason, too, the traditional reward and punishment methods of child training are no longer effective, regardless of the regularity with which they may be employed by parents. Force, power, and dominance must now be replaced with more equalitarian methods and techniques of parental influence.

In situations where reward and punishment *are* used, the child comes to feel that, "If you have the right to hurt me, I have the right to hurt you." This can lead to a progression of retaliation and revenge. The more mother or father punishes, the more the child retaliates. But because many children are far more resilient and tenacious than many adults, they may out-plot and out-last their parents. To neutralize this condition, the authoritarian concept of punishment must be replaced with a sense of mutual cooperation and respect.

Even though children are no longer in an inferior position, they remain both inexperienced and untrained. It is for this reason especially that they need our leadership and guidance and will accept it if we treat them with respect and dignity. If we as parents can create an atmosphere of mutual self-respect and consideration, we can provide an opportunity for each child to live comfortably and happily with others. To do so effectively, it is necessary that we *arrange learning situations,* which include demonstration of respect both for ourselves and for the child.

The child's provocative behavior is part of his goal, which is to gain our attention, engage us in a power contest, or retaliate for what is seen as previous injustice. When we punish a child, we should realize that we have done so only to relieve our own feelings of tension and frustration. When a child constantly defeats us, perhaps we feel we are entitled to the short moment of victory when we beat him in some way at his own game. Such occasions do occur; we are all human and, hence, imperfect. When they do occur, however, we need not feel guilty about them later.

In training our children, guilty feelings are a luxury that we can do without because they tend only to pacify our reaction to our own acts. Much better is a frank and honest admission to ourselves, for example, that "While I did hit him, in some sense, he asked for it. And while I may regret it and know it is a useless training method, it at least made *me* feel better." Such a frank self-admission on the part of a parent after having lost his or her temper with a child can help to forestall future outbursts. It can also add greatly to that adult's own courage and feeling that he or she can both improve self-control and cope with the child on future occasions.

The practice of granting rewards to young people for good behavior can be just as detrimental to their psychological growth as a system of punishment. Since humans reward their inferiors for favors or good deeds, the same lack of respect is demonstrated through the granting of rewards as is true in punishment. In a system of mutual respect among equals, a job is done because it needs doing with related satisfaction resulting from a mutual helping effort. But because young people are attention-centered, they can very easily develop a "What's in it for me?" attitude. When this occurs, the child's developing social interest can be stifled by the mistaken idea that he has a place or belongs only if he gets a payoff in return for each of his actions.

Because this is true, it is not a good idea to pay children for household chores. They share in the benefits of family living, including clean clothes to wear, shelter, and food. If they are the equals they desire and often claim to be, they are obliged to share in the toil necessary to sustain and maintain the family enterprise. Through use of rewards and punishment, however, many children develop the idea that they need not do anything unless there is something in it for them as individuals. Under such circumstances, it is not possible for children to develop a mature sense of responsibility.

Children who learn to place undue emphasis on rewards soon learn that their parents may run out of sufficiently satisfying "prizes." Eventually, such a child may find that no reward will seem totally satisfying. For this reason, it is crucial that children learn to share in all aspects of family life and work. They should definitely have and share in spending money, usually in the form of an allowance. The allowance represents their share of the family's money, and as such, they should be allowed to save or use it as they choose. Parents should not establish a connection between the allowance and the chores or work expected of the child. Children do family chores or work because they—just as every other member of the family—contribute to the welfare of the family unit. They receive allowance money because they also share in the benefits of the family's endeavor.

Parents should not try to win the cooperation of their children by offering any type of material gain. Children actually want to be good. Good behavior during childhood springs from the child's desire to belong, to cooperate, and to contribute usefully. Parents who bribe a child for good behavior are, in effect, showing that they do not trust him, which is a form of discouragement. A reward will never give the child a sense of belonging. As soon as we run out of rewards or as soon as a reward is withheld, acceptable activity by the child is interpreted by him as a waste of his effort. The "What's in it for me?" child soon learns to wonder why he should bother to do anything if he does not gain something special in return.

As this progression occurs in the life of the child, his attitude of materialism grows. Soon, a completely false sense of values may become established as the child learns to assume that the world owes him anything and everything. If what he desires is not automatically forthcoming, he feels he has been cheated; he must retaliate and take what is his. Why, for example, should this child upon acquisition of a license to drive his father's car follow rules to preserve lives since following rules has no place in his set of values? Why should he follow rules made by others? Where is the reward? It is much more fun to experience the thrill of defiance. And, "Who cares about a little punishment if I do get caught? Dad will take care of it anyway."

The end result of use of reward and punishment with children is development of the attitude, "They did not reward me, so I will punish them—but if they do punish me, I'll get back at them." In our mistaken efforts to win the cooperation of our offspring, we too often deny them the basic satisfactions of autonomous responsible living. True satisfaction comes only from a sense of meaningful contribution and participation.

We have been attempting to point out that the primary fallacy of the theory of punishment and reward is that both methods are based on the mistaken assumption of parental power and superiority. Parents who expose their children to such methods may teach them to behave favorably under adult pressure but will rarely teach them to do so on their own accord. Since conformity achieved through either pleasant or unpleasant pressure results only in superficially "good" behavior, any cooperation which may be achieved in this way will not be based on social interest and a genuine desire to adapt or conform. Just slightly beneath the social veneer of such behavior lies a thinly veiled rebellion, which will inevitably lead to antisocial attitudes that may lead in turn to social deficiencies, including disruption of cooperation, order, and law.

Through these dynamics, young people learn to regard society as a tyrant to which they must submit and not as their own domain that they have helped to create and to which they belong as equals. As a result of the development of this viewpoint, many of our children and youth display cooperation which, because it is not based on a recognition and acceptance of a social order, is not genuine. It is for this reason that large numbers of our offspring are willing to conform only when they can avoid hardships or when they can gain personal advantages. The value of cooperation and peaceful order cannot be taught using the methods of punishment and reward because this approach conceals the real issue by presenting social adjustment as a submission and order as an imposition.

Careful observation of children within family units has revealed that the only really workable inducement to childhood social adjustment is use of the natural consequences of disturbed order—i.e., letting the child learn from experience, which will be discussed later in this chapter. This approach is successful because it stimulates both recognition and acceptance of order, regardless of favorable or unfavorable circumstances and because it is independent of the actions of other persons. A danger, however, in the case of parents who are accustomed to use of retaliation is that they may misuse logical consequences. Probably the most common such error made by parents involves a reintroduction of their own strength and power into the social order. Statements based on "authority" which suggest "If you do this, that will happen" only threaten the child. Then, as the parents carefully watch and monitor the child's behavior, the child often surprises them by reciprocating through some form of retaliation designed to punish them for what he thinks they have done or are doing to him. As each party then attempts to even the score, a characteristic power contest develops, having grown directly from inappropriate procedures employed by discouraged parents who may already have felt overpowered or defeated by the behavior of their children.

Parents who are prone to employ punishment or reward or both in child-training are in many cases not aware of their own motivations in continuing to use even those methods that they may recognize as ineffectual or futile. For this reason, parents must (1) learn to understand the significance of their own actions, (2) monitor their own behaviors, and (3) find help, if necessary, to replace ineffective methods with more productive approaches to child training and management.

Consider the following example: mother calls Johnny from the back porch. Johnny is slowly swinging and eating a popsicle. She calls again, but he does not respond. Soon she becomes angry and shouts a threat. Still nothing happens. Later, in boredom, Johnny slowly walks to the back porch. Mother has gone inside the house. In this situation, Johnny displayed a complete lack of respect for his mother and her request. He responded with open defiance to her clearly evident expectation for compliance. In this power contest, mother lost by making what to Johnny was an unreasonable request. Why should he go to her when she would not come to him?

In this situation, mother not only got what she deserved but also what she, in reality, asked for and should have expected. From Johnny's point of view, there is no good reason why he should comply and stop playing on the swing. When his mother attempted to show her authority and then failed to act, Johnny played stubborn and "won." Her words were used only as weapons. Her threat, which was "to tell daddy when he gets home," was also to no avail. One would guess that Johnny may have heard that one before. Such a threat is always ill-advised. Neither father nor mother should be put into the role of having to or be expected to exert superior authority since the authority role no longer really works for parents in our society.

Attempts to use authority should be replaced by reasonable requests characterized by respect for the child and recognition of the need for order. Since adult superiority is no longer accepted by most youth in highly industrialized societies, the child who feels dominated may become determined to be disobedient as a matter of principle. Most children who feel either bossed or imposed upon will retaliate with disobedience. To avoid such conflicts, parents must learn to make only reasonable and necessary requests in a nonauthoritarian manner. But many parents simply fail to recognize their own attempts to maintain a superior-inferior relationship, even when it is pointed out to them. Often, they follow a pattern of increased anger when a child refuses to obey, followed by increasingly unreasonable requests or demands in an attempt to control the child. At the same time, it is likely that the child is becoming increasingly "mother-deaf" or "father-deaf," depending on which is involved. The child simply ignores the words of his parents. At this point, the power struggle is on in full force. Exceptions to this pattern do occur, however, which involve children who comply even to frequent and unreasonable demands because of an intense desire to please. Such a child is not learning to function as a self-determining individual.

Some parents attempt to treat their children, much like servants. However, to ask a child to do what we ourselves would not like to be asked to do implies gross disrespect for the child's rights. And one can always be suspicious of situations in which parents demand that the child do something immediately. Such an authoritarian approach nearly always contains an unreasonable request. Only when requests are infrequent—and when parents request the child's help rather than demanding his obedience or service—can friendliness and satisfactory interpersonal relationships be successfully encouraged. As parents, we must be sensitive to the capabilities of each of our children as well as to the situation when we make a request of a child.

Within this context, children enjoy special responsibility and its related recognition. The activities involved when another child takes care of younger children in mother's absence may serve as an example. However, there should always be agreement before the responsibility becomes necessary as to when and under what circumstances such responsibility is to be assumed. Of course, if mother occasionally finds herself in an unforeseen situation where she really needs extra help, she may feel free to call on one of her offspring for assistance. This should cause no real problem, however, in a family where mutual respect has allowed harmony and cooperation to evolve.

Be Firm, without Domination, and with Respect

The differences between firmness and domination at times seems difficult for some parents to comprehend. Children need firmness in their relationship with adults since it provides limits without which they feel uncomfortable. If no limits are set, the child will go further and further with his behavior to see how far he can go before he is stopped. Psychologists often call this "reality testing." Some parents, as they attempt to avoid stifling the creative development of their children, become overly lenient with lively children who in turn come to feel that "anything goes." The usual results of these patterns of behavior include a point of parental outrage, an unpleasant scene, and disruption of family harmony. When parents permit violation on one occasion and explode in anger on the next, they succeed only in teaching their children that it is necessary to obey only when parents become loud and/or violent. Parents need to learn to be firm without dominating. Domination means imposing our will or telling others what to do. When parents attempt to impose their will on children, they dominate and succeed only in evoking rebellion.

Firmness, on the other hand, is an expression of personal action. Mother can always decide what *she* will do and carry out *her* plan. Firmness without domination requires practice in mutual respect and cooperation. Parents must learn to respect the child's right to decide what he or she wants to do. But we must also respect ourselves in situations of conflict or confrontation. Such self-respect is gained by parental refusal to be placed at the mercy of unruly children. For example, a parent may decide that he or she simply will not drive the family automobile while the children are unruly. Each time they become overly boisterous, the parent merely stops the car. The parent may then say something, such as, "I cannot drive as long as you continue to argue and fight." He or she then need only sit quietly until order is restored with no other explanation necessary. In this case, the parent has taken a clear stand and remains firm in that decision.

Parents must realize that their children have the right to make decisions, and they must respect those rights. But in their desire to be "good" parents, they must not assume the role of slave. Mother and father can learn to be firm in what they do, and in most cases, still allow their children to take care of themselves. But within this context, respect for the child's wishes and needs is essential. The requirements of the total situation should be our guide as we develop the sensitivity to recognize the difference between needs and impulsive whims or desire.

The child having a tantrum on the street while walking with his mother is a case in point. Mother wishes to continue home, but her son sits down angrily and will walk no further. If mother calmly and quietly continues the walk toward home, without looking back, a predictable series of events will occur. At first, the child will probably double his stubborn efforts, perhaps with the addition of screaming. As mother remains firm in her resolve, however, the child will begin to follow, then run to catch up. Soon they will again be walking happily together.

In this rather typical predictable situation, mother indicated clearly by her action that she had decided to continue toward home. She neither gave in to the child's behavior nor did she harass the child with explanations or arguments. When the child saw that mother was firm in her resolve, he decided she really meant to go home, respected his mother's decision, and joined her. Parental firmness includes refusal to give in to the undue demands of the child or to indulge his every whim. The child will soon catch on. Once a parent or parents have made a decision—in line with order, however—it must be maintained. Children learn limitations only through firm insistence.

If the child is excessively noisy and will not stop, he can be asked to leave the room. If he is not willing to dress properly on a cold day, parents can prevent him from leaving the house. The maintenance of order often does require a certain amount of firmness and quiet pressure, especially with younger children. When mother says "no," she must mean no, which means that she must see that logical and reasonable restrictions are carried out. However, such acts of pressure must always be accompanied by giving the child a choice. The choice of "You may stay if you are quiet" can be followed by a choice of going alone or being carried out if he is not quiet. To order or even to ask him to leave will appear dictatorial.

However, if the relationship between parent and child is friendly, and if parents do not artificially inflate the matter with apologies, long explanations, or preaching, the child is likely to respond with minimal resistance. Quiet insistence is particularly necessary and effective with young children. Sometimes only a glance is required. Children read their parents well. They sense when we mean it, but they also know when we are weak or unsure in our positions.

As parents display firmness in their response to the behavior of their children, they must also be very sure to show their respect for the child and his rights. Living in a democracy is based on mutual respect, but there is no equality if only one person in a relationship is granted respect. This display of respect requires sensitivity in reaching a balance between expecting too much on the one hand and expecting too little on the other. Only when we have and display confidence in a child and his ability can we show genuine respect. This, of course, does not mean that we may make undue demands. Humiliating a child for any reason whatsoever reveals intense lack of respect, and as such, is a most inadequate device for training the child. Respect for children means that we regard them as individuals who have the same rights to make decisions that we have as adults. However, similar rights do not mean that a child may do what adults do since each member of a family has a different and unique role to play. Our point is that each individual has the right to be respected in that role, which he or she is expected to play as a member of the family unit.

Use Logical and Natural Consequences Effectively

The most effective single method that parents can use to preserve order is to let the child experience the natural or logical consequences of his or her behavior. This works well with difficult cases. The more frequently used method of direct intervention is almost always less effective because spanking, scolding, exhortation, and command work from outside the child, thus forcing him into certain molds of conduct from which he may or feel he must try to escape. However, when the child spontaneously and voluntarily adjusts his own behavior to meet each situation, he develops proper impulses, allowing correction of behavior from within. Until the child is prepared to observe order within himself, parental education and training efforts will usually be of limited and temporary value. Until the child realizes that having respect for rules of conduct is more satisfying than violation of these rules, he will not yet be ready to arrive at his own inner acceptance of order.

When mother forgets her meal on the stove, it burns. This is the natural or logical consequence of her having forgotten. Similarly, when we allow children to experience the consequences of their acts, we provide a real and honest situation from which they can learn. For example, when the child forgets to take his lunch to school, the natural consequence will involve hunger. If this becomes habitual, his mother on each occasion can hurry to rescue him or she can simply tell him that she no longer feels responsible to remind him to take his lunch to school. Then, when he forgets, she simply ignores his complaints. It is now his problem, not her problem. Initially, when this change occurs, the child will display anger because he thinks it is his mother's duty to take responsibility for his actions. If mother simply replies, "I'm sorry you forgot your lunch," perhaps with the enlisted aide of school officials so that someone else will not give him lunch money, a valuable lesson can be learned. However, if mother lectures to teach him "a lesson," she will immediately turn the natural consequence into a punishment. It is important that children learn that they have it in their power to deal with their own problems.

We do not have to assume the responsibilities of our children nor do we have the right to take on the consequences of their acts. Although parents do not desire to see their children suffer—and in our previous example, hunger *is* unpleasant—such discomfort can be effective in stimulating responsible behavior. Further, it clarifies the roles of parents and children, which can serve to eliminate much friction and lack of harmony within the family.

A healthy child who displays a poor appetite at mealtime does so to keep his parents busy. Eating supports and maintains life; it is a normal individual and personal function. Hence, it is the child's business to eat, and parents should mind their own business, not the child's. When a child does become a feeding problem, we always look for a controlling parent who is usually very easy to identify. Such a parent must learn that the simplest way to teach a child to eat is simply to let him eat. If the child refuses, parents should refrain from verbal reminders, retain a friendly attitude, remove the unfinished food when all have finished the meal, and allow the child to find out what happens. Only at the next meal, and not before, should food again be offered. If we do not eat, we become hungry. No threat of punishment or bribe should be offered. If the child dawdles, nothing is said; friendliness prevails during the meal.

If the child is hungry during the meal, food is available. If he does not choose to eat, the logical assumption is that he is not hungry. The food should be casually removed if the child plays with it. Later, if the child complains of hunger and begs for a snack, mother need only point out that dinner will be at six and that it is too bad the child will have to wait so long. Regardless of the pressures or pleadings of the child, mother may allow her child to experience the natural consequences of not eating. We eat not just because we are hungry but to keep from getting hungry. The discomfort of going hungry is not imposed by the adult but is simply the logical result of not having eaten. The suffering imposed by the mother who spanks her child, on the other hand, is a punishment because it is inflicted by the parent.

Most parents feel deeply responsible for managing the lives of their children. Many would feel accused of being a "bad" parent if they let their child go hungry as suggested in the preceding example. Such parents have learned to feel overconcerned and anxious about their children. However, what many parents feel to be a sense of responsibility for their children is in reality a desire to control them. It is this authoritative control, which their children are fighting. When their authority is removed, the child no longer has anything to fight against. It will take time and patience, but when there are no benefits in not eating, the child will probably eat.

Children are quick to discern the differences between punishment and logical consequences. They respond to logical consequences, but they fight back when punished. When consequences are imposed or used as a threat, they cease being logical consequences and become punishment. The secret of success lies in the manner of application. It is the wisely planned withdrawal of the parent that allows the logical consequences of an event to occur. In our previous eating example, the consequence works both ways. While the logical consequence of not eating is discomfort, the logical consequence of eating is comfort and satisfaction.

Many parents have difficulty getting their children up and off to school in the morning. Here again, if this becomes a chronic problem, it is the technique of natural or logical consequences that may be employed. The best approach in such a case is to buy the child an alarm clock, teach him to use it, and tell him that from then on it will be up to him to set his alarm and get himself up on time. If mother wants her child to take this responsibility himself, she must give him that responsibility and withdraw completely. Then, if he decides to shut off the alarm and continue to sleep, that is his affair. When he finally does wake up, he, of course, must be required to do his duty and go to school, no matter how late it might be, there to face the consequence by himself. In such difficult cases, if he has missed his ride, it will be necessary that he walk or make other arrangement since mother is busy with her household or other duties.

To make her training effective, this mother must be consistent and follow through with her decision, day after day, with no leniency. When her son finds that he can no longer engage his mother in a struggle to get him up, he may become willing to accept *his* responsibility. In each case, parents must arrange a consequence which will fit a particular disruption in the order and responsibility of living. Each must be tailor-made.

The first time Peter goes into the street, his mother should tell him he must stay in the yard where he must remain to be safe. On the second occurrence, she should quietly and without anger pick him up and firmly carry him to a play area in the house. When she has done so, she should say, "Since you do not want to play in our yard where you are safe, you may not go out. When you are ready, you may try again." The first phrase of mother's statement indicates Peter's right to his own feelings. No mother can make her child want to stay in the yard, but she can establish both limits and consequences. As soon as Peter expresses willingness to try again, he should be allowed to do so. If he then again runs into the street, he can be taken into the house for the remainder of the day. To prevent this from becoming a power contest, after the third or fourth such occurrence, mother may choose to keep Peter in for a day or a few days.

Within the context of situations such as the one illustrated in the preceding example, it is most important to continually give children a chance to try again. This allows them to feel they still have a chance and indicates the parents' faith both in the child and in his ability to learn. Peter will probably protest being taken into the house. As he expresses his feeling of rebellion at not getting his own way, his mother should simply remain calm. She can only deal with one problem at a time. Later, as Peter learns to play safely in his yard, his mother can express her pleasure that he now knows what to do.

This process, which should involve no personal humiliation or submission, is the only means by which the child can willingly learn to accept unpleasant responsibilities and modify his own desires when the necessity arises. Then, within his context, unless false pity leads the parent to spare him such experiences, opportunities will arise in the natural course of events to allow the child to experience the unpleasant results of his transgressions. Unless parents allow themselves to be misled by pride or distorted sense of shame to help the child or to do for him what should be his own duty, the child will learn from his experiences. Natural consequences can have their proper effect *only* if the adults of the family do not interfere with their behavior-shaping qualities/characteristics.

The natural consequences of violations, which will impress the rules of conduct on the child's mind without further action being required, are encountered frequently enough so that special effort on parents' part to create them is usually unnecessary. To assure that the child will learn fully from his experience, however, it is important that parents restrain themselves so as not to destroy any of these valuable opportunities through miscalculated zeal to protect their child from discomfort he may very much need as a *direct experiencing of life*. Often, it is just such restraint which—while difficult—will subsequently save both parent and child numerous annoyances, while at the same time, they teach the child responsibility for self, self-discipline, and self-management. If Johnny is slow, he will miss some of the activity. If Sarah puts her left shoe on the right foot, it will pinch.

In the few cases where it may seem necessary to contrive or arrange certain experiences, the parent can devise harmless means of showing the child, for example, that a chair may fall over backwards, that a needle pricks, or that the oven door is hot. Use of a casual method of calling such realities to the child's attention is always far more impressive than intimidating him with profound or dire warnings, even in situations where the parent feels an intense need to see to it that certain consequences will be invariably forthcoming. If

Peter fails to gather his playthings to put them where they belong, he could fail to find them the next day. If his brother, Harold, is unpunctual for meals, Harold may find that the next meal has already been served for everyone but him. If Jane is too slow in getting ready for walks and excursions, she may benefit from discovering that mother has gone without her.

Although such measures may at first seem harsh, they are designed for difficult cases and, to prevent future disorder, in the best interest of the child as well as other family members. And again, it is important that the child not consider these unpleasant effects of his nonconformity to be parental punishments or hostility. The parent should strive to maintain a perfectly passive, benevolent attitude, which may of course involve expression of regret that the child has had to go through painful experiences. In no event, however, should the parent assume these consequences of the child's acts for him. Wide-ranging experience of implementing this method with hundreds of families has revealed that the child will not consider the parental attitude outlined above to be hostile or mean *if* the parental logic is obvious, *if* beyond his parents' attitude he can recognize a consistent order which regulates his parents' conduct as well as his own, and *if* the consequences are not imposed in an arbitrary way through the strength or "authority" of an adult.

Although this method is recognized as one of the most powerful available to parents, for many, it is one of the most difficult to acquire and use since most parents have not been trained to think in this way. For many more, the fine distinction between "consequences" and punishment may be difficult to establish. While the use of natural consequences is just as uncomfortable for the child as is punishment, from a psychological viewpoint, the difference is very great. Consequences are acceptable to the child, while punishment is at best only tolerable because (1) children are far more responsive to psychological influence than to physical punishment and because (2) the common sense of the child will soon make him realize the logical reason for the result he has experienced.

The successful application of this method of education requires imagination, thought, and deliberation. Consequences must have an inner logic understandable to the child. For example, if a child does not come home from swimming at the pool on time, he may be told he cannot go next week, but telling him he may not go if he does not eat his dinner has no inherent logic. Consequences are *not* retaliations but rather the natural result of misbehavior. To say, "You did not behave, so you must…" is to punish; while to say, "As long as you misbehave, it will be impossible for you to…" is not. The latter statement is an invitation to improve since it emphasizes what will follow in the future more than it emphasizes what did happen in the past. Instead of closing the issue, it opens the door for future improvement and adjustment.

The loud and unruly child is punished when mother says, "Go to your room and stay there. I can't stand your behavior anymore." He is shown the consequences of his behavior when his mother says, "I'm sorry that you cannot stay here with us if you disturb us. Please go to your room until you feel you can behave properly." If the child were to hesitate, mother might add, "You may either go alone or I will take you." While in both cases mother must insist that her child leave the room, in the punishing method the isolation is final, ending the episode. The logical consequences method, on the other hand, allows the child to return as soon as he feels ready, leaving to him the decision to change the situation.

It is extremely important to leave a choice for the child, particularly in tense situations when he refuses to comply. Although adults who act logically instead of psychologically may feel that for them this difference is of little importance, for the child, the difference is very important. If dad asks Jimmy, "Do you want to leave the room by yourself? Or shall I carry you out?" he allows his son to feel more important and less reluctant because he is given a choice. While from our adult viewpoint the unpleasant duty of leaving the room remains in either case equally unpleasant, this is not the case from the child's point of view. If the child does not answer in such a situation, the parent can always say, "If you do not want to go by yourself, I will have to carry you." Such an approach will usually save the situation in cases where the child is not yet excessively hostile or stubborn. If he is adamant or large enough so the parent cannot carry him out, the choice then becomes one of either the child or the parent leaving the room. However, the child will usually respond to the first choice he is given if he knows from previous experience that his *parents mean what they say.*

The tone of voice used by parents also distinguishes consequences from punishment. When an adult speaks in an angry, harsh voice, the result is punishment from the viewpoint of the child. However, if the adult maintains a friendly attitude, he or she is emphasizing that it is the logic and order of the situation rather than the adult's personal desire or power which has to be observed. In the first case, one takes a stand against the child leading to his feeling of rejection, while in the second one objects only to the child's behavior without threatening his feeling of personal value. The distinction between the tone of voice used in each case expresses a difference in relationship. The punishing tone disrupts the relationship while that which requires order through consequences maintains the feeling of friendliness and sympathy.

Within this context, especially in difficult cases, parents should be wary of exaggerated or misplaced sympathy since it may weaken them just at the moment when their child may learn by experience. For example, promises, whether solicited or voluntary, are pitfalls to be avoided. Such misplaced sympathy is often the cause of parents succumbing to the clever efforts of their children to talk themselves out of their predicament. Hence, in the critical moment of pleading or promising, the child should not immediately be given another chance. However, because the past should never be held over him as a weapon, once the consequence has taken place, he should always have another chance at another later time. The moment when the natural consequence technique is being employed is not the time for talking, but rather for action.

Perhaps we should now make a distinction between two of the key terms we have been using. Sometimes, it is possible to allow the natural flow of events to occur without interference from parents. This result is known as a *natural consequence*. In the example cited above, which involved a child who oversleeps, that child would just naturally be late for school and have to face the displeasure of a teacher or principal if he took no action on his own behalf. However, at other times, adults may need to structure events that logically follow a misbehavior. The outcome here is called a *logical consequence.* Since natural consequences represent the pressure of reality without any specific action by parents, they are nearly always effective and beneficial. Logical consequences, however, cannot be applied in a power struggle, except with extreme caution because they may very easily deteriorate into punitive acts or at least be interpreted as punishment or retaliation.

The use of either logical or natural consequences requires a significant reorientation in typical adult thinking. When appropriate consequences are accurately and consistently applied, they are found to be remarkably effective and can result in significant reductions of intra-family friction as they increase harmony within the family. Children seem quick to see the justice of such consequences and usually accept them without resentment. Often a natural consequence to fit an act will occur to an adult after just a bit of thought. We may only need to ask ourselves what would happen if we did not interfere. In some situations, of course, there may be no apparent consequence, so parents must wait for another occasion or attempt to create an appropriate situation. In such cases, it is often productive to simply discuss the problem with the child to see what he or she has to offer. This suggestion can, of course, be helpful in any family problem situation.

Too often, however, when parents feel exasperated by disturbing behavior, they are inclined to brush it aside with a "be quiet," "don't do that," "stop it," "quit it," or "hurry up" kind of admonition. This sort of response has been called "shooing flies" because parents wave the problem aside much as one might a bothersome insect. While such behavior may seem to reflect an apparently natural reaction, it is ineffective as a training method. In most cases, such behavior terminates only after the parent has finally become either forceful or violent. When we as parents act in this way, we succeed only in training our child to believe that she does not have to mind us until we become angry or violent. Since this is not what we want, we must learn to avoid this reaction in our response to a child's bid for attention. If a parent truly desires that the child either do or not do something or that she in some other way comply with order, it is necessary that the adult give the matter his or her full attention from the outset and then stand by until the requirements of the situation have been met. This is simply a matter of taking time to train the child correctly.

If little Jerry continues to punch and hit his brother as mother drives them to the party, it will not help the boys to learn order if mother repeatedly asks them, tells them, then shouts at them to stop. Instead, her quiet insistence or use of an appropriate consequence will be much more effective as a training method. No words will be necessary as she stops the car along the curb to await the return of order. Very simply, her sons must behave if they want to continue their journey. If mother had earlier taken time to point out that she cannot drive while disorder prevails in the car, she can now quietly insist on such order. On other occasions, other appropriate consequences may be just as effective.

It does no good to attempt to change a child's behavior by nagging since that child will merely tune out what his parent is saying or shouting. Words are not our only means of communication, and in some cases, they may be the least effective. Again, at risk of repeating, if parents *truly* intend to bring about desired results while training the child to recognize and respect order, they *must* be conscious of the influence of their own behavior. To change our child's behavior, we, as parents, must very often use ourselves as tools to bring about specific results.

Parents must continually realize that they no longer live in an autocratic society that can control children, but rather in a democratic society designed to guide them. Within our democracy, there will be many times when parents will experience excellent opportunities to allow the consequences of their child's behavior to take effect. Due to feelings of sympathy or pity and the desire to protect the child, however, many parents deprive their offspring of the opportunity to experience appropriately helpful consequences. Then they may compound their error by punishing the child. To replace such faulty parental behavior with carefully selected natural or logical consequences, most adults will need to reorient their own thinking concerning child guidance. As adults, parents have no right to punish other persons having status equal to their own, but they do have an obligation to guide and direct the emotional and personal development of their children. And while they have no right to impose their will, they do have an obligation to refuse to give in to the excessive demands of the young.

Learn to Avoid and to Manage Conflict

Parents can avoid and/or manage conflict with their children if *they stop and think, remain flexible,* and *display restraint* in their response to childhood misbehavior. When conflicts do arise, mothers and fathers should work to *relieve* the *pressure* and *tension* of the situation, *arouse* the child's *interest,* and in other ways endeavor to *win* the child's *confidence.* Probably the most potent tool the parent has in dealing with conflict, however, is to *withdraw* from the conflict situation.

(1) To avoid conflict, stop and think:

Parents who act on impulse or permit themselves to be carried away by momentary notions or whims will usually feel at a loss when dealing with problems of childhood. This is because most children are persistent and deliberate in devising new and effective ways and means of achieving their purpose of evading unpleasant duties while at the same time soliciting parental attention and concern. Since children are astute observers, they are quick to discover and take advantage of the slightest indication of weakness in their parents as well as in other adults. As the child adapts himself to each individual and each situation, he will know how to vary his tactics to suit mother and father and to have his way with both. In one case he may coax and beg, in another he may display self-pity through use of tears, while in still another he may turn to stubborn defiance.

To determine the methods of training that will be best suited to any specific set of circumstances, parents must first carefully observe the child's behavior. Then, having decided on the best procedure to follow in a particular situation, an adult will find that he or she can move to change the bad habit most successfully by recognizing and giving free rein to the unpleasant consequences which logically result from it. Since the sequence of cause and effect must be made obvious to the child, this process must always be based upon careful thought and reflection. Having first considered what the child's reaction may be, his parents will realize that he may not calmly accept unpleasant experiences without crying, a struggle, or perhaps some new mischief-response. Probably the most important principle to remember at this point is that one can work productively on only one aspect of the child's behavior at a time. Parents who attempt to do more may find that they seem unable to accomplish anything.

Child training is most effective when employed persistently but sparingly. To do so requires that the means of intervention be created using clear common sense. For this reason, it is essential that parents be helped to eliminate the emotions of worry, irritability, and anger—however understandable they may seem—because they are expressions of weakness and futility. Most actions that result from the sense of weakness which accompanies these emotions are almost certain to be wrong since they arise only when we are at our wits' end or when we feel we have yielded too much ground and must now take a firm stand. While it is understandable that malice or hostility in children may move parents to indignation or anger, the parent who gives vent to these emotions is only defeating his or her own purpose. For example, the parent who becomes sufficiently enraged to slap a child must realize that the slap was not the act of an educator but rather that of an infuriated human being. Although some parents may in some cases justify such acts to themselves, they should realize that neither the act nor the justification will be of any lasting value in training the child.

Unless the parent—or educator—is confident in both his method and its efficiency, the education or training which he or she imparts will lack effectiveness. Parental loss of control indicates clearly to both child and parent the latter's loss of self-confidence. For this reason, when the parent becomes overexcited by a child or is for any other reason in danger of losing self-control, it is advisable to simply drop everything for the moment and leave the room. Only when the parent has regained her poise and calm will she be capable of reflecting objectively and deciding rationally what should be done. This will take time from the busy schedule of the adult—a hurried mother, for example, who may feel that she is so overburdened with worry and work that she has no time to think. In reality, however, this procedure takes much less time than is required for continual reprimands, admonishments, and punishments which are not only ineffectual but also harmful. Use of small segments of time for reflection may not only exempt the parent from a great deal of turmoil and agitation but will conserve her valuable time.

The preceding advice does not apply, of course, in genuine emergency situations that require the parent to avert acute danger by immediate actions. Since nothing an adult may do will have lasting educational value in such moments of danger, the parent must bear in mind that opportunities for instruction and discipline will come later when the crucial moment has passed. Since situations that involve real danger are far less frequent than parents in their anxiety for their child may be led to believe, parental reprimands usually function more as a release for parental tensions than they do as a means for training for future prevention.

(2)   To avoid conflict, be flexible:

Parents who fail to observe and reflect before they act tend to follow set routines which include use of rigid methods that were either (a) absorbed from their own parents or (b) continued through sheer force of habit and inertia from earlier similar or related occasions. Since inflexible parents frequently respond predictably to their children's misbehavior with the same old routine of scolding, coaxing, shouting, or threats of physical punishment, the child usually knows well in advance how his parents will react to any given behavior he may display. As the child learns to take the attitudes of his parents for granted, he adapts himself to them with the end result that parental effort and admonition makes no real or lasting impression on the child. Within this context, the reason why rigid methods fail so often is that they neglect the specific needs and requirements of each individual child since the same child cannot always be treated in the same way. To be effective in influencing the child, a parent must learn to adjust himself to the different stages of the child's development.

By watching effects or results, by experimenting with new approaches and by varying and adapting methods, a parent can determine the most adequate means of influencing each individual child. But even the amount of attention the child requires is not a stable quantity. During some periods of the child's life, for example, he will flatly refuse to listen to advice, while at other times he may be very amenable to instruction. While on some occasions he will voluntarily seek parental advice, under other circumstances he will insist on making his own decisions. Parents often need help to realize that (a) a rigid attitude on their part will not allow for the varying needs of each child and that (b) really effective methods of training must always be adjustable to each specific situation and change, which may accompany that child's pattern of growth.

The suggestion that parents remain flexible, allowing their methods to change frequently, does not contradict our earlier statement of the importance of parents remaining consistent. Standards and social requirements must be firmly established, remaining definite and constant, while at the same time parental efforts to aid the child to understand and comply must be allowed to vary and adapt as necessary.

(3) To avoid conflict, display restraint:

The need for parents to exercise the greatest possible self-restraint in their attempts to influence children is a basis for child training and management which is very seldom fulfilled. The most effective methods of education are those that make themselves superfluous as soon as possible. Such methods have as their purpose the transformation of the child from an irresponsible object of discipline into an independent individual who displays a matured sense of personal responsibility. Parents who follow a policy of observation, which includes a minimum of intervention in the child's activities, find that when they do exert their influence, its effect will then be more beneficial. In addition, of course, they will not run the unnecessary risk of interfering with the vitally important growth of self-reliance in the lives of their children.

Whenever possible, it is best to allow children to learn from experience, which can be done only to the degree that parents learn to exercise restraint. The tendency of parents to fail to recognize that it is not their duty to do everything for their children springs either from undue fear or from desire to prove their own power and importance. The fact that a child can assume duties of his own at a very early age, which he can carry out on his own initiative is, of course, not to suggest that children should ever be neglected. All children need tenderness and love as well as encouragement and stimulation. The parent should never be aloof but instead should take positive action while exercising care to intervene no more than is absolutely necessary.

(4) To avoid conflict, work to relieve the pressure or tension of the situation:

Since innumerable situations occur that have potential to incite a child to hostility and defiance, parents need to know how to overcome resistance without conflict. Probably the most effective method, especially with young children, consists of diverting the child's attention from the point of controversy. One of the most successful means of doing so is through use of humor, which should not be confused with buffoonery. The successful use of wit with children seems to lie in the manner of speech employed, often not so much in the area of meaning as of inflection. As a parent, our goal must be to help the child laugh with us. Needless to say, the joke should never be on the child.

Since so much depends on attendant circumstances, the turn of a phrase, or the tone of one's voice, examples are not easy to present. The parents' own feeling of merriment or appreciation of the amusing side of a situation is often enough. In other cases, a funny story, droll grimace, or humorous gesture may break the ice. Regardless of the circumstance, however, the adult should always remain friendly and under control, regardless of how rebellious, sulky, or obstinate the child's initial behavior may be.

Since obstinacy, rudeness, insolence, and disobedience are often only attempts to conceal a feeling of hurt, loneliness, or neglect, warm parental expressions of understanding and empathy often work wonders in softening the child's repressed defiance. Often, an overt sign of willingness to help the child will almost immediately relieve hostile tension, but not unless that child has faith in the honesty of the desire of the adult to render genuine aid. Unfortunately, since many children lack just such confidence in their own parents, the first order of business must become the reestablishment of a sense of trust and confidence. When parents truly care about their children's feelings to the point where they desire to establish or reestablish a genuine sharing of trust and mutual confidence, the parent must openly display her feeling of empathy, congruence (honesty), and positive regard (caring).

(5)   To avoid conflict, arouse the child's interest:

Since children respond much more readily to influence when parents are able to arouse their interest, much depends on the adult's body language and the tone of voice used when speaking to children. A lively natural expression will prompt the child to take notice while the deadly monotony of repeated explanation, commands, or reproval is sure to lead to an apathetic reception at best. Further, attempts at baby talk often bore the child who may soon come to see them as ridiculous. Dull, lifeless, or even harsh tones usually provoke either unresponsiveness or a response that clearly implies a desire to be left alone.

On those occasions, when it seems *impossible* to effect rapport with a child who seems so *obstinate* that no amount of effort seems to influence him, a parent may be inclined to lose self-control because of an inability to manage her own feelings of helplessness. The one course of action that can be pursued in such a situation when a parent is *completely at a loss* as to what to do or to save a situation which may seem completely out of hand consists of first determining what the child expects the parent to do next and then doing just the opposite. The adult can detect what the child expects by observing what she herself feels inclined to do. Since the parents' own reactions usually correspond completely with the child's expectation, they will often reveal exactly what he wants and will try to provoke. When the parent then does the opposite of what is expected, the child is caught off guard and moved off balance, which not only arouses his interest but also forces him to reconsider his own attitude or position.

Displaying indifference when the child expects annoyance or an outburst, acknowledging his superiority when he expects to be subjected, praising him when he expects scolding, and giving him a free hand when he expects to be stopped are tactics that both release tension and make the child more receptive to further actions. At the very least, parents can use this approach to gain the time necessary to permit new approaches to both the child and the situation. In many cases, it is possible for the parent to use this period of mutual relaxation for friendly talk to which the child may now be more willing to listen.

(6) To avoid conflict, win the child's confidence:

As parents become increasingly successful in gaining the confidence of a child, their influence over the child will become correspondingly stronger. However, the parent has not won over the child until that child is no longer in opposition and voluntarily accepts parental guidance. Before this can occur, parents must realize that the child's obedience will depend not only on his belief in the parent's firmness and consistency but also on his faith in that adults' goodwill and practical reliability. Although the child may feel greatly attached to the parent, he may remain hostile and inflexible, making cooperation impossible if he detects any indication of a struggle for power on the part of his parent.

Especially in disturbing situations, it may take more than the surprise tactics outlined in the preceding section to win the child's confidence. The best means to this end must always involve benevolence and genuine friendliness. Children are exceedingly perceptive and will quickly distinguish between that which is true and honest and that which is not. For this reason, a friendly but genuine tone must be maintained, especially during trying or critical moments. To do so it is essential that parents avoid personal punishment and reprimands and that they allow the child to learn from the purely impersonal and logical consequences of his behavior. While harsh words will repel the child and only increase his antagonism, the policy suggested here will allow a parent to avoid the necessity of placing himself in an unfriendly light.

Any adult who displays a friendly, active interest in a child can usually be assured of that child's willing attention and ready response when necessary. However, mere indulgence will not gain the confidence of the child nor will laxity impress him as goodwill since from the child's viewpoint, it is seen only as a sign of weakness. Experience reveals that a child can be won over most easily when the parent displays a real interest in that child and in those of his affairs which he chooses to share with his parent. Parents who will participate in joint activity with a child as wholeheartedly and intently as does the child himself by conversing with him, playing with him, taking him for walks, telling him stories, or whatever else may seem appropriate—without any kind of condescension or possessiveness—are likely to move with their child beyond the reach of serious conflict.

(7)   To avoid conflict, withdraw from the situation:

In some cases, the approaches discussed in the preceding paragraphs are insufficient or for some other reason fail to generate the desired effect. Since most childhood misbehavior is for the benefit of parents either to keep them busy or to defeat them, the act of withdrawal or physical removal of the parent from the scene often yields dramatic results. Mothers who learn to extricate themselves from the undue demands and pressures of their children soon learn that the behavior of the child does change when they refuse to continue being that child's unwitting victim. For example, the so-called dependent child is usually a very demanding child who uses a real or assumed weakness or inability to put his mother into his service. However, if mother refuses to play this role, the child often overcomes his weakness or inability and begins to function on his own. Since the disobedient child is usually also a tyrannical child, he is probably very well prepared to resist parental pressure while remaining capable of forcing his parents to do what he wants rather than giving in to their wishes. For this reason, (a) he can learn the futility of force if his parents are careful not to yield to him, but (b) all parental attempts to force him into submission will serve no useful purpose.

A common childhood behavior well designed to stifle the best of parental efforts is the temper tantrum. But since even the best tantrum is worthless if there is no audience to be frightened or impressed, the simple expedient of leaving the child alone is one of the most effective means for correcting such inclinations. The same is true of fighting among children, which is usually for mother's benefit. If she can learn to stop interfering and refrain from her attempts to first separate the children and then to judge, the children will learn to get along with each other and to solve their own conflicts. The mother who will remove herself in any conflict situation, preferably by withdrawing into the bathroom behind a locked door until the turmoil has subsided, as we shall point out later in detail, can contribute to the harmony of her family. This sort of tactical retreat is particularly advisable when mother feels she is no longer able to control herself or to "stand it" because she is "at her wits end." If such a mother can place a closed door between herself and her child before she loses her temper and becomes involved, she can later emerge from her voluntary retreat—again the warm, friendly person she both wants to and ought to be.

Eliminate Criticism, Minimize Mistakes

When parents center their attention on a child's mistakes, they direct his attention from the positive to the negative. The child becomes afraid to make mistakes, which leads to more mistakes. Parental emphasis on mistakes in dealing with children leads directly to discouragement. This emphasis is seriously counterproductive since in dealing with children we cannot build on weakness, only on strength. For this reason, when children attempt to perform any activity, we should make the emphasis of our response to it as positive as possible. In doing so, we give the child both pleasure and encouragement. In response to such encouragement, the child will be inclined to perform again in positive ways. Unfortunately, however, many parents expect too much of their children, and may seem to expect perfection. As Johnny displays his laboriously written note to his uncle, for example, father should comment on his thoughtfulness and well-formed letters, not on his poor spelling and penmanship. Parents who (1) center their child's attention upon that which he or she can do well, (2) give encouragement, and (3) express confidence in their child's abilities may make childhood mistakes seem to fade away through lack of nourishment.

Many parents seem to almost constantly correct or admonish their children as they continually supervise them in attempts to prevent mistakes. Such behavior reveals fear that the children will develop poor attitudes and bad habits as well as lack of faith in the children. From the child's point of view, it is both discouraging and humiliating. As a child focuses his energy on negative attempts to avoid making mistakes, he saps the energy needed for progress toward achievement. Such a child will also gain the impression that unless he is perfect he will be unloved and will have no value. As he is constantly corrected, a child not only "learns" that he is wrong but also becomes increasingly afraid of making errors. Such fear can lead to an increasing reluctance to try since in so doing he might do wrong. For this reason, as a child grows and develops, he or she must learn that we all make mistakes and that very few are disasters. Perfection is an unattainable goal, and striving for it during childhood leads much more often to feelings of despair and giving up than it does to improvement.

It is important for parents to realize that adults as well as children often have to make a mistake to realize what the mistake is and to realize how it is a mistake. For this reason, we as parents must not only have the courage to be imperfect ourselves but to allow our children to be imperfect as well. It is only in this way that our children can maintain the courage necessary to minimize their fear of mistakes as they direct their attention toward positive achievement. Parents who maintain the attitude of "If you make a mistake, make a good one so you will never have to make that mistake again" (i.e., have courage to act, then learn from your mistake) will help to minimize fear and discouragement in their children.

The act of making an honest mistake is not nearly as important as what we do about it afterward. When your children come to you in tears to report "I burned the cookies," an appropriate and encouraging reply might be "Yes, I can see that. I know you didn't want to do it and it won't help to cry. Of course you feel bad, but let's find out why it happened, okay?"

Faced with a noncritical direction in which to move in his or her response, the child can stop crying and examine the situation. Upon discovering that the youngster miscalculated the time on the automatic timer, mother might say, "Let's clean off the table so you can try again."

Often, when a child makes a mistake, it is the result of faulty judgment or inexperience. Since the child may already be distressed over the results of his behavior, parents only add insult to injury when they punish or condemn his efforts. In the example cited above, the mother turned evidence of failure into a learning situation for the child. She did not scold over the wasted food nor did she criticize for error. Rather, in a matter-of-fact way, she demonstrated to her child that mistakes need not be considered disasters and that the real need in such a situation is to discover where the mistake in judgment occurred and correct it. While she did acknowledge her daughter's dismay and frustration, she did so without appearing overly concerned. This tact allowed the mother to quietly lead her daughter out of the situation by joining her in a search for the reason for the mistake. Finally, she dissipated discouragement through an offer of sympathy and support as she simultaneously encouraged her daughter to try again.

When parents display a generally critical attitude, they may unknowingly promote an incidental deviation from desirable behavior into the beginnings of a serious and potentially permanent fault or deficiency. For example, many children stutter occasionally, but the defect disappears if no issue is made of it. However, since parents often feel responsible for preventing or correcting undesirable behavior, they may feel something must be done, so they press the child for change. But far from providing the incentive to change, such parental response will in many cases increase the difficulty. When this happens, it occurs for one of two reasons. It either brings the child added attention or the child can use the situation to win and be victorious in defeating adult pressure. When this sort of thing occurs, criticism does not teach the child constructively but rather stimulates the child to maintain his deficiencies or objectionable behaviors. In cases of this sort, it is important that parents provide *instruction without criticism* coupled with encouragement directed toward the child's self-discovery of his or her abilities.

As was suggested earlier, many acts of wrongdoing are the result of mistaken goals. When an objectionable act has a purpose, however, it is no longer a mistake; it is now a fault. The shy child, for example, has a purpose in his shyness. For this reason, it will be futile to tell him to stop being shy. And by paying attention to the fault, which is really a mistaken approach to finding a place in the group, we merely reinforce it.

By identifying himself as the shy child in his family, little Mark is able to achieve a certain distinction. As people try to get him to respond, he becomes the center of their attention. For him, this result of his shyness is a reward for certain behaviors, which he has displayed. Since shyness pays off for him, why should he stop it? He will squeeze all the attention he can out of the situation.

Parents who desire that their child overcome a fault must discover the purpose which motivates that behavior. Then, without talking about it, they must act in such a way that the purpose of the behavior is no longer fulfilled. Such "actions" might in fact involve doing nothing or it could involve avoiding first impulse or perhaps failing to respond as expected. Suppose Mark, in our previous example, were to fail to receive overconcerned reactions. If this was the case, there would be no point in his continuing to be shy in his reactions to others. The payoff would be gone. But how could this result be best achieved? His mother, for example, could introduce him in a casual manner but with pride and, when he failed to respond, could simply continue her conversation with her friends. By taking such action, the boy's shyness would be ignored or, at best, minimized. If the friend were to upset mother's plan by saying something such as, "My, he is a shy boy, isn't he?" Mother need only respond by saying, "He isn't shy. He just doesn't feel like talking now, but he will later." The same general procedure should be used every time Mark is shy in a group.

If the child was to use crying as a technique to gain attention, casual acceptance of his right to cry together with a statement that he may join the activity of the family when he is ready would suffice. The purpose of many a "crybaby" is to gain undue attention. If the child is in some way physically hurt, his parents must provide the necessary medical treatment; but if his purpose is to only gain adult attention, they must act in another way. In the latter case, they must refrain from talking about the crying and must not identify the child with the crying. In other words, they must ignore it. To be of maximum effect, this technique of removing the results of attention-seeking behavior and minimizing fault-finding must be accompanied by the practice of paying genuine attention to the child when he is happy and cooperative.

As we deal with such behavior in our children, we must make a particular effort to separate the deed from the doer because of the unfortunate habit many people have acquired of labeling or name-calling. Children are not liars or scatterbrained or tattletales or crybabies. They are misdirected children. When we label a child, we see him as we have labeled him, and so does he. He identifies with our label that reinforces his faulty self-concept, which in turn further prevents him from moving in a more constructive direction.

Children need to be recognized not as bad children but as good children who misbehave because they are unhappy and have found that their misbehavior pays off for them. When adults can recognize that it is not the child but rather his behavior that is unacceptable, the child may sense this recognition and respond to this shift in expectation. As children become increasingly aware of our faith in them, that awareness provides added encouragement toward overcoming difficulties, which in turn grow less as both parents and children learn to minimize them and replace them with more productive acceptable behaviors.

Encourage the Child

It has been said that encouragement is for the child's development what water is for a plant since neither can grow well without the appropriate form of nurturance. The difficulties of childhood are always based on some form of discouragement. They may stem from persons in the child's environment who have disheartened the child or from unsuccessful attempts to master certain tasks or to acquire certain abilities which may have caused the child to lose faith in his own capability. Whatever the reasons for the child's difficulties may be, however, and regardless of the guise in which they appear, it is the duty of the child's parents to bolster his self-confidence.

We now know that a child who misbehaves is a discouraged child. Hence, encouragement is more important than almost any other activity when raising a child. It is so important that its lack can be considered to be the primary cause of misbehavior during childhood and adolescence. However, in hundreds of very subtle ways, parents indicate that they consider children to be unskilled, inept, and generally inferior. By tone of voice and by action, this message is clearly transmitted to children who want to be an integrated part of the family. Unfortunately, in their attempts to gain recognition to find a place and to make their mark in life, many children meet with frequent if not almost constant discouragement.

Rather than allowing children to test their strength and performance, parents constantly confront young people with prejudicial doubts concerning childhood judgment and ability. Having done so, the adults then attempt to justify their behavior by establishing standards at various age levels at which their children may be trusted to undertake various activities. Johnny wants to help or try something new. "Let me do it myself," he cries. "No, you're too young. You'll have to wait until you're older," his mother replies.

A bit at a time, little by little, again and again, we stifle the child's attempts to find a place in his family through being useful. In so doing, we discourage our children without realizing the significance of our acts. We reject our children's efforts as weak and inferior. It is our attitude that produces this atmosphere of discouragement. We lack faith in our child's ability to perform and function now. We assume that since he is now so small, both physically and mentally, he is incomplete, hence incapable. We assume that he will be able to do things only when he is older. And, of course, parents are busy and they do have nice things that break.

As we observe the child's behavior, we are given direct clues to his evaluation of himself—his self-estimate. The child who doubts his own value and ability will clearly demonstrate it through his deficiencies. He will no longer seek to belong through being useful or through participation or by making contributions. In his discouragement, he will turn to provocative and/or useless behavior. As he becomes convinced that he is inadequate or cannot contribute, he determines that he will at least be noticed in one way or another. There is some distinction in being known as a bad boy, just as there is in being of value. To be spanked or otherwise disciplined is better than to be ignored. Such a child has now become convinced that for him, there is no hope of gaining his place through cooperative behavior.

All human beings make mistakes. When a child makes a mistake or fails to accomplish a certain goal, adults must very carefully avoid words or actions which indicate that they consider him to be a failure. Again, parents must separate the doer from the deed. A statement such as "I'm sorry it didn't work out for you" focuses on the event and not the individual. Both parents and their children must clearly realize that failure only indicates lack of skill and in no way determines the value of the individual. We all need courage in our encounters with life. Such courage is found in those who can fail or make mistakes without a lowering of self-esteem. Without courage, discouragement and defeat are inevitable.

Parents must learn to encourage their offspring effectively. As they do so, they must be especially careful to avoid discouragement by overprotection and humiliation. In fact, any act or word that undermines a child's faith in himself is discouraging. Conversely, whenever we in any way support a child to continue to develop a more confident and courageous self-concept, we offer productive encouragement. As parents act, however, they must continually take note of the results of their efforts to enhance self-concept. Such encouragement must then become a continuous process devoted to giving the child a clear sense of accomplishment and self-respect.

The first demand made upon any human being is to be self-sufficient. A child needs to learn how to take care of himself, and this process begins at birth. In their honest efforts to be good parents, however, some mothers/fathers* become severely overprotective. Often, in an effort to encourage their children to be happy, they unknowingly discourage the child's efforts to be self-sufficient. To remedy this, mother must stop and examine her own behavior. If the child displays temper tantrums, for example, she must stop falling for such behavior. When a tantrum occurs, mother may let the child cry if that is the child's decision. Mother need only provide toys for the child to play with and then leave that child to his own resources. This would be encouragement. A definite training time should be set aside each day when the child can be left to take care of himself, perhaps during morning hours when older children will be in school and mother will be busy with household or other tasks.

Of course, it is very difficult to ignore a crying child, but a mother can reinforce her own courage by realizing that love for the child means advancing that child's best interests. To be "a good mother," it is not necessary that she give in to all of the demands of her child. In fact, the child who seems happy only when he or she is the center of attention is not a truly happy child. In children, as in adults, genuine happiness arises from within the self as a result of self-sufficiency and is not dependent on the attention of others.

---

* Just as the pronouns he and she are interchangeable in this text, the label father and mother can also be interchanged.

Healthy children display much courage and will eagerly try to do the things that they see others doing. Listlessness and apathy, on the other hand, are symptoms of deep discouragement. Since living does have its bumps and hurts, children need to learn how to take pain in their stride. A bruised knee will heal, but bruised courage or a bruised self-image may last a lifetime. Mother needs to realize that determined efforts to overprotect her healthy children from being hurt will only indicate to them how incapable she believes they are. By so doing, a mother increases the child's fears of danger and feelings of inadequacy. Children need autonomy to grow and test their ability to cope with wide varieties of situations. Of course, mothers should not be careless; they can be near if the task or risk is too great.

The stimulation of competition between children does not encourage as some adults seem to mistakenly believe. Instead, it emphasizes the hopelessness of the situation to the discouraged child while it creates feelings of apprehension in the successful child who fears he or she may not be able to stay ahead. For this reason, in a competitive situation, the discouraged child may give up while the successful child may become overambitious and set impossible goals. Then unless the successful child is always ahead, he may also learn to consider himself a failure.

Each child can function only in his own right, not as a copy of someone else. Hence, all comparisons are harmful. Unless mothers have faith in their offspring and express it, they will not offer the encouragement that is necessary for healthy personality development. The performance of a discouraged child will improve only if and when his confidence is restored. This is why mothers must avoid the tendency to compare and criticize. Instead, they must learn to point out and acknowledge accomplishments, even those that may seem very small and insignificant in the beginning.

There is, of course, no definite rule or pat answer for encouraging children. It all depends on the child's response since each child identifies what he is with what he does. Any action that supports the child's overambition or his self-estimate of failure will increase his discouragement. But even when discouraged children succeed at something, they often consider it to be only an accident. For this reason, these young people need to have their attention diverted from the perfection of accomplishment to the satisfaction of contribution. However, many children learn to feel that unless their contribution is perfect it is a failure. Parents must work to change this mistaken concept.

Each discouraged child needs help toward a reevaluation of himself and his place in his family. Discouragement and related perfectionism do not come from nowhere. Parents often set excessively high standards of accomplishment, at least in the eyes of the child. They may tell their child that she does not need to be perfect but then, by their example, contradict their own words. For this reason, families need open discussion with all of their children concerning how good one has to be to be "good enough." The child's self-concept is reinforced by her parents' expectations, by their faith or lack of it, and by the words they choose to use. Children who behave in unfriendly (discouraged) ways do so because they lack confidence in their ability to get positive attention from their parents or others. Such children doubt their place in the group and for this reason often feel compelled to make a nuisance of themselves as they seek ways to gain positive attention.

A bully is a child who as a result of having become discouraged assumes that a person is significant only when he can display his power. Here again, we must distinguish between the doer and the deed. Such a child is simply discouraged, not cruel or mean. In his misbehavior, we see a mistaken approach brought about through his discouragement. The most helpful reaction to such behavior is to avoid all discouraging remarks or comments in responding to him. To do so, we must display a faith in his ability to interact fairly and democratically, which can be accomplished most effectively through communication of an attitude, rather than through use of words.

For example, if while visiting neighbors with his mother, little Billy continues to bully the young son of the family being visited, his mother might say, "I'm sorry you feel so cross today, Bill. Since you do not feel like playing, we will go home." Although this procedure will make it necessary for mother to cut short her visit, it will reveal to her son that he may come again only if he is willing to manage his behavior. If mother can demonstrate her love for her son, even though his behavior is unfriendly, she will offer encouragement without condoning misdeeds. When she grants him the right to do wrong, she places upon her son the responsibility for his behavior and indicates that he will have to bear the consequences of his choices and decisions.

Since we cannot protect our children from life, it is essential that we prepare them for it. Condemning misbehavior, overprotecting from the results of misbehavior, and feeling sorry for children as they assume the consequences of their choices are among the most seriously damaging attitudes parents can develop. To do so demonstrates to children that we lack faith in them and their ability to cope with the realities of their lives. Again, parents can build only on strength and not on weakness, but to do so in child-raising often requires much parental courage and discipline. As they work to help each child, parents must recognize each child's need to become self-sufficient in terms of his or her own needs as well as the needs and expectations of others. And they must not expect everlasting effects from one act of encouragement. Encouragement must be continuous to prompt lasting changes in the mistaken self-concept of the discouraged child.

And the use of recognition and encouragement may be used just as effectively in development of character and moral qualities. If any child is to develop a healthy personality, that child must be courageous. This means again that his parents must avoid both actions and statements that might force a reduction in the child's self-confidence. Statements such as the following are encouraging, not discouraging.

"Don't give up."
"All beginnings are difficult."
"Good program."
"Much better."
"We learn from our errors."
"Practice makes perfect."
"Everyone makes mistakes."
"No one was born perfect."

"Good work."

Further, while direct allusions to the child's age may sometimes produce a good effect in this context, they should be used with caution since the child may easily learn to feel he is unable to do something he should have mastered. Experience has revealed that general comments, such as "There's no longer any need for me to help you dress, you can do it," nearly always are preferable when it is possible to use them. Perhaps the best suggestion that can be made in this regard is that parents keep a close check on each child's response to their words to see how that particular child accepts them or rejects them, i.e., whether their effect is encouraging or discouraging.

In pointing out the mistakes in child-raising practice that seem common among "modern parents," we in no way mean to suggest criticism or condemnation of adults who are currently struggling with the role of parenthood. It is an especially difficult and often frustrating role to play in our society because the parents of today are victims of many circumstances beyond their immediate control. However, unless we all learn from our errors, we will be unable to make significant progress. Parents need the courage to be imperfect. We are all going to make mistakes. For this reason, we must acknowledge our errors without a sense of loss of our personal value and worth. Parents, too, need large amounts of courage as well as patience. Each small improvement is a step forward. Each step forward is the source of further encouragement. Above all, we must remember that our goal can never be perfection, only improvement.

Take Time for Training

Sufficient time for training must be an important part of the daily routine of any family, which includes young children. Although the child will pick up much knowledge through observation, he will also need much specific guidance. Training in activities such as how to cross the street safely, how to behave acceptably when with others, how to work, or how to bathe and dress himself properly will, of course, depend on the child's level of development. At no time, however, can effective training be provided by scolding, threat of punishment, or through incidental rewards.

To be maximally effective, each instance of training must be specific and carefully done. Parents who fail to take time for training when it is needed will eventually find that they will be forced by events to take even more time to correct their untrained or poorly trained children. Constant corrections also fail to teach the child because they are criticism and as such provoke and discourage the child. As a consequence of such conflict, the child will become determined not to learn. Instead, he will usually discover the "usefulness" of appearing helpless to get special attention or will initiate a power contest.

Afternoon playtime is usually an ideal time for training in a new skill. Such training can be made part of a game. Wide variations of training aids can be found on the toy market, but a mother can easily make her own. For example, Montessori schools have taught us that large holes punched in cardboard upon which a picture of a shoe has been drawn can serve as an excellent model upon which lacing and tying can be taught. Or a row of large buttons and buttonholes from worn-out clothing can be tacked to a board as an aid to learning and mastering the coordination necessary for buttoning clothing as the child dresses himself. The child who is allowed to participate in the creation of such items can become doubly interested. By involving her child in the preparation of most aids, a mother can appeal to the child's ingenuity and in so doing can foster her developing creativity.

Behavior in automobiles or on buses or airplanes can be taught by devising pretend rides. Similarly, table manners can be taught at doll tea parties. It is also wise to provide children with training in and understanding of unpleasant situations or contingencies. Training in any skill or situation, however, should be repeated in a specific routine sufficiently often until that particular skill is mastered. Also, each skill should be learned separately with the adult displaying confidence and patience in the child's ability to learn. Learning occurs best in a happy, pleasant atmosphere. The use of encouraging phrases such as "Try again, you'll get it," and acknowledgment of each accomplishment will help to make this learning process increasingly enjoyable for both parent and child.

In some situations, it becomes necessary for the parent to teach and then step back to allow the child to work out a difficult part for himself or to let the child practice alone. It is also helpful to show the developing child that there are several or even many ways to cope with certain problems. The child whose wagon is caught by a wheel on a post, for example, may howl and pull with frustration before he is helped to see that by first backing the wagon, he can free it to move ahead. With appropriate help, children can learn to evaluate situations before choosing the appropriate action to take.

When guests are present or even when the family is out in public are *not* times when training should be attempted. In such situations, the child will always act as he or she is accustomed to acting in similar circumstances. If parents want their children to behave properly in public, they will have to train them to do so *at home*. If the child's behavior is not appropriate for the situation, the only practical solution for the parent is to quietly remove the child.

As the family grows, the training needs of younger children may easily be neglected. Parents should be careful that they or older children do not do what younger children should do for themselves. It is necessary to watch for this possibility since older children may use such opportunities to establish a feeling of superiority over those who are younger. Each child needs and deserves his or her own period of training, not only for the skills acquired but also because success during this period leads to a sense of personal accomplishment and satisfaction.

Provide Effective, Creative Guidance

Because it is best for a child to learn by his or her own effort, the practice of introducing the child to new tasks or responsibilities requires special care to avoid discouragement. Each new accomplishment should be a tangible step forward, but if the child is guided too painstakingly, he may easily acquire the impression that the task or responsibility is too difficult for him. Since it is important that he not get the idea that his parents doubt his ability to do the job, it is advisable to give him only a start and then let him try by himself until a result, perhaps the desired result, is produced. When doing so, one must use words carefully since talking is worthwhile only if the child is in a receptive mood for listening and may become counterproductive if it is seen as haranguing.

Immediately after he has done something wrong, a child will appear either rebellious or downcast. For this reason, such times are not good for discussion of that misbehavior. Probably the most productive time for discussion is a quiet, meditative moment when the parent and the child are alone. Quiet time spent sitting together or strolling in a quiet place or the ten or fifteen minutes just before bedtime are occasions which may be used to good advantage.

In all such discussions, the parent or parents must carefully avoid demonstrating superiority over the child, remembering as they do so that their guidance and instruction will be wholly ineffectual in the absence of friendly goodwill. Regardless of the suggestion made, it will be much better received if the parent indicates it is something that *they* can do or work on together, although this spirit of cooperation ought never induce the parent to relieve the child of his responsibilities. More generally, regardless of what is being taught, the adult must make clear that those rules of conduct that the child must learn apply consistently to everyone.

The reason a child will often listen more willingly to persons other than to his own parents is that others often talk with him on a completely equal footing while his own parents may be inclined to stress their own superiority. The more parents tend to do this, the less readily their children will accept their advice and guidance. Children are more willing to recognize parental superiority the less it is brought to their attention and the less parents demand such recognition. For this reason, parents should not only feel free to treat their children as equals but should recognize the wisdom in doing so, in spite of their own obvious advantages in experience, knowledge, and perspective or judgment.

It does no harm for the parent to admit personal weaknesses and failings. We are all human. Parents who are frank to admit that they do not know everything will avoid giving their children false answers or incorrect information, which is probably among the surest of ways to lose their respect. Since the perception and insight of children is keen, and since their understanding of their surroundings is more acute than many parents often suspect, they will often consider any efforts by parents to gloss over their own frailties as simply an additional parental weakness or limitation.

A helpful technique is to appeal to the child's initiative since it makes him feel grown up and stimulates him to concentrate his efforts in a definite direction. This means of reconciling the child to the necessity of education or training can be employed whenever it is necessary to correct his behavior, introduce him to a new task, or break him of a bad habit. By standing aside, while taking a benevolent friendly "I'm sure you can do it if you'll just try" attitude, and while displaying a willingness to cooperate whenever necessary, the parent can avoid conflict while guiding the child. Faults, defects, or other elements of the personality that can be subject to educational influence may in this way be transformed into more tangible, hence solvable problems.

Although the desired results may not be produced immediately, this position allows the parent every opportunity to encourage the child and, in so doing, to strengthen that parent's position as a concerned friend. Regardless of the nature of the difficulty and no matter how long or tedious the process may be, using this basic approach, the parent will be able to sustain a friendly bearing by acknowledging and emphasizing each sign of progress, however delicate it may appear. As this attitude serves to clear away conflict-laden and conflict-generating elements of the parent-child relationship, opponents may become allies who can work together cooperatively toward mutually attainable goals.

Earlier in the chapter, we pointed out that reward and punishment are no longer commonly accepted as standard methods of child-raising because we now realize that both are merely arbitrary expressions of parental authority and as such are injurious to healthy childhood growth and development. Although the child may eventually submit to oppression, in doing so, his antagonism will be aroused.

While it is true that every child must eventually learn to subordinate himself, this subordination must never be to the autocratic power of any individual. The only conformity that we can legitimately expect of a child in a democratic society is a conformity to the social scheme that binds all members of the society equally. The general laws of natural social order will be sufficiently strong and definite to impress the child with the unpleasant and pleasant consequences of his behavior, only if his parents refrain from interfering by unnecessarily protecting the child. This, of course, does not suggest that parents should assume a completely passive and indifferent attitude, especially when danger is involved.

The role of parents necessitates that they be available to assist the child in her efforts to recognize the requirements of any given situation and to adapt herself to it. Beyond this, however, each child needs the experience of learning to manage her own life, which means making choices and decisions and taking responsibility for them. In implementing this position, it is best for parents to eliminate the word *must* from their conversation with children, replacing it whenever possible with the words "you may." To fail to do so will deprive the child of the sense of being a free agent who can act voluntarily to frame her own destiny. The word *must* suggests the arbitrary dictation of individual authority, while the word *may* suggests the natural order of things.

More specifically, if one considers the reaction of a five-year-old to the order, "You must set the table" as opposed to the statements such as "Please set the table" or "You may set the table if you wish," the possible difference in effect may become more obvious. The point here is two-fold: (1) Parents should emphasize correct procedure rather than that which is unacceptable, and (2) they should do so by avoiding negative commands while providing friendly encouragement. An appeal to desire for recognition and self-respect will often prove to be effective in guiding the child toward the desired end. And a little friendly encouragement, especially when one can point out a discrepancy between the child's potential performance and his current achievement—perhaps with a statement such as "I am sure you can do better, Bobby"—will often provide additional impetus.

The mutual confidence born of complete comradeship is always the best means of winning the trust of a child. As suggested earlier, parents who freely and frankly admit their own imperfections are able to create a closer relationship with their children. But it is not enough for a parent to allow the child to regard fathers and mothers as vulnerable human beings; parents must consider the child in the same light. Some parents disregard even the most obvious social rights of their children by such acts as prying into the older child's secrets or correspondences, humiliating him by making light of his opinions or sentiments, breaking promises, or betraying his confidences. Yet these same parents may express amazement and act offended when their children fail to confide in them.

Parents cannot demand confidence nor can they take it forcibly, since it must be earned. Mothers and fathers have no one to blame but themselves if their children do not regard them as trustworthy friends. In circumstances that reveal lack of mutual confidence, parents should not be surprised to find that their influence over their children is purely superficial and that the children may choose to turn for guidance to other persons who inspire that confidence. And since genuine trust must be mutual, each child needs demonstrations of parental confidence. For example, all children, even before they reach school age, can be entrusted—not ordered or commanded—to do many useful duties around the house as part of the ongoing effort to meet family needs. As the child grows older, his contributions may grow from running errands and doing minor marketing chores to more responsible contributions, which may involve requests to talk things over or provide his opinion and advice on key family matters.

As both parents and child benefit from growth in mutual confidence, parents should—and many will—begin to revise their belief that it is in the child's best interest that adults know all they think and do. As parents grow with their child in mutual trust, they should learn that the more they force or insist on frankness, the less likely they will be to receive it. As incessant inquiry becomes inquisitiveness, the child's life will close to parental view with continued pressure often forcing the child into lies and hypocrisy. Although treatment of children with proper discretion and tact can lead those children to a willingness to confide implicitly, as a result of the wrong approaches and attitudes so frequently used by parents, relatively few have any real notion of what does go on in the minds of their children.

Within this context, parents often ask the following question: To what extent should a parent reveal to a child what he or she knows about the child? We know that it is generally futile to ask a child the reason he performs certain socially unacceptable acts or otherwise misbehaves because he most often simply does not know the real reasons. Although parents are often infuriated when the child says he does not know why he did what they just saw him do, in most cases, he in fact does not know because he has followed his impulses without any clear realization of his own motives. Even when the child seems to try very hard to answer truthfully in explaining his behaviors, his parents should realize that the explanations given are mostly rationalizations and excuses and not the real cause. For this reason, instead of asking the child to explain his actions, it is much better for the parent to tell him the reason. Such information about his goals and the purpose of his conduct can be of great help to the child. Why? Because in order to change his attitude, the child must first understand himself and his behavior. But care must be taken to make these psychological discussions effective.

One major consideration should always be the optimum time and place to conduct these discussions. Perhaps most important, they should never take place immediately after misbehavior when both the adult and the child are upset and excited. Another fundamental requirement is that such talks should always be factual and unemotional in their conduct since even the slightest implication of reproach or criticism will evoke opposition, and hence, may fall on deaf ears. Because psychology can be a powerful tool of great potential value, it can also become a weapon of tremendously destructive power. For this reason, when applied to punish or humiliate, its results can be devastating. No matter how correct a psychological interpretation may be, its effects may be worse than futile if it is given at the wrong time or in a belligerent way. Effective discussion of psychological interpretation requires calm, friendly conversation conducted at a time of personal closeness when exchange of opinion will be acceptably and openly shared by both parties.

Attempts to dig into deep sources of motivation or to pry into the unconscious should not be confused with psychological interpretation, which is concerned solely with present attitudes and immediate purposes. Detailed psychological analysis and psychotherapy is the province of the highly trained clinician, and as such, is very different from the psychological interpretation of childhood behavior, which everyone who deals with children should be able to provide. It is very important that all parents and educators have at least a basic psychological knowledge and understanding of the nature of the childhood personality. However, in difficult cases, which may require the service of a child psychiatrist or child psychologist, it is also very important that the detailed analytical knowledge gained from such consultation never be used as the basis for conversation between parents and children. Correct professional utilization of such knowledge will involve its use only as a guide to aid parents in the management and guidance of the child.

As parents make use of their understanding of a child's actions in their attempts to influence that child, they will find that discussing the questionable action with the child may often become one of their most successful methods for changing his behavior. However, as a parent engages the child in effective discussion, he or she should not seek to investigate the underlying reasons why a child acted in a certain way but rather should only explain the immediate purpose for which the child acted as he did. This distinction, although it may seem superficial, indicates the very real difference between emphasis on past and on present goals. While there may be hundreds of reasons which lead to the child's present attitude, there is only one purpose possible for his or her actions.

A child will respond in a different manner to an explanation of causes as opposed to explanation of the goals of his or her actions. Explanations of causes—such as lack of self-confidence, jealousy, feelings of guilt, self-pity, or feelings of being dominated, neglected, or rejected—may be accurate in explaining the child's behavior but will be accepted by the child with friendly indifference *at best*. This is because such information only tells the child what he is, at least in the eyes of others. His reaction will be quite different when he is told what he wants, which may be to get attention, to demonstrate his power to show his superiority, to get even or to punish others, or to display his inadequacy.

Correct interpretations of the child's true intention will immediately evoke a very definite and characteristic automatic reaction on the face of the child called a "recognition reflex." This reflex, which has also been called a guilt reaction, consists of a characteristic twinkle of the eyes and a roguish smile which at once reveals the correctness of the adult's interpretation. Although the child may not say anything or may even deny the interpretation, his facial expression gives him away.

Discernment of a child's psychological attitude or goal, when it is revealed to the child, usually leads to an immediate change in the particular behavior under consideration. This is especially true in the case of young children. Children as young as two years of age, as soon as they are able to comprehend the meaning of words, are capable of conscious understanding of their intentions and are inclined to change their attitudes when made aware of them. Although this does not imply a complete change of lifestyle, it may eventually lead to changes in the child's basic concepts in relation to other people.

These psychological interpretations must, of course, be used with care since if repeated or overdone, they no longer serve as revelations. In no case should they ever have a belittling or humiliating effect nor should the child ever be allowed to translate them as criticism or fault-finding. Definite statements such as, "You do that because you want to" are not advisable; while remarks of vague conjecture such as "Could it be that you" or "I wonder whether you might really want" are much more effective. Such conjecture may often be preceded by the question, "Would you mind if I told you the real reason?" which will almost always be answered with a "Yes" or "Okay."

Even if the parent is on the wrong track, his discussion with the child can do no harm. When this happens, the parent will know it because he will not get a reaction. The parents can then make another inference or informed guess with confidence that the child's reaction will clearly indicate if it is correct. When a voiced interpretation encounters a blank or expressionless face, the parent may simply go on probing.

Behavior that means one thing in the life of one child may mean something very different in the life of another, since for each child, it is only a tool to reach a particular goal. In the same vein, the change in behavior that usually results from a correct interpretation does not necessarily lead to a basic or immediate attitude change, although attitude change may be expected over time. What a change in behavior does mean is that the particular method which was being used is no longer useful to the child once its purpose has been recognized.

For example, when five-year-old Bobby repeatedly threatened to hit other children, especially his playmate, Sally, our first impression was that he wanted to show his power and how strong he was. When our voiced interpretation encountered a blank stare, we went on probing. Perhaps Bobby felt neglected and wanted to hurt in order to get even. Again, we got no reaction. On the third try, his face beamed and twinkled as he looked like the cat who swallowed the canary in response to the question, "Could it be that your mother gets upset about your threats, and you want her to talk to you about it and tell you that you shouldn't do it and make a fuss over you?" This same behavior in another child, of course, could have meant something very different. For Bobby, it was clearly a tool to keep his mother concerned with him.

Although the preceding example focused on one individual, the technique of disclosing personal goals and attitudes is also a very effective means of influencing entire groups of children. Here again, the objective is the revelation of attitudes and goals within a context of the significance of the purposefulness of all human actions. Group discussions, which can be of great help in changing the attitudes of individuals within the group as well as those possessed by the group as a whole, can be used in school classrooms as well as in the family council (which will be discussed later in this chapter).

Within this context, as the child grows older, it becomes increasingly important that he have companions of his own age. The exclusive company of one or more adults is not a satisfactory substitute since with most adults, the child will be either over or under-stimulated. In either case, this causes his position to be out of keeping with accepted concepts of the developmental tasks that are essential to various life periods. To the degree that either situation is characteristic of a child's early life, the probability will increase—with age—that he will develop into an eccentric, uncongenial type of individual.

Nor is a continuous association with a single sister or brother enough. This dual pattern of companionship, when not supplemented by other peer contacts, often turns into a relationship of superior to inferior, often older to younger, which generates feelings of power and weakness that tend to persist over time. Nor is it enough for the child to play occasionally with chance companions in the park or street. A child needs regularly available companions of his own age beginning very early in his life. These playmates are essential to development because it is only with other children that a child can feel himself to be an equal among equals. This aspect of the child's self-concept allows him to adjust properly to the social scheme of the society in which he lives.

The very best opportunity for natural and free adjustment of a child to the social order may be provided through an organized group of children under competent supervision. For this reason, and within the context of the prevailing practice of keeping families small, it is advisable to enroll children in a carefully selected nursery school or prekindergarten beginning in their third or fourth year of life. Later, but usually not before age six, the child may also profit from involvement in summer recreation or day camp activities. Once these decisions and proper arrangements have been made, parents should then refrain from meddling in the internal affairs of the group of which their child has become a part.

Although all such formal or semiformal groups have their faults or limitations, the parent must remember that never in his life will the child belong to a completely perfect group. For this reason, each child will have to learn to manage himself or herself within the context of certain periodic intragroup imperfections. And of even greater importance is the need for parents to refrain from using their own anxieties as a pretext for securing special privileges for their child since such action would interfere directly with the socializing purpose to be achieved by the activities of the group. Stating this principle more broadly, adults should interfere as little as possible when the child is interacting with other children since it is the child who must find out for himself how to accommodate his interests to those of others and, more generally, how to share and get along with them well.

Mistakes or missteps will quickly become apparent and may be recognized by their consequences. In those situations where the child's play is unsupervised, a parent or other adult may watch but should reserve comments until the two are alone. Then, when discussing the child's behaviors, the adult must be careful not to inoculate this developing individual with the adult's own timidity, distrust for others, egotism, or antisocial tendencies since none of these qualities will in any way improve the child's character. As the child grows, he must be taught to regard his playmates as companions and friends—and never as enemies—in whose company he may enjoy himself completely.

Most parents seem to agree that quarrels should be prevented whenever possible and that serious ill feeling should never be permitted to arise among children. They may assume that this attitude is completely correct, but is it? What is the ideal parental attitude toward fighting? Scuffles, quarrels, and brawls will occur among children as long as they feel the urge to match their strength and powers and, of course, they must be prepared to defend themselves if attacked. Parents who prohibit their children from fighting—particularly their sons in our society—will succeed in driving away his adversaries, but when the child is older, his parents will not always be available to protect him. For this reason, the child must learn to look out for himself, which means learning to "fight" like the rest if necessary.

With correct parental guidance (summarized in this chapter and that which will follow), as the child grows older, a peaceful disposition will express itself through an acquired ability to find other more peaceable means of settling differences. But this will not occur through a dread of fights. Within this context, parents may need to discourage tough, rowdy, or bullying tendencies, and they may also need to keep the child away from certain exceptionally rough or undesirable individuals during the formative years.

Listen to Your Children

Many parents are so busy talking and doing that they too often fail to really hear what their children are saying. A part of this phenomenon seems to be a general prejudice against children. Parents not only take children for granted but may also assume that they know what children mean without really listening to their words. Here again, as suggested in earlier sections of this volume, parents often underestimate the intellectual development of their children. Our children *are* adept at sizing up and understanding the implications of the situations they experience with us, and they often *do* have intelligent and informed suggestions or solutions to offer. They also have a fresh perspective on life, which many adults could use to advantage *if* they would make an effort to listen and understand the words and ideas of children.

Our children often know exactly what we are doing wrong as parents—and as human beings—and will usually tell us in a very straightforward fashion if and when we are willing to listen. Yet, it is we who feel so sure that only we as adults have the intelligence, maturity, insight, and the right to tell them what they are doing wrong. We could profit from the sensitivity of our children if we could learn to treat them as equals and if we would really listen to them; but our pride too often prevents us from doing so.

One Saturday, Julie, David, and Joan were arguing over what program to watch next on television. David wanted a cowboy movie while his sisters preferred a cartoon. Finally, in exasperation, mother ordered David—who was shouting—to go to his room. His question, "Why do you always have to pick on me?" was answered by his mother's repeated order to leave the room coupled with a demand for, "No back talk, young man! There will be no trip to the beach for you this afternoon."

"I don't care," was the boy's angry and sullen reply. Of course, David does care—very much—but his pride and hurt feelings will not let him admit it now. His reply is an extension of the defiance he feels and is designed only to get back at mother.

David's mother should have listened to him since he asked a very good question. Why *does* mother always seem to pick on him? If mother were to listen to her son, she might learn two things. First, she might discover how she helps to keep the family fights going. Second, she might learn that she easily falls into the trap prepared by David's two sisters to keep their brother in trouble with his parents.

Parents need to learn to listen for the meaning behind the words their child uses. In the case of David's "I don't care" response to his mother, what he really meant was, "Even your punishment doesn't bother me. I refuse to be hurt unfairly." Or when a child screams, "Mommy, I hate you," she may really be telling us that she feels angry when she can't have her own way. Finally, when a child resorts to a series of "why" questions, he is really asking his parents to pay attention to him.

Although most children give us decreasing opportunities to overhear them as they grow older, they are very frank and open with each other. Because parents tend to make an issue of much that they overhear, most children become increasingly cautious in their communication with adults with each passing year beyond age seven or eight.

Ten-year-old Scott, for example, may confide to his friend Sam that he told his mother he felt sick to his stomach the previous day to avoid going to school. He would not be likely to make such a statement to his parents or to his friend's parents, however, because his parents would make a fuss, and his friend's parents would either repeat his story and cause him trouble or moralize. But Sam accepts what Scott has done as a part of life. He does not moralize nor punish, and he can be "trusted." Sam realizes that children can make themselves feel sick to escape what they dislike.

There is a sense of equality and trust among children that too rarely seems to exist between the generations. From the child's point of view, it seems that adults often do not even try to listen or attempt to understand. Instead, they continually try to control, manipulate, moralize, and reject that which has meaning to the child. There is much that adults can gain if only they will take the time to listen and try to understand their children.

Many parents—and mothers in particular—seem to lose this ability as their children grow older. When her child was an infant, mother learned to distinguish the many tones of his cry. She knew when he was angry or happy or distressed, for example, by simply listening to his sound. But as her child grew older, some of mother's attention became directed elsewhere. She no longer discriminated among his sounds in this way. Still, at every scream or each time he cries out, she may continue to dash to her child to determine the trouble, not realizing that her response is now often the purpose of the screaming or crying. Perhaps she could avoid a response that serves her child's mistaken goal if she would stop for a minute and listen. Again, through listening, there is *much* that we as parents can learn from and about our children.

A child first senses and then learns his environment and how he can manipulate it to his own ends. For example, the event of a child crying or screaming and his mother coming to pick him up and cuddle him is repeated in thousands of households each day. This ritual may be repeated each time he screams or cries. As a consequence of this ritualized response to the sounds he makes, the child soon learns that if he wants to be picked up, he needs to only scream or cry. By picking him up and holding him each time he does so, the parent succeeds only in encouraging the child in his attention-demanding behavior. This sort of parenting prompts the child to even further demands for attention and service as a way of feeling wanted.

By resorting to this ritualized response each time her "baby" cries, a mother may deprive the child of needed self-originated activity. But of even more importance, she will give him a mistaken idea of how to find his place in the world. A much better method involves establishment of a set routine that will include time for self-directed individual activity as well as for shared family activity. Such a routine should help the infant to discover regularity in life and the comfort of an established order. To do so effectively, it is essential that parents avoid their first impulse. Instead, they must stop to consider what the situation requires of them.

This principle of avoiding first impulse and doing even the unexpected holds true for older children as well. The child who feels dethroned by other older members of his family, for example, may assume he has no place in the family. Such a child might express his feelings by disrupting family activity in an attempt to force a display of the rejection he feels from others. What would you do in this situation?

Suppose daddy, Bert, and Samuel are building a snowman. Samuel, who is the youngest son, may continually collide with the snowman as he slides on a strip of packed snow. After several such collisions, father could become very angry, and on impulse, shout and send Samuel into the house. Or in a more constructive move, he could suggest that they stop building the snowman for a while and join Samuel in a sliding game. Father might even suggest that Samuel lead the group in tramping a wider and longer path so everyone could slide.

Samuel's cooperation is increasingly likely under these changed conditions since it will forestall his attempts to avoid being "rejected" and reverse his role into that of leader while simultaneously promoting family fun. In this way, disturbing behavior can be turned into constructive behavior. This father "listened" with his eyes as well as his ears. Experience with children reveals that whenever parents respond on impulse to what a child does, they are very likely to be doing exactly what the child wants them to do, although the child's goal may be a mistaken goal and the child himself may not be consciously aware of it.

If we fasten Johnny's coat for him, at his insistence, we only place ourselves in his service and reaffirm his self-concept of helplessness. This, of course, is the strength of a child who has learned to see himself as weak or unable. If Alice interrupts and whines while we are talking with a friend on the telephone, our response is likely to be to her desire for our full attention. When mother feels provoked into scolding Peter for tracking mud onto her freshly scrubbed floor, he probably has succeeded in involving her in a power contest.

If parents look at their own response, they may discover what the child gains from it. If they then cease to respond as formerly, the child's efforts may appear futile, and he or she may then seek a better and more useful method. This will be doubly true in cases where parents also make the effort to provide attention on other occasions as well as means for the child to gain status in more constructive ways. This is true because from early infancy, children explore both ways and means of finding their place and of feeling and being significant and important.

Regardless of how many times we scold or punish children, when they discover techniques or methods for reaching their goals, they cling to them. Children will stick to their successful results. As long as they continue to find success, almost any degree of unpleasantness of parental reaction will not diminish the satisfaction they find in feeling important, even in very socially unacceptable ways.

Because the child is seldom aware of the purpose of his misbehavior and disturbance, neither force nor "reasoning together" will change his approach to life. For this reason, to plan constructive action, parents must keep clearly in mind that the child's behaviors are part of his or her attempt to find a place, to be accepted, and to belong to a group. When the child's behavior violates order and disrupts cooperation, he is simply using faulty methods to reach his basic goal.

Unless we pay careful attention, and unless we carefully analyze our own reactions to a child's behavior, we as parents may react only on impulse and succeed only in reinforcing the child's mistaken assumptions about himself and his situation. When parents allow this to occur, their child will not only become further discouraged but will also become more convinced that there is no other way for him to behave if he is to feel worthwhile.

Confront the Issue of Television/Social Media/Mobile Electronic Devices (Finding Balance in a Tech-Driven World)

First, an editorial comment, then our observations and suggestions. It is impossible to dispute the many ways technology has positively affected the world. Tech has made interacting and collaborating with people from all corners of the planet as convenient as conversing with a next-door neighbor. Technology also has changed the face of education, making it possible for students from all walks of life to easily access a wealth of information at the click of a button.

But for all of its many attributes, technology has its drawbacks as well. One of its notable detriments is the "always on" reality of tech as well as the ability to become addicted to such instant gratification. Few adults and children can spend more than a few minutes without checking their devices.

According to a recent report in the *Daily Telegraph*, on average, people are online twenty-four hours a week, twice as long as ten years ago. One in five adults spend as much as forty hours a week online. According to Common Sense Media, teens spend an average of nine hours a day online, compared to about six hours for kids between the ages of eight and twelve, and fifty minutes for children three years old or younger.

Technology also has blurred the lines that distinguish work and personal time. Gone are the days of the parent leaving the office behind when the workday ends in early evening. Today's workers can take work home, work remotely, and even check work e-mails or put in some hours while on vacation, making less family time for necessary parenting. Children, too, can pay a price as a result of engaging with technology. For example, various studies indicate more than half of adolescents and teens have been bullied online.

Since it seems that television, social media, and mobile devices are here to stay, we must learn to solve rather than resent or fear the problems they present. Some other issues relate to criticism of the content of radio and television programming, plus that on other social media, which convey impressions and concepts of which parents may disapprove. Information technology using direct market advertising based on personal information is also upsetting for parents. All of this can also lead to neglect of bedtime as well as homework and behavior, generally, but also to intrusion into individual and family privacy and belief systems.

During the recent past in many families, mealtime was somewhat consistently regulated by TV program schedules as families changed their dining habits to eat in front of the set. More recently, even though "at will" program availability has evolved, some conflict may remain. Further technological development of computers, cell phones, or other electronic devices may cause more interruptions. These habits, of course, also isolate each individual in his or her own private absorption while listening, viewing, or otherwise interacting through those electronic media. When this occurs, parents understandably become concerned over time lost for mealtime or other family activities employed to promote family unity. To deal with these situations as well as other similar modes for disruption or isolation, many parents may feel compelled to resort to authoritarian methods as they attempt to regulate their children's screen time and other social involvement. The result, of course, too often involves family dissension and/or fighting.

Let us first consider the issue of social media access. One of the most frequent problems may still occur when young children disagree over access to media. In this situation, as in others which involve arguments, parents may simply choose to stay out of the fighting. However, they might also decide to restrict access until the children have reached an agreement. This situation becomes doubly complicated, of course, when the quarrel evolves to involve both children and parents or grandparents (e.g., grandpa wants to watch the 5:30 news while cartoons are on). The problem here is not whether "parents" do or do not have the right to dictate program choice nor whether it is their responsibility to give in to the rights of other family members. This problem is a family problem which involves all family members and for that reason must be solved by the family as a unit.

The question is not, "What must I do to regulate our family's TV watching?" but rather, "What are we as a family going to do to resolve these problems?" Since all members of the family must come to a joint agreement, this subject and others like it may require group examination in a family council (more will be presented concerning the family council later in this chapter). In cases where emotions run high and dissension is severe, the situation may be handled much like an industrial strike during which no work is done until the argument is settled. In this case of television viewing arguments, the set may be unplugged by an adult so that no one, including the parents, may see any program until an agreement is reached. In the case of social media/mobile devices, the equipment, which is family property, may be removed until resolution is achieved.

An understanding may be reached concerning a neglected homework problem through individual discussion with the child involved. Here, the child should be allowed to offer a solution. He may choose for himself what time he will watch television or play on his phone or other social media/mobile device and what time he will do his homework. Since school assignments are a part of the child's "work" responsibility, just as is the parents' work for pay, it is a total family responsibility to work with each individual's and the family's special needs.

The family council, for example, might decide to designate a quiet place for study and perhaps a "quiet time" when the distraction of radio, TV, or other media devices are not allowed. Then, when the child has made his or her decision regarding study and viewing times, the parents may remain firm and hold the child to these agreements but with action and not an excess of words. As the child grows older, he or she may desire to renegotiate the agreement. This, of course, may be done, but the basic question remains one of deciding what is to be done to find an equitable solution.

When children demand to watch television or interact on their mobile device after their bedtime, parents must remain firm in order to maintain routine. The act of simply taking the young child to bed without words will not precipitate a power struggle if mother or father do not have a personal stake in "making" the child maintain his routine. In doing so, they are merely maintaining order and following the demands of the situation.

In the case of the older child, too, parents and child must come to an agreement and then follow through on what has been agreed upon. But this may not be easy if the parents have failed to develop a relationship of trust and cooperation with their children. This point is made to indicate that problems of TV watching and social media/mobile device involvement may merely highlight a much more inclusive pattern of lack of cooperation between parents and children.

Within this context, it is foolish for parents to passively wait for the networks, media companies, or the nation to solve the problem of content and quality of programming on TV or mobile devices/social media. Although this has been and continues to be a subject of national concern, since it is a problem that occurs in our own homes and families, it is there that we must act. But how can this be best accomplished? As parents, we should realize that we only invite a power struggle when we insist that a child not watch a specific program or use certain social media/mobile device content. We already know that in a power contest, it is the child who wins, and there may seem to be no more powerful argument for the child than "All the other kids see it" or "All the other kids do it." Since the child will only seek revenge in other ways, if we continue to deny his desire, again, what can be done?

Parents must first come to the realization that they cannot protect their children from television or other electronic media nor from the impressions—including violence, sexual content, or horror—which they receive from watching. What parents can do, however, is prepare their children by helping them to develop resistance against bad taste and poor judgment. But this cannot be done by preaching since words in today's "modern" culture are often used as weapons rather than as means of communication. As we pointed out in an earlier section, the child becomes "parent deaf" as soon as the sermon begins.

Experience has revealed that a discussion in which a parent asks questions and then listens to the replies of the child can serve as a very profitable beginning. Parents can share their impressions in a game-like atmosphere after having watched a questionable program or other electronic media content with their children. Questions related to attitudes, values, and feelings, such as "What did you think of (the program?), "What else might the people have done?", and "How do you think the others felt and why?" can help a young person take a critical look at a program and think and decide for himself or herself concerning its content and meaning. Questions like "Could it really be fun to beat or hurt someone else?" and "How would the victim feel?" may be balanced by questions like "Do you know any good or kind people?" and "How do you know they are good?"

However, if we as parents try to correct the child's expressions of his or her impressions, we risk losing all we hope to gain. But if we can learn to educate and trust the child and his judgment, we will be able to accept what he says as he says it, noting as time passes that the child will develop an increasingly critical sense of value. During this process, a parent may occasionally choose to contribute his or her own thoughts, perhaps in the form of a provocative question such as, "What do you suppose would happen if…?" If the parent will then listen, the child will have an opportunity to learn a valuable lesson that he too has the ability to offer acceptable ideas.

Children will not learn to think for themselves if we do all of their thinking for them by handing them ready-made ideas. As we discuss with our children, we develop rapport with them when we avoid imposing our own ideas while simultaneously encouraging and assisting each child to think for himself. To the degree that a good relationship can then exist between the generations, the child may feel free to be candid in his replies and tell us what he really thinks and feels. Parents who through mutual trust and respect can allow their children to be this open often express both amazement and pride in the knowledge and astute judgment of right and fair play, which their children will in turn express.

When we know what to do and have confidence in our ability to cope with the problems which electronic media poses, exposure to its content need not be a source of continuous worry and frustration to parents. Those parents who will approach their children as has been suggested here will find that children can take TV and other electronic media in their stride. When parents avoid conflict over television watching and electronic media exposure as a source of power struggle, interest in such conflict will most often simply fade away. Hence, we can neither take away the child's privileges to experience electronic and social media nor can we dictate all aspects of media programming to which she would be exposed. This is a form of imposing our will, and as such, will eventually lead to our own defeat in a struggle for power. But we can successfully guide our children if we offer them experiences of even greater interest to stimulate and influence their development. Overconcern with either too much passive entertainment on the one hand or an excess of inappropriate material on the other can be successfully offset if we make sure that other forms of family fun, entertainment, and interaction are not only readily available but actually planned and undertaken on behalf of all members of the family.

Now, a final editorial comment. It was not too long ago when reasonable people could agree to disagree without it turning hostile. That was a time when people talked face-to-face. A recent survey discovered that 69 percent of respondent's blame social media and the Internet for the current state of divisiveness.

Technology has made it possible to instantly voice our opinions from the anonymity of a computer screen or telephone keyboard. That has made it easy to say things we would never say in person.

Social media allows us to disagree with others, and the emotion involved often makes an enemy on the other side of the argument rather than an opposing point of view which can be considered in a rational way. There was a time not too long ago when we took time to organize our thoughts before blurting them out on social media. All of this influences our children.

These tips may help adults and children regain control and find balance in a tech-driven world:

(1) Set strict usage time. Being plugged into devices on an almost continual basis directly affects the brain by keeping it in a state of constant stimulation. This can make it difficult for the brain to get the downtime it needs to

recharge. Limit hours of screen time, and wind down at least an hour or so before bed.

(2) Put devices on silent. If you or your children cannot resist the lure of those devices, set them on silent or put them out of sight and out of reach at key times during the day.

(3) Emphasize in-person socialization. Instead of texting or e-mailing, speak with friends, family, and coworkers in person.

(4) Increase exercise. Time spent outdoors away from computers or other devices can be beneficial to the mind and body at any age.

(5) Find alternative solutions. Rather than running an Internet search every time you have a question, look up answers in a book, travel to learn about new things, experience hobbies, and immerse yourself in the physical world with renewed vigor.

Tech has changed the world, but it doesn't have to consume people's daily lives. With some mindfulness, individuals can find the right balance.

Use Religious Interest Wisely

As human beings, our highest aspirations, ideals, and moral values emanate from and are upheld in our "religion," whether it be formally institutionalized or simply a subjectively experienced set of unrefined feelings and/or beliefs. For many people, religion serves as an inspiration in their striving for the good life; hence, it may seem difficult for some to imagine how religion could be detrimental to the developing young personality. Consider, however, the case of Peter who has been in a cross mood all morning. Mother is busy, so she gives her son a crayon and paper and sends him to his bedroom with instructions: "Draw me some nice pictures, Peter."

Later, when she looks in to check his progress, she finds that he has emptied the contents of his dresser and closet into a pile on the floor. Furious, she jerks and swats him. As she marches him into the kitchen to sit on a chair, she points out in an angry tone that "God doesn't like bad boys. He will punish you if you don't learn to be good."

Peter then denies making the mess and says his sister did it.

This obvious lie upsets mother still more. Mother begins to lecture Peter on the dangers of lying by pointing out that "Heaven has no place for liars. Truth is goodness. When a boy lies, he is not good."

Parents clearly admit their own defeat when they threaten a child with punishment from God or from heaven. And by suggesting to the child that they are shifting the entire problem to a higher authority, they are also preparing that child to take pride in their defeat. Since no punishment from God may be immediately forthcoming, the child may learn to scoff at the threat. As this occurs, he may be learning to feel and believe that no good power or influence can match his will to do as he desires, not even that of God. For this reason, the practice of using religious beliefs as a punishment is not only a useless training technique but can be and often is counterproductive.

As suggested in previous units, unless a child has encountered obstacles in his environment that have caused him to become discouraged, he has no need to turn to misbehavior as a way out of difficulty. It is so much easier for a child to be "good" that he will have no need to be "bad" unless he encounters such obstacles. Further, anxious moralizing will neither change nor remove such an obstacle since the child does have a purpose in his behavior. Such moralizing will add only one element, and that is discouragement.

When we as parents hold up an ideal which all persons should strive toward and point out to the child how far he or she falls short, we succeed only in adding to the discouragement that made that child fall short in the first place. What a child in this situation needs most is help out of his difficulty, including sincere encouragement, and never the condemnation implied in moralizing over his mistaken behavior. The child clearly realizes that he is expected to be "good," but because the real purpose of his behavior is unknown to him, he has no real idea of why he is "bad." Then, from his discouragement over his "failure" to reach the ideals held out by others, a conflict develops between what he finds himself doing and what he feels he should do. Since the child feels he cannot do both at once, he learns to pretend.

Whenever moralizing is used by adults in an attempt to stimulate "good" or "appropriate" behavior, we find children with false fronts. Such a child learns to hide behind good intentions when his real purpose or goal may be quite the opposite. He develops an intense but often well-hidden fear that the "worthlessness," which to him seems very real, will show through this veneer of acting. As he attempts under any and all circumstances to put himself in the best possible moral light, he expends increasingly large amounts of time and energy on appearances. The more energy he expends in this attempt to deceive himself and others—really to hide his fear—the less he will have to expend in solution of the real problems related to his growth and development.

A related issue involves the child's attendance at a "Sunday school." Many parents insist that their children attend while they themselves either remain at home or engage in certain recreational or other activities. This practice suggests to children the existence of two parallel but unequal moral standards—one for adults and one for themselves. In a very real sense, the child feels, "If I need this training to be good, why should my parents who sometimes do bad and unjust things to me be privileged to have fun on Sunday instead of attending religious services?" As the child's sense of equality is again abused, his sense of oppression by adults gains in weight. To the degree that this interpretation of the child's experience tends to make "Sunday school" (under its various labels in various religious denominations) seem to him to be an increasingly unfair and disagreeable chore, it may defeat the very purpose of such formal religious training.

As a child grows older with these sorts of frustrations and confusion, in addition to parental suggestions of threats of punishment in heaven or the hereafter, he may develop a morbid fear of the future, perhaps including all that he is unable to experience directly, including death. This fear is in no way helpful since it generates anxiety related to the unknown and to the passage of time. In so doing, it denies the child the strength and feeling of freedom which he or she will need as it becomes necessary to assume the increasing responsibilities of increasing maturity.

Looking at this situation realistically, if the child were not already in trouble, he would not need to misbehave as he does. And as his parents' behavior toward him generates a fear of certain unseen forces, which may punish him for his unhappiness, it is possible that this fear will lead to an unspoken or unacknowledged hatred for a God who punishes. The problem of dealing with these sorts of feelings—that are probably, for the child, beyond expression—then adds another layer to the false front which he shows to the world. To the extent that such a pattern does develop within the experience of the child, the conflict between pretense and the real intentions which that pretense contains can lead only to further maladjustments in the child's life.

All human beings periodically get into difficulties. When this happens during childhood, children need help to see that they—like adults—must seek ways of restoring harmony, which is the ultimate good regardless of the name by which it is labeled. Within this context, religious teaching can be most helpful as adults attempt to show children that certain types of behaviors and interactions were long ago found to be wrong because they damaged or destroyed good and happy relationships between people. Religious stories and principles, especially, can serve as invaluable aids to such parent-child communication when they are designed to restore friendship and harmony through exploration of various possibilities for and ways of resolving human conflict.

Have Fun Together

Cultural changes that pit children against their parents are due at least in part to our lack of skill in living together democratically. Many parents feel so deeply concerned with providing the best for their children that they neglect to join them and to share with them. It is tragic to see so many modern families so divided that the children have nearly all of their fun and enjoyment apart from their parents with the latter perhaps supplying the means but little or no personal participation. *Much* can be learned, shared, and enjoyed in family group activity.

At earlier times, when families were large, children were forced by circumstances to depend more upon each other for fun and recreation-based learning than is now the case. This custom was handed down from one generation to the next and prevailed until introduction of mass entertainment through radio, television, etc. A closely related factor is the loss of common interests between parents and children, which has also become more prevalent during recent generations. This phenomenon seems related directly to parents' inability to enter the child's world as an equal but also to the rather frequent rejection by the older child of at least segments of the adult world.

It *is* difficult, if not impossible, to have fun together when a state of undeclared war exists, and in many homes, as suggested in earlier sections of this volume, this is virtually the case. Many children, as they grow older, no longer want their parents to play with them; yet, when they can enjoy recreation or games together, levels of hostility are reduced, giving family harmony an opportunity to grow and develop. But many parents simply do not take time to share common fun experiences with their children. Some feel pressure of the work-a-day world to such a severe degree that their primary desire is simply to be left alone. As parents, we all need time alone or with our adult friends to recoup our strength and perspective, but we cannot sacrifice our children's basic interpersonal needs to do so.

It is part of the role of parents to foster an atmosphere of mutual concern and family solidarity through play and other recreational activity. Our advice is to have fun together. Parents who do so help to engender a spirit of sharing and mutual respect among the members of their family. By making the effort, they may be able to change the conception, which many of our children have unfortunately developed from that of busyness, arrogance, and fighting to one involving a group of mutually concerned individuals with common interests.

Our children desperately need this form of participation. When they were babies, we probably were more responsive to this parental duty, but as they grow older, we seem to lose our interest in and knack for doing this well, if at all. Probably our most frequently used excuses are that we "just don't have the time or strength," are "too busy," or have "something else we *have* to do." However, a more honest statement might be that we "just don't have the inclination" or "there is something we would *rather* do." We all find time—or perhaps more correctly, we make the time—for those things that we really want or feel we should do.

The play hour, or "family time," can become a focal point for development of mutual understanding and harmony between the generations in any family. At home, children can learn that games can be a source of fun rather than of bitter competition. At home with parents and family, the child can learn that one can have fun and gain satisfaction from simply playing the game and that one does not always have to win to enjoy mutual interaction and cooperation.

Since most children are accustomed to winning or at least to wanting to win, in whatever they do, this may be a difficult but very valuable lesson for each one to learn. Observation of both individuals and family activity suggests that if this lesson does not begin at home, it may never be learned. For this reason, each family should plan group activities geared to each child's level of development. A definite time for family "play" should be planned as part of the family's regular routine. Evidence exists that if it is not planned, it will probably not occur.

Family activity may involve everything from participation in games and family outings to various other shared experiences. Young children may enjoy creating their own family entertainment, such as putting on a play they have created themselves. Some children particularly enjoy having their parents take the roles of children in a story while they themselves play the parts of adults. On some occasions, a fairy tale or a legend known to all may be acted out or the family may choose to make up the play as they go along or all may simply guess what each is pretending to be. Various projects can also be used for family activity, such as making paper baskets for May Day or paper ornaments and decorations for Christmas or some other holiday.

Other family activities may involve discussion of and planning for family summer vacation trips, outings, or field trips, family collections of various sorts, or even family conversations or song fests while doing the chore of evening dishwashing. On this last point, many mothers report that they have had and continue to have many of their most intimate conversations and mutual learning experiences with their children while doing the dishes. It is during the simple act of washing and drying dishes many parents report that they "really get to know" their children. The advent of the automatic dishwasher, unfortunately, has ended this potentially valuable activity in many households.

Those family projects that are selected by a family will depend, of course, on the interests of the individual members of that family. During the early 1960s, for example, the Kennedy family displayed their interest in this philosophy, particularly through their open participation in family sailing, skiing, touch football, and lively family conversation. Although parental enthusiasm can be contagious, children also often display marked eagerness and ingenuity as they indicate activities which they find to be of interest.

Parents who are alert and who listen to their children will discover all sorts of activities that interest them. With imagination, these interests—coupled with the parents' own—can be developed into family projects sufficiently enjoyable and challenging to meet the needs of all family members. Various church denominations report that "families who pray together, stay together." There seems to be some good evidence that this is true, at least as it pertains to attendance at religious services. We also now find evidence to support the thesis that families who play together may stay together—at least in terms of a lower divorce rate—more than other families.

Feelings of group stability develop through games and family projects in which all can share. That which individuals enjoy as members of a family group not only brings them together but also provides warm feelings for the other participants. Such family solidarity is important for the atmosphere of equality it promotes, but also for the feeling of harmony, relaxation, and trust that it creates as part of the family's pattern of living. This wholesome atmosphere and mutual feeling of goodwill nurtures the self-confidence of each child while it simultaneously provides each member of the family with an inner strength and resilience in times of trouble, if and when that too might occur.

Establish a Family Council

Both the growing number of rights which society bestows on children and their awareness of their status as equals make it essential that they be accepted as equal partners in the affairs of the family of which they are members. Equality, in this sense, of course, does not mean equal function since each family member can and must perform different duties and roles. And in addition, these differences should not imply any lowering of status, which might inevitably lead to feelings of resentment and unwillingness to discharge those functions that may imply lower social prestige.

The greater freedoms that our contemporary democratic society provides for each member of the family in turn requires that each assume an increasing share of the responsibility for the welfare of the entire family as well as for each family member. But unless the experience of freedom—which means self-determination—also includes a sense of responsibility, it will lead only to confusion, disorder, and chaos. This means that as long as the parents—and particularly the mother—take on all responsibility, while the children enjoy all the freedom to do as they please, an unbalanced state of equilibrium will be inevitable. Within such a setting that deprives the children of roles which allow useful functioning, young people will tend to become increasingly demanding and tyrannical.

The purpose of the family council is to give each family member an opportunity to express himself or herself freely on all matters that pertain to the family and to the home. In a very real sense, the council is a learning laboratory for educational democracy that provides important educational experiences for parents as well as for their children. At a council meeting, any family member may criticize or object to whatever he does not like, but these objections should be coupled with his suggestion for a solution. This right to criticize carries with it a responsibility to share in the contributions that all must make to the maintenance of a secure and happy family life. Since tradition has not provided us with specific guidelines for living with each other in a rapidly changing society, it has become necessary for most people to establish them by trial and error. In this sense, every family is a pioneer family in the adventurous enterprise of learning to live with each other as equals.

Experience in working with members of the modern American family has shown that children who fail to learn to live democratically in their own families often have very little chance to learn it later. Study of human growth and development reveals that as an individual's arbitrarily developed sense of inferiority and superiority become well established, he or she often tries to demonstrate superiority while simultaneously feeling fear of being inferior. For these reasons, the family council format can be very helpful in providing each family member with the very important sense of equal status concerning both rights and obligations. In this way, it can be used to facilitate the application of democratic principles to family life.

The family council is no more or less than a meeting of all members of the family in which problems are discussed and solutions are sought, just as the name implies. As such, it is one of the most important tools a family may use to deal with and settle troublesome problems in a democratic manner. The council should become a regular part of the family routine with an agreed upon specified hour on a definite day of each week set aside for this purpose. Every member of the family is expected to be present at the agreed upon time with the meeting hour not to be changed without consent of the entire family.

Although the details of the family council can be worked out by each family unit to suit its own needs, the basic principles to be followed remain the same for all. In the council, the vote of a parent is given just as much weight as that of a child. Further, each member has the right to bring up a problem, and each has the right to be heard. Then, together, all seek a solution to the problem with the majority opinion upheld by all. Decisions made at the council meeting hold for one week until the next meeting. Following each meeting, whatever course of action has been agreed upon takes place with no further discussion permitted until the next meeting. The answer to each complaint between meetings is "Bring it up at the next council meeting." If at that time it is discovered by the group that the solution of last week did not work well, a new solution may be sought. Again, it is the responsibility of the group to decide, "What are we going to do about it?"

At a first meeting of a family council, an individual need only present his or her problem. Perhaps it will be mother who should then ask each other family member, including each child, what they think could be done about it. The first time this is done, some children may act puzzled or perplexed. This may simply suggest the degree to which they feel overwhelmed by an opportunity to contribute and by an inability to completely trust such openness.

Some children are at first very quiet at a family council meeting, feeling that they won't be given a real chance anyway. But as we pointed out earlier, children catch on quickly. If there is no immediate suggestion for solution to her problem, mother—after waiting for all to have time to think—may then present her suggestion. In doing so, it is always wise to propose an idea as a question such as, "What would happen if…?" or "Do you suppose it would help if…?"

Parents can help sullen, angry children to participate if they will show their understanding of that person's viewpoint. A statement such as "I'm wondering if Billy feels he just doesn't have a chance? He doesn't seem to like the arrangement very much as it now stands. What do you think, Billy?" is often of great help. The sullen child at first may not even be willing to discuss the problem, but if mother (or father) continues to display genuine interest in what he thinks, he may overcome his conviction and begin to participate. Then as further discussion about what could be done ensues, perhaps for a while, Billy should be the first to be asked for suggestions. However, if the parents are the only persons who present problems and offer solutions, the meeting is not a true family council. *All* family members must participate to make it work. Each child must be stimulated to contribute his or her full share.

A favorite story of Adlerian psychologists—often used to illustrate the family council—involves a mother, a father, and three school-aged daughters. At a family council meeting, the girls reported their joint decision that the family should buy a new house. The oldest—aged ten—offered twenty dollars from her savings bank, while the eight-year-old offered fifteen dollars, and the six-year-old offered ten.

The parents were shocked. What could they do? Assuming their daughters had no real idea of the cost of a house, they raised the issue only to be told that the girls would guess the cost at about ninety thousand dollars, which seemed a reasonable estimate. Now what could be done? Because of the importance of the issue, the family decided to discuss it further at the next council meeting.

During the seven-day period between meetings, these parents sought the advice of a family counselor. At the next meeting, daddy and mom (with dad speaking for both) agreed to contribute 550 dollars with the suggestion that the girls buy the house. This ended the matter, but suppose the girls had insisted that he provide the full balance? If so, he could have appealed to their sense of fairness (1) by educating them concerning the amount of family money needed each month for food, fuel, payments, etc., and (2) by pointing out that since there were five family members, it would have been unfair to expect any one person to raise nearly the whole amount. Again, daddy (and mom) could have agreed in the desire for a new house but have asked that the girls raise the money. (Later, the family decided to make some changes in the house in which they were living.)

A parent can always state what he or she is willing to do or how far he or she is willing to go in a plan and then return the problem to the group for further discussion and statement of intent by the others. To deal effectively with problems of this sort, parents must make creative use of their imagination within a context of consideration of what they might do if it were their adult friends who presented such ideas instead of their children. Since the problems being considered are not the problems of individuals but of families, and since living together in a family unit requires multiple interactions, each solution must be as much a family procedure as is the difficulty or problem itself. This is true because democratic family living rests upon a foundation of mutual sharing, mutual respect, and equality. The shared approach to problem solving, which is implicit in the family council, promotes family equality and develops both mutual responsibility and mutual respect. For this reason, the secret of success in organizing a family council lies in the willingness of all members of the family to approach problems as family problems and not as individual problems.

Some families add on an annual family business meeting to the family council concept. Corporations must have an annual meeting each year to bring together stockholders, thrash out problems, and report on profits and losses and other matters. Sometimes the results of such meetings are negligible since they are mere formalities, but often, the stockholders do get a chance to express themselves, learn about the company, and contribute ideas. Families that arrange such annual meetings do so in order to give a sense of participation to all members, to benefit from a cross-fertilization of ideas, and to make plans for the coming year.

In one family with which we are familiar, at the annual meeting, the family members set so many expenditures one year that nothing was left for vacations. This, however, was quickly solved by an eleven-year-old. "Let's go camping," he said. The thought had never really occurred to the parents, both of whom were in their thirties. They tried it, enjoyed it, and came home refreshed in spirit and financially solvent as well.

The extent to which each member of the family is involved in such a yearly financial meeting may vary greatly. Some families elect officers, plan budgets and allowances, assign responsibilities, and even establish a family bank. Such things as income, expenditures, cash flow (the amount one regularly receives and spends), and budgets are discussed. Even the youngest may be put on an allowance, the purpose not being to bribe but to show that with income comes responsibility. If a member of the family has a special objective for which no money is budgeted, he or she may—with approval of the others—borrow money from the family bank at a specified rate of interest so that the bank operates at a profit.

The bank idea is an especially good tool for teaching money management in particular and responsibility in general. The youngster can earn money in the bank (interest), but he also learns that it costs him to spend beyond his income. The potential borrower is never turned down abruptly. He is told that the bank will consider his request for a loan but that he will be expected to repay on certain terms and that this, therefore, reduces his ability to purchase other things. It's his (or her) choice.

In many families, parents begin family councils with good intentions and a high level of enthusiasm. However, if either they or their children violate the basic promises of democratic procedure, the council will lose its meaning and function. This difficulty of establishing and maintaining a democratic relationship of equals is the reason most often responsible for discontinuance of the family council. The maintenance of a family council requires courage to chart new courses without distrust or fear and with the conviction that others also want to live in peace and harmony but may not know how to achieve this goal.

Such maintenance requires cooperation, persistence, and a willingness to see one's own mistakes as well as a willingness to examine and possibly change one's own attitude while respecting the attitudes of others. Unless one has and displays respect for and confidence in the other members of his or her family, there will be little chance for meaningful and productive discussion of conflicts and difficulties, which means even less chance for finding mutually acceptable solutions. The specific principles developed in the paragraphs to follow from points made earlier are designed to help facilitate both the conduct and maintenance of family council meetings.

Perhaps the most basic recommendation is that the family set a specific time, date, and place for the council to meet each week. Although it is possible to establish procedures in a regular council meeting for emergency situations, it is not advisable to call a meeting whenever one member desires to have one. Such a sense of urgency on the part of an individual usually means a clash of interests or a conflict situation has erupted, but such situations are rarely, if ever, so urgent that they require immediate settlement. Further, the moment of anger or upset is not the time to talk since words used in conflict situations are used as weapons and not as means of communication.

Although participation should not be compulsory, all members of the family must be invited to participate. If one member of the family does not choose to attend, regardless of who that member may be, his or her absence may involve the remainder of the family reaching decisions that he or she may not like. This procedure is usually sufficient to induce the uncooperative member to attend the next sessions, during which he or she will have a chance to try to alter the previous decisions.

The chairmanship of the council should be rotated either weekly or monthly so that all participating family members may experience this responsibility and privilege. Even children—given proper training in the conduct of meetings in a democratic manner—are often able to function adequately in the role of chairperson. All members then participate in the council on an equal footing with each having one vote. If and when parents or other more mature members of the family see that the course of action being taken by the group is uncomfortable, however, they must still abide by the decision, bear the discomfort, and allow the natural result to take place. Parents who will do so will soon realize that children often learn more from these experiences than they will ever learn from parental words or impositions.

Any age requirement for participation will depend entirely on each child's ability to understand what is discussed. Even very young children are usually able to contribute and express at least some of their ideas. The maintenance of parliamentary order provides each member with the opportunity to express himself or herself freely but also justifies the obligation of each to listen to all other participants. Any members of the family who choose to disrupt the session can, under these rules, be asked to leave if that is the consensus of the group.

Each parent, like any other member of the family, may merely submit his or her viewpoint to the group. The primary objective of each meeting should involve willingness of all to listen sincerely to what each has to say. Simply stated, when the council fails to remain democratic, it fails in its purpose. For example, when the family council is used by parents to scold, preach, over-explain, or otherwise impose their will on other family members, the council is bound to fail. Regardless of the problems to be confronted and before any solutions can be found, the habitual procedure of listening to each other with the goal of understanding what the other means must be firmly established.

Parents who are inexperienced with the conduct of a family council most often express their fear that wrong or improper decisions will be made against their more mature judgment. It is, of course, possible that this may occur. However, such wrong decisions—usually proposed by children—can be used to great advantage. Since in most cases not much harm can result, instead of attempting to prevent such decisions, parents should allow them to develop to let the children see what will happen, i.e., experience the consequences of such decisions as was suggested in the house-buying illustration cited earlier. Usually, at the next meeting, the children will not only be more careful but will also agree on a better solution.

Establishment of the council as the only family authority in conflict situations means that no individual may lay down the law nor make decisions for others, except in a physical emergency. It also means that no one person must assume the full responsibility for the management and adequate functioning of the household. Most parents, particularly mothers, find this to be a most difficult lesson to learn because they are often overimpressed with a sense of responsibility and obligation. For example, if for some reason Mrs. Brown fails to take care of the needs of all, she is very likely to feel negligent with the result that her children will be given little if any opportunity to take on responsibilities for themselves. Many parents fail to realize that it is much more important for children to learn to accept responsibilities than to have family life run smoothly at all times. Further, mother will *not* have to feel guilty if things do not always go ideally *if* she is willing to accept the council as the supreme family authority.

Organizing and beginning a family council requires both time and effort to get all family members oriented to democratic procedures and to realize that a fundamentally new and untried course of action has begun. Because the council format is new to parents as well as children because they are usually not well prepared for it, and because many family members may not fully trust each other, some may not display much initial faith in any project that will require their cooperation. Parents are often afraid that decisions and demands made by their children will lack maturity, judgment, and responsibility while their children are simultaneously afraid that the family council is just another adult "trick" to make them behave or do things they do not want to do.

In some families, it may seem difficult to get the sessions organized or underway, while in others the enthusiasm of a first meeting may seem short-lived. For these and possibly other reasons, early council sessions may seem to be a burden to all. However, although working to create an effective family council may impose hardships on parents at the beginning, if the difficult early periods can be tolerated without giving up, this method of managing family conflicts can and very often does grow to be of great value in child-rearing.

3

Avoiding the Most Common
Errors in Child-Rearing

No parent can avoid making mistakes in the raising and training of children. This is, of course, true because no one is perfect. Parents who demand perfection in themselves are bound to become discouraged and, as a result, to become less adequate and effective than they might otherwise be in rearing their children. The various dilemmas of parenthood, which were discussed in chapter 1, make it very difficult to find adequate solutions to many of the problems encountered in the education and training of children.

To find success in their efforts to be successful parents, mothers and fathers must first learn to accept their children as fellow human beings—despite their inevitable imperfections—if they hope to maintain harmonious relations with their offspring while simultaneously helping them to remedy faults or weaknesses. But the same is true for the parents themselves. Adults, too, may improve if they first make peace with themselves, learn to accept their own limitations, weaknesses, failings and faults, and then determine just where they intend to go from that point on. For parents as well as children, it is important for each individual to realize that an indication that they have erred is not an indictment to be taken defensively as a criticism.

Instead, it should be viewed as helpful information to be used in a program of self-improvement.

Any effective method of learning to act correctly must involve avoidance of incorrect activity. This means that parents who are looking for answers to difficult child-rearing problems should first stop and think of what they should not do in their attempts to do right. This is true because errors are always specific, which makes it much easier to point out and define mistakes than success. While it is possible to follow advice literally about what not to do, one often cannot be literal or exact about positive suggestions since correct attitudes usually depend to a large extent on imponderables such as tone of voice, imagination, and emotional conditioning or sensitivity.

Because a correct answer to a problem can usually be found in many different ways, explicit and seemingly constructive suggestions may turn out to be restrictive in the sense that they may prevent the individual from seeking other, perhaps preferable solutions. Any parent, for example, might learn to believe that spanking children is not good. Such a parent could very easily grasp this bit of advice and follow it exactly if he or she were to decide to do so. Although any such decision regarding the proper handling of children may be followed literally, it may at the same time offer no real solutions or may under certain circumstances be detrimental. It is for this reason, especially, that it seems advisable for adults to acquaint themselves thoroughly with details of incorrect as well as correct techniques of child-raising.

It is also important that parents not allow themselves to become discouraged because it is when they act on the basis of discouragement, guilty feelings, frustration, and defeatism that they are most likely to make their most serious mistakes. This is true regardless of how hard they may try to act in a correct fashion. In this connection, it is again important that parents realize that they as well as all other parents are bound to make many mistakes in the process of child-rearing. The crucial point is that by being aware of their own feelings as well as the nuances of the situation in which they find themselves, they may minimize the number and influence of those mistakes that do occur. Finally, it is important that adults recognize the strength of human nature, which provides young people with an ability to withstand many if not most of the bad influences that we as parents impart—often unwittingly or unconsciously—to our children.

All errors in child-training arise from three primary sources. Either (1) the child is not required to observe order, (2) the parent allows himself or herself to be drawn into conflict with the child, or (3) the child is discouraged. In most cases, however, elements of all three are present. Some parents try to force their children to observe order under all circumstances and, in doing so, allow themselves to become involved in a bitter struggle. Others attempt to avoid conflict with the child by giving in, thus neglecting his education for social conformity. Both procedures lead to failure and disappointment since laxity and lack of orderliness on the one hand will eventually force the parents into conflict with their child while the act of conflict on the other can never move the child to a proper observance of order. This leaves parents with only two unacceptable alternatives—disorder and conflict or order without conflict.

Selection of a proper procedure necessitates recognition of a fundamental principle called "the rule of cooperation." All mistakes in childhood education occur as a consequence of violation of this principle that suggests that maintenance of proper human relationships require a mutual respect for the dignity of each person who is in any way involved. Those parents who either refuse or fail to demonstrate respect for their child succeed only in frustrating, humiliating, enslaving, or overprotecting that child. If, on the other hand, parents indulge their child by making themselves his servants, or if they allow the child to boss them, they not only disregard their own dignity but also fail to earn respect for themselves or for their role as parents. A great variety of child-rearing mistakes are rooted either in parents disregard for their own dignity or in their disregard for the dignity of their children with a vacillation between forcing and giving in being the direct result of this disregard or neglect.

Talk *with*, Not *at* the Child

Although psychologists often recommend that parents conduct discussions with their children about mutual as well as individual problems, it has often been noted that very few adults know how to talk with children. Unfortunately, although parents may be friendly to their children, they often talk to or at rather than with them, so that instead of two-way communication, the child hears a sermon. Much of our ability to converse effectively with a child depends on our skill in communicating our respect for that child, even when we disagree with his ideas. Our children *can* think. They *are* able to make astute observations. They *are* able to organize their observations into systems and then act on conclusions.

As adults, we as parents are much too often so concerned with trying to impress young people with what we think that we fail to show respect for their thoughts and feelings. We neither listen as well as we should nor do we give our children credit for having ideas of their own. From the child's viewpoint, our apparent attempts to mold or program his mind, character, and personality—as we might attempt to shape a piece of clay—is little short of tyranny and as such is totally unacceptable. While this, of course, does not mean that we should not or cannot attempt to influence or guide our children, it does mean that we cannot and should not attempt to force either his behavior or his ways of thinking into our mold. Because each child is a unique individual, he must be trusted to respond and react to what he encounters in his life on his own terms.

As parents, our job is to guide the development of our children. In doing so, we can only be truly effective when we clearly realize what we are doing, how we are doing it, and why. We can gain such understanding by observing the behavior of our children—and our response to it—to learn the child's hidden purpose. And we can learn even more if we are willing to find out what our children think and feel. Because most children are very free in expressing their thoughts and feelings, this is not nearly as difficult as it at first might appear.

To the degree that we admonish, rebuke, criticize, or find fault with what children think and tell us they feel, they will slowly close the doors to intercommunication so as not to expose themselves to such uncomfortable and unpleasant experiences. On the other hand, to the degree that we freely accept a child's ideas and feelings, examine them with him and explore with him possible outcomes, the child will gain a sense of success and accomplishment in the business of solving life's problems. The asking of leading questions such as "What may happen then?" or "How will you feel?" or "How do you suppose the other person would feel?" remains one of the best methods for parents to convey ideas and perspective to their children. Parents who act as if they expect that a child will have only "right" ideas or parents who seem always to be telling him that they are right and that he is wrong merely terminate their communication with him while teaching him nothing. Parents who make these kinds of mistakes are parents who talk *to* and not *with* their children.

Consider the example of six-year-old Beth who says in anger that she hates her younger brother. If her parents can retain their objectivity, i.e., if they do not get involved, they can be of help to their daughter by talking with her. Mother's question, "Why would a girl hate her brother, I wonder? Do you have any ideas?" is designed to prompt discussion of the daughter's feelings.

Beth's response that, "He always gets in the way when my friends come over to play" tells mother much. To prompt further discussion in this case, the mother might then ask Beth what else she might do instead of hating him. It is the "what" and the "why" of the child's point of view which must be brought into clear focus in such an interchange. It is mother's job to acknowledge her daughter's spontaneous feeling of intense emotion, which Beth displays as anger and labels as hate but without moral implications of good or bad. How different this is from the typical "Shame on you, you really don't hate Johnny, you love him. He's your little brother. We all love him." type of response we so often hear from parents. This, too, is talking to and not with the child, and as such, succeeds only in alienating and never in helping that child.

Parents who recall the pain and frustration of their own early years may vow not to allow the same to happen to their own children. Adults, often with the best of intentions, may become inclined to presume that they know both what their children think and how they feel. When we perceive this feeling in ourselves, we must recognize that our child may have an entirely different viewpoint from our own. Mother, who remembers feeling angry and jealous because her younger sister seemed to get most of their grandmother's attention—perhaps because she was so cute—may decide that she will not allow the same to happen to her own daughter. Mother's approach to solving this problem may include an intention to be a good or even superior parent. However, the immediate situation may be and probably is quite different from that which mother may remember. Her own daughter may *not* be letting her cute baby sister get all the attention. Instead of the resentment, which her mother had displayed in the earlier similar situation, the daughter may—for example—strive to outdo her sibling, but in an unpleasant way.

Our point is that it is never wise to assume that we know our child's mind and emotions. If we are wise, we will find out what he thinks and feels, and to do so, we must listen and communicate. To retain perspective as parents, we must be willing to admit that our way of seeing things is not the only way. There is always the possibility of more than one point of view.

While remaining ready to acknowledge that a viewpoint different from our own may have merits, we must be prepared to use extreme care in our response to the discovery that our child sees things differently. We immediately close the door to further confidence when our response causes him to feel embarrassment or to lose face or to feel disgrace for any reason. Even if we are surprised or shocked, we *may* choose a neutral response such as "I don't know, you may be quite right. We will need to think about it and see what happens." Or we may choose to disclose to the child that we do not agree with him. When this choice is made, it is also wise to point out that he has every right to his own opinion but that we would like to watch with him "to see how it turns out."

It is important that parents remain willing to reevaluate their own thinking in keeping with practical results and not only according to their own definitions of "right" and "wrong." If parents truly desire that their child change certain opinions, which also means being able to accept the change, their only alternative is to lead that child to see that another way would work better. However, in a situation of equals, children must be allowed to present and defend their own opinions. Perhaps in some situations, it is we as parents who need to be led. Parents who listen *do* learn from their children. It is always important that parents accept their children as partners in the business of creating and maintaining family harmony and order. Each child's ideas and points of view are important since each child will act only in accordance with the world as he or she sees it. These very personal ideas form the child's "private logic," which is the sum total of the unconscious reasons for that child's behavior.

Because every child feels he has a right to his own opinions, adult attempts to tell a child not to do what he already knows is wrong are futile. This is true since the wrongdoing, whatever it may be, is the child's means for attaining a mistaken goal. Because his opinions cannot be disproved by our logic, adult admonitions succeed only in increasing his determination. We must listen to each of our children to discover that child's logic. When we do so, we learn that to a child, even unpleasantness can be desirable if it brings desired attention or power or if it otherwise reinforces a false self-concept. For this reason, helping such a child must always involve guiding him to a viewpoint from which he can see or experience advantages not seen before.

Consider the example of the child who wants power but who also wants to be liked. A parent of such a child may choose to discuss with the child the difficulties of getting both. In doing so, the parent may help the child to begin to see that he will not be liked if he wants to be a bully and that he will have to decide which he prefers. If the parent were to simply "tell" the child, point blank, however, that parent would only invite further hostility. In such a situation, carefully phrased questions, such as, "How do people feel toward a bully?" or "If a bully wanted to be liked, what could he do?" or "Does such a person have a choice?" could lead the child to discover what had been happening in his life and what he could do about it. By approaching the problem in this way, the parent may plant seeds for thought.

In situations that involve two or more children, the same indirect approach can be used. Suppose mother hears two of her sons fighting because one cheated in a checkers game. She decides to stay out of the fight, but later at a time of quiet friendliness, she decides to initiate a discussion of cheating. Here, she could again phrase her question in such a way as to elicit evidence of how each child thinks. Then, after each response, she could ask the other child what he thinks of his brother's answer. This mother would be helping her sons to recognize what was going on in their minds. Having planted her seeds, this mother need not say anything at all about what she thinks should be done. Having led them to see for themselves what the problem may be and what possible solutions may exist, she may then decide to let them think it over and see what happens.

Most people are much more willing to discuss the problems of others than they are their own personal difficulties, particularly if the problem is initially presented as an accusation. No individual—adult or child—will want to examine a situation in which he or she may be at fault. For this reason, if parents speak in general about "people" or as if the focus of their remarks was someone other than the persons involved in the discussion, they may create a distance which will not alienate while it simultaneously promotes objectivity. Of course, there are also times when it does help to be very direct. For example, mother may say, "Judy, when I am trying to get dinner on the table and you want me to help you with homework, I get very nervous and upset trying to do two things at the same time. What do you think we should do about it?"

Any and all information that parents are able to gain from discussion with their children may become the basis for future action on the part of the parents. However, when we as parents attempt to correct what to us seems to be an obviously faulty idea by moralizing, we not only fail to get the information we need, but we also defeat our own attempts to be useful. As long as we attempt to impress a child with our impression of the wrongness or incorrectness of the ideas which he presents, that child simply cannot and will not feel free to engage in open exchange of ideas with us. For this reason, we must learn to accept, at least temporarily, the ideas which the child presents, including those which to us seem obviously unacceptable. Note that we have *not* said that parents should agree with or approve of or believe these ideas. We say only that parents must be accepting of their child's ideas, which means that we should listen and hear out the viewpoints expressed by our offspring.

Rather than precipitating an argument that will only alienate the child, a much more productive approach could involve a statement such as the following: "I see. You have a point there, but I wonder how it would work if everyone chose to do the same thing?" In cases where a child shows reluctance to continue in a discussion with his parents because they have not—or he believes they have not—been receptive to his ideas or because they have implied that his ideas are not practical or workable, it is best to simply put aside the discussion temporarily. Here, a neutral statement such as that which follows may work best. "This is a complex problem. Let's all think about it some more and then talk again in a few days. We'll all have a fresh perspective and maybe even some new ideas by then."

Ideally, each member of a family unit will assume a creative part in the construction and maintenance of family harmony and order. To do so, each must be helped to realize that he or she does contribute to the whole. Forcing acceptance of adult thinking, which involves such elements as obedience as well as approaches to getting things done, detracts from this ideal and, unfortunately, is accomplished when we talk *to* our children. When we talk *with* our children, however, we can work together in a search for ideas concerning solutions of problems and improvement of situations. This does not mean that children have the right to run the family according to their ideas. Those readers who may feel that the approach suggested here will mean a giving in to children and a giving up of adult leadership are in error. In fact, the opposite is true.

Cooperation cannot be demanded; it must be won. The best way for parents to gain the cooperation of their children involves joint exploration for better ways of dealing with family problems as well as those of individual family members. This can only be done when each and every family member feels free to talk about what he or she thinks and feels. Such a discussion is the key process through which family members can identify and refine the best possible solutions to any problem that may confront the group for the benefit of all concerned. When we fail to listen to our children, when we fail to sit down with them to talk over current problems, and when we fail to allow them to express their opinions, we not only end up doing what they want us to do, but we also lose our very important influence over their behavior.

Stimulate the Child's Sense of Independence

Parents who fail to stimulate their child's independence may do so out of love. "I want to do everything for Sara," says mother. "I love her and I love taking care of her. She's everything to me. And she's so little; she's only five years old." These statements are the words of a woman who sees herself as a loving mother whose life is dedicated to the service of her child. This mother fails to realize that her love for her child is actually self-love. This mother who dresses her child, brushes and combs her hair, and in dozens of other ways pampers her and does things to and for her daughter would be shocked if she could realize how she is damaging the development of the girl.

This child has begun to behave like a mechanical doll. She is charming and delightful, but she has not learned to fasten her buttons without help nor can she tell her left shoe from her right. This child is being methodically taught that she is helpless, inferior, inadequate, dependent, and useless. She will learn that she has a place only as long as everything is done for her. Next year, when she enters school, her courage may be undermined greatly, and her helplessness will probably increase. Because there will then be no mother present to do everything for her, she may flounder as she encounters crises for which she will be almost totally unprepared. Although the preceding anecdote involved a girl, it might just as easily have involved a boy since in this example, as in others cited throughout this volume, the gender of the child makes relatively little difference.

Children find pleasure in having things done for them because they receive a feeling of power from being able to command adult services. However, when parents do for a child that which he can do for himself, they discourage him as they deprive him of the opportunity to experience his own strength and success. Whenever we do for a child what he can do for himself, we demonstrate our assumed superiority and his supposed inferiority. As we behave in this insensitive manner, we clearly show our complete lack of faith in the child's ability, adequacy, and courage. We rob him of his sense of security, which grows from his realization of his own capacity to both meet and solve problems. All this we do to maintain our own image of indispensability. Then we wonder why our son or daughter feels incapable and deficient. We have taught him ourselves as we have displayed our immense lack of respect for him as a person of worth.

Children learn as infants that being helpless and incapable brings the attention and service of mother. If the child has older brothers or sisters, their more mature abilities simply add to the child's discouragement. Such a child will need a great deal of unhurried encouragement and personal success. He or she will need help to develop a new concept of self as a capable individual as well as help to discover new ways to find a satisfying place in the family unit. What such a child does not need is the continual service he or she has been receiving and enjoying.

In helping her child, mother may use words of support combined with refusal to accept the child's self-evaluation of inadequacy—her pleas that "I can't do it."

"Yes, you can, Becky, you are five years old" is a proper response. A child badly discouraged may play the situation to the hilt by crying pitifully and making no further attempt—to get dressed herself, to play in the snow, or whatever else may be expected or desired. In such cases, mother must avoid her natural impulse to feel pity and to give in to the child's self-proclaimed weakness. If others are outside playing, for example, and Becky sees that she is missing the fun and that no one is any longer impressed by her pitiful situation—of being "unable" to pull on her own coat or whatever—she may change her mind and decide to solve her problem alone.

The same sort of situation may occur near the age of three when children continue to insist that their parents take them to the bathroom. Although most children at this age can manage alone, they may use temper tantrums as tools to elicit their parents' service. Jerry, for example, said, "I have to go to the bathroom."

"You can go by yourself," was his mother's gentle reply.

"No, I can't, and I have to go now. I want you to go with me."

"No, I'm sorry, I can't. I'm mixing bread dough."

"But I can't do it alone."

Mother said nothing more, and Jerry threw himself on the floor to scream and kick. Before long, he simply lay still, then he got up and went to the bathroom by himself. In cases such as this, a mother may quietly and gently refuse to do for the child what he or she can do for himself. Mother should also refuse to engage in a contest of words. In the case just cited, Jerry is learning to respond to life situations with a growing sense of independence and self-sufficiency.

Our children show us that they want to do things for themselves from earliest infancy. As children grow and develop, parents may often hear statements such as, "Mommy, I want to do it myself." Even the infant may reach for a spoon in an attempt to feed himself. At first, this is seen as cute behavior, but all too often, parents dissuade these early attempts in an effort to avoid a mess and more work for themselves. This they may do, but by their actions and attitudes, they also succeed in promoting discouragement and a false self-concept in the growing child. Very few parents recognize the potential seriousness of this error. They fail to realize how much easier it is to clean the baby or the floor than to later restore the child's lost courage or to bolster his damaged self-concept.

As parents learn to recognize this reality, they must also realize that many more opportunities exist for the child to help himself and others than most of us may realize without stopping to reflect on the details of a child's daily activities. If we as parents hope to encourage a child and help him to learn satisfactorily, we must allow that child to take advantage of natural learning experiences and let him learn through experience whenever possible. As soon as the child demonstrates a desire to do things for himself, we must refrain from interfering to as great an extent as possible. Simultaneously, however, we must supply the help, supervision, encouragement, and training which the child may require. To make this distinction wisely, we as parents must slow down in our busy lives at least enough to observe and gather information necessary to make informed rather than impulsive decisions.

Parents have no more right to stop a child from making useful contributions, which he is eager to make, than they have to do everything for the child. Children enjoy their ability to do and contribute if they are given opportunities to be helpful. As the child develops, he will display his natural inclination to try to continually do more and more for himself and for others. However, this inclination may be smothered by the fear, protection, and service of his parents. When this happens, the child will become discouraged, which may lead him to quickly discover the positive value of "weakness" or apparent inability. Such a child will develop a low opinion of himself and his ability and will increasingly assume that he is inadequate and unable to do things for himself. Then, his already weakened self-confidence and self-reliance are further undermined as he gains comfort in gaining service from others.

Parents can prevent this sort of detrimental progression by following a simple rule: *Never do for a child what he can do for himself.* Parents most often fail to follow this rule when they are either in the habit of doing certain things themselves or when they feel hurried to get them done. In so doing, parents tend to magnify the child's helplessness while minimizing his abilities. Most parents underestimate their child's level of development and readiness and for this reason are unaware of what their offspring has become capable of doing for himself. In this context, it is important that adults become sensitive to the subtle differences between expecting too much of a child, which is a form of imposing demands upon him and having and expressing confidence in his abilities, which is a form of respect.

When a mother is able to say, "Sally, I am so glad you can do it yourself," she is doing her duty. As she refuses to do for Sally that which Sally can do for herself, she gives her daughter room to develop. In such a case, the child's gain is her growing independence while her mother's gain is a satisfaction in her own effective stimulation. Psychologists know that very few parents would, with conscious intent, damage their child's self-sufficiency. But to avoid doing so, parents must become aware of the dangers of overprotection while at the same time remaining alert to opportunities for the stimulation of independence. We must be alert so that we do not ask too much, but we must recognize the steady development of each child's ability. When parents can step back to give the child room, when they can deny their own unnecessary assistance, and when they give proper encouragement, they will be doing all that is necessary to stimulate independence.

Be Firm; No Means No

As suggested in the preceding section, some parents seem to feel a compulsion to satisfy their child's every whim. Such a plan might work at least tolerably well in some theoretical situations if the child's parents were able to do so throughout life. In the real world, however, there is a need for children to learn to cope with life's constraints and frustrations. As long as parents satisfy the child's every whim, there is no need for that child to learn to cope with life's problems. Under such conditions, parents simply allow their tyrant child to continue (1) to disrupt order, (2) to fail to develop respect for other persons, and (3) to develop a well-defined concept of self as a powerful person with rights to both demand and receive.

Parents of such children literally assume the role of slaves to their offspring who often become very skillful in using anger as a control mechanism. Such children may also learn to manage their parents through winsome actions combined with logical presentations of requests or demands. Such behavior may be exceedingly well presented to play upon parental desire to please. When parents refuse a request, however, the badly spoiled child will usually retaliate and punish by being unbearably unpleasant. Such a child then often gets his or her way—again. Parents who are careful observers will quickly realize that it is the implied threat in many of their child's requests, which make them dictatorial demands.

When parents are unable to say "no," they show lack of respect, not only for themselves, but for their children's needs and for the necessity for routine and order as well. Parents who keep account of the number of times they acquiesce to a "just this once" plea will note the regularity of their children's success in parent training. Although many parents learn to feel obligated to please their children, this is a mistake. Parents who allow their children to manage adult members of the family succeed only in arousing a servile attitude or role, which will in turn promote self-centeredness in the child. Through the experience of such a situation, the child will learn to regard life as competition through which the strong or devious get their own way or else. The abilities of such a child to develop skills and attitudes of cooperativeness are, in this way, undermined. The child does not learn to fix his attention upon the needs of the situation but rather— and mistakenly—upon himself and his own desires. This so-called "spoiled" child will acquire a felt need to make others suffer when he cannot have his own way. Because such children have not learned to manage frustration, they are not able to accept a "no" graciously and to make the best of it.

Parents' own shortsightedness may make it difficult for them to recognize the long-term results of yielding to the child's every whim since by pleasing, they may have learned to bring temporary harmony to the home and family. For this reason, it is wise to use care in gratifying or pleasing the child. It is important that children learn to manage frustrations. If they fail to do so with minor frustrations during their youth, they will not have acquired the skill, the insight, or the resilience to do so when encountered with the more complex frustrations of later life. Finding a balance between pleasing and not pleasing requires careful consideration by parents. The routine and order of family living sometimes does require denial. If parents acquire the courage to say "no" in those situations that require it, their children can acquire the skills that they will need to tolerate the frustration they will certainly meet in life. A child who has not been helped to acquire these skills will be seriously handicapped as he meets situations in life in which no one will be concerned with pleasing him.

Consider the example of a mother and son at a supermarket. The son, Peter, enjoys rolling canned goods between the feet of passing shoppers. When his mother asks that he stop, he does not; when she insists, he simply screams. She angrily swats the boy, replaces the cans while mumbling an apology to people in the area, and then returns to her shopping. As she does so, she tells her son, "Now be a good boy, Peter, while mommy finishes shopping. Then I'll buy you some candy."

Soon the cans are rolling again. This mother's behavior suggests that she lacks the courage to say "no" with conviction. She may also report that she "can't stand to hear him scream." This mother has trained her son to feel justified in his demands and to get his own way no matter how outrageous his behavior may be. He in turn has trained his mother so well that she is both ready and willing to submit to his tyranny. Such a child may violently express his resentment at being denied. The parent, however, is obliged to maintain order. If the boy chooses not to manage his behavior, he should simply be removed from the store. This may require that the parent return later to complete her shopping alone. In any compilation of family priorities, parents must make these sorts of decisions.

Suppose the boy was not rolling cans but instead was squirting shoppers with his water pistol. Mother might go through the same ritual of asking, shouting, or hitting and apologizing, perhaps in unison with her son's screaming and stomping. In this situation, mother must take his toy since she cannot allow him to squirt others. Since he is not willing to restrain himself, mother cannot let him hold the pistol. She may choose to say something like, "When you are ready to keep your pistol in its holster and leave it there until we get home, you may have it again." Although mother must respect Peter's right to express his resentment, both must respect her right to say "no" and mean it.

Parents must learn to be concerned with the demands of the situation and to be unconcerned—or at least less concerned—with other less central elements, such as in this case "what people might think." People will stare, and this is unpleasant, but the training and development of the child is much more important. Here, a parent must make a choice between her pride and vanity—which may be temporarily hurt—and her obligation as a mother.

Let us return again to the supermarket, this time in the toy department. Lisa wants a toy doll. Mother says, "No, it is too expensive."

An argument and crying ensue. Mother compromises and buys a less expensive toy, a puzzle. Lisa wants it now; she wants to unwrap it.

Mother says "no" again, thinking that all the parts will fall out onto the floor. More temper and pulling prompt mother to "let her carry it home." Soon mother is scrambling to collect pieces that have fallen. Her daughter has torn open the cellophane window. Mother and daughter angrily leave the store. Again, we see a mother who lacks courage to say "no" and face her daughter's displeasure. Lisa has her mother well-trained, under her thumb. Mother would show much greater concern for her daughter's welfare if she were more careful in pleasing her offspring and if she would maintain an attitude of "no" to random buying. There is absolutely no reason why parents should buy a child every toy he sees and thinks he wants, nor is there any good reason to buy him something each time the child accompanies his parents on a shopping trip.

The toy itself will have little value to the child and will probably soon be discarded. It is making the parent give in, which is important to the child. The child in this situation is not nearly as interested in the toy as in proving that his parent must constantly give and that he or she can control the parent's behavior. The practice of buying a child something on each shopping trip only pampers his whims and teaches him to feel that these purchases are his right, prompting an "If she doesn't buy me something, she doesn't love me anymore" mistaken attitude. Further, if there is no limit to what he can demand, he will assume that the family's supply of money is limitless. As this occurs, his sense of the value of material things becomes progressively more distorted.

Shopping should be purposeful, and toys should have a useful purpose or meet a specific need. They should be given on days when presents are expected or seasonably, such as indoor toys in the winter, jump ropes or roller skates in the spring or baseball equipment or water toys during the summer months. When parents lack the necessary courage to establish this sort of order, they often do so because they feel afraid of the child's reprisal. To allow this to occur is a serious mistake that deprives the child of necessary discipline. As parents, we need not be arbitrary in refusing to give the child what he wants, but whenever his desire or request is contrary to order or to the demands of the situation, we must have the courage to stick to the "no," which expresses our own best judgment. It is natural that we want to please our children and to feel the satisfaction of satisfying their desires. We need to be alert to the dangers of this action, however, and to the ease of reaching a point where we try to please the child at the expense of order and give in to his demands unduly out of fear or embarrassment.

Learn to Withdraw from Conflict

When a power struggle is in full bloom, it is usually impossible for a parent to utilize natural consequences effectively. And in a full-blown power struggle, the best structured logical consequence will degenerate into punishment, with the parent simply using it as a weapon. When a child's immediate goal is power, the child will arrange to display his ability to do as he chooses and, in doing so, may engage his parent in a battle. Perhaps it is the battle of bedtime, which occurs in so many homes. For example, four-year-old Craig may refuse to stop his play activities, then dawdles in his bath, then romps on his bed, then wants a drink of water, then returns to the living room for a goodnight kiss or to watch television, then gets up to go the bathroom. The list can go on and on. Perhaps after his mother loses her temper and Craig has burst into tears, daddy will come to the door to scold mother. Perhaps later, there will be peace. Perhaps.

Some parents allow their child to remain with them if they are engaged in a quiet activity such as viewing television (the influence of television, etc., was discussed in greater detail in chapter 2). In the case of a young child who may want to lie on a sofa to watch television, her or his mother (or father) may hold the child's feet on her lap and gently rub them—or the child's back—until the child falls asleep. Then the child may be carried to bed. When the child is small, this may work well; but it is likely to become habitual. In the case of the older more reluctant child, more stringent methods may be required. Consider the following example:

Gordon is stubborn. He should go to bed. He needs his sleep, but mother does not know how to persuade or otherwise induce him to do so. There may be several productive methods, which she could use to solve this problem, but one of the most effective is to withdraw from the conflict, which Gordon is provoking. To prepare Gordon, she may tell him during his afternoon play hour that his bedtime is eight o'clock and that she will tell him when it is time. At 7:45, she tells him that when the big hand points straight up to twelve, it will be eight o'clock, his bedtime.

At eight o'clock, mother and father enter his room, where he is playing, to inform him that it is now bedtime. Firmly but with a friendly manner, they may help him to dress for bed if he chooses not to do so himself. After kissing him goodnight, they will help him into bed, talk with him briefly, and leave. Later, if he begins to use his techniques to gain attention, mother and father will be too absorbed in their television watching to notice. They will act as if he is already in bed, fast asleep. Gordon may return to bed or he may fall asleep on the floor, perhaps crying himself to sleep.

Gordon's parents have not been cruel. They have been firm on his behalf. Very little of this sort of behavior is usually necessary to influence a change in the child's pattern of "spoiled" behavior. Although this pattern of response is often difficult for parents, it does work, and with no lasting damage to either the child or to the family relationship. In this case, mother and father have said goodnight and then assumed responsibility only for what *they* would do. They have withdrawn and left the field to Gordon.

In the beginning, Gordon's parents should expect that he will probably desperately double his efforts to engage them in fighting to get him to go to and stay in bed. If their firmness holds, even while he plays on their pity by crying, this mode of training will have begun to alter his relationship both to his parents and to the order necessary for cooperative family living.

But what about the next night? Suppose on the next night, after his parents tuck him in and leave him, he again gets up, demands a drink, wants another kiss, or whatever. Mother and father should again act as if he were asleep. He may then go back to bed. The chances are good that within a week, Gordon will readily accept eight o'clock as the end of his day. If not, his parents should continue to avoid the power struggle by putting him to bed firmly but without excessive words. As before, they could take him by the hand at the proper hour, undress him, and bathe him if that is part of standard procedure in this family and then remain totally aloof when he disturbs, this time retreating to their own bedroom and locking the door. This last addition is not always necessary.

Many children go through a whining phase that they will eventually outgrow. However, it is not necessary to endure this bad habit since there is something that can be done about it. Simply stated, the parent can refuse to meet a whined demand. To do so effectively, the parent may state his or her desire that the child not whine. Then, when whining occurs, the parent must withdraw *without talking*. If the parents were to remain, he or she would make a steady target and would almost surely yield to the child's pressures. Here again, it is of value to all concerned to take time out from a ritualized "game" for productive training.

This time, the withdrawal—probably by the mother—should be to an interesting book or magazine and her portable radio or telephone. Where can she go? She should go to the bathroom and lock the door behind her. This is the one room in the house that is an absolutely ideal retreat because by custom, it symbolizes privacy. The bathroom should be stacked with reading materials to entertain her and a radio to shut out the noise of whining. Whenever junior whines, mother disappears into the bathroom. She says nothing. It isn't necessary, and junior may soon change his tone of voice.

Most mothers first refuse to respond but then give in. As the child manipulates his mother, he gains strength as well as confidence in his power to do so again. Mothers or fathers can make whining or temper tantrums futile by simply retreating from the scene. Let junior do his whining or have his tantrum in a vacuum. He will soon stop. Why? Because no tantrum or episode of whining has a payoff without an audience. If mother returns to her work in five, ten, or fifteen minutes, we would expect that she would probably find her child contentedly playing or otherwise engaged. Usually, a mother will not need to resort to this technique more than a few times. Children learn fast!

Even infants will try to get their own way. For example, eight-month-old Bruce must be trained to accept order. His mother should respect his decision to try a temper tantrum to get his way. When she yields the field to him, however, she does not give the desired service or attention. Although this withdrawal is an impassive act on mother's part, it in no way implies rejection of the child since her feelings and expressions of love, affection, and friendliness will continue. In fact, the act of withdrawal at the time of conflict actually helps to maintain a good family relationship.

In moments of anger, what we say to or do to our children is often very harmful to the relationship. The exchange of shouted insults and/or blows can only be damaging.

Parents who become skilled in immediate withdrawal often find that their children respond very readily to this simple act. Once this practice has been established in a family unit, children very quickly sense the new limits of the situation. Because they have a deep desire to belong and because an empty battlefield can be most disconcerting, they very quickly modify their behavior to avoid a now useless exhibition of ill temper. The situation now becomes predictable. As the child now accepts the limits of the situation, his parents indicate a desire to again cooperate. In this technique, parents have an excellent procedure by which to win cooperation, which is the goal of their training.

In utilizing this method, we are not allowing the child to get by with misbehavior since his motive in most conflict situations is either to engage our attention or to involve us in a power contest. Parents who become involved in the child's game succeed only in succumbing to his scheme, and by doing so, they strengthen his goal. For this reason, it is always futile to attempt to correct a child's misbehavior through use of words.* Instead, we must act to induce a change in attitude. When the child finds that he has failed in his attempts to have his own way, he will learn to adjust to the requirements of the situation and eventually will learn how much more he can gain through cooperation. As this occurs, the child develops a respect for his parents who represent the existing social order and the reality of life situations.

It becomes much easier for family members to deal with conflicts in public once training through withdrawal has been well established at home. A severe test must be met by parents when their children misbehave in public because by doing so, sons and daughters put their mothers and fathers in the position of being seemingly inadequate parents. Extensive experience with children has revealed that they behave in public as they have been trained to do at home, with the possible exception of those who do even more misbehaving in public because they sense parental vulnerability.

Because children are extremely sensitive, they will feel the withdrawal and noninvolvement of the parent in any context as can be clearly seen in the case cited earlier of a child who—while walking with his mother on the street—decided to go no farther. The mother simply walked on as her child displayed stubbornness and temper. As she did so, she found he soon began to follow along to keep her in sight and then ran to catch up. In this case, the mother withdrew from the conflict, using a mental withdrawal-to-the-bathroom technique that could include bystanders. As parents, we will always have the key to any such problem situation when we have learned to focus our attention and behavior upon the demands of the situation rather than upon our own personal prestige.

Don't Overprotect the Child

Parents who seem to be continually "doing things" for their children provide many services for their children that are entirely unnecessary. These same parents often report that they do so to pro-

---

* When parents do not know what to do, they talk or yell.

tect their children from harm, which is a natural and normal desire. However, many adults simply overdo it. They see potential danger lurking everywhere. They are overprotective. In reality, we cannot protect our children from life nor should we want to do so. While it is important that we as parents train our children in the strength and courage needed to face life, an overly fervent desire to protect them from harm may have a discouraging effect. It may also keep them helpless and dependent on adult supervision.

Many parents have developed a mistaken attitude. They place themselves in a superior and prominent position, which tends to keep their children submissive. As today's children grow and learn about life outside of their families, they become increasingly intolerant of such efforts. In time, they will rebel against them. In many cases, under the pretext of concern for the child's welfare, parents attempt to keep the child dependent and relatively helpless, often so they may appear powerful, protective, and necessary in their own eyes as well as those of their children. Many parents fail to realize the extent to which they exploit their children because of their own need to be needed. A closely related reason, which also fosters parental overprotective efforts, is the self-doubt present in many adult personalities. For these reasons, parents who doubt their own ability to manage and solve problems foster a corresponding lack of confidence in the ability of their young offspring to take care of themselves as they too meet problems in their lives.

The way in which any child deals with an overprotective parent depends upon that child's goals. The most dangerous response is that of helplessness or inadequacy—the fourth goal defined in chapter 2. The child who feels completely discouraged may give up and expect to be continually protected from all of life's difficulties. For example, parents of a child with an organic disability such as diabetes may strive to maintain for that child a life which is as normal as possible. However, lies and evasions will seldom serve this purpose. Rather than calling his medication "vitamins," meeting out of the child's presence to discuss his disorder, and lying to him about his condition, parents of such a child should share both truth and responsibility with him. Sooner or later, this child will have to know and understand his condition because eventually, he will have to deal with it himself.

In the past, if the child had contracted a childhood disease such as measles or chicken pox, for example, his parents would have told him the nature of his illness as they worked to help him live through it as comfortably as possible. More recently, ear infections, pink eye, or urinary bladder infections are frequently seen. But because children soon recover from such common childhood diseases, they may seem less formidable than a chronic disease such as diabetes, which—because it is likely to be a lifelong problem—may be much more difficult to explain to a child.

Experience with this sort of problem has revealed that by the time children enter kindergarten, they are usually mature enough to understand the importance of medicine in helping the ill body to function. Parents who assume a casual attitude early in the child's training will help him to develop a healthy attitude on his own. After all, it is his problem and will be all his life. Such a child needs to gradually become aware that he has a specific disorder that can be managed so that he can live a very normal, active life. Such a child needs training, help, and encouragement to face his problems, with the best encouragement being acknowledgment that he *can* deal with it.

As the child matures, his knowledge of his disorder can be increased. Parents will be able to provide their child with the necessary approach for meeting such a problem if they themselves don't become overwhelmed and overemotional about it. Parents who shield their child from such a problem succeed only in denying him his right to learn to cope with it himself. The same is true of parental overprotectiveness in all other areas of living. At some point in his life, the growing youth will have to learn to cross the street or get to the store alone. Sometimes he will have to learn to choose appropriate clothing for various weather conditions. As some point in time, he will have to learn to manage his own life if he is to become a secure, self-accepting, confident, competent individual. As parents, we can no more completely arrange and control the lives of our children than we can our own. It is the desperate attempt to do so which accounts for much of the misery that we encounter in our lives.

If we attempt to protect our offspring from all discomfort and hardship in life, they will not learn to resist the inevitable. Then, to the degree that the child accepts this implicit assessment of him, he will learn to believe that he should be able to continue to have things his way. But the realities of life do not allow this to occur, with a resulting disillusionment not only against parents but also against life itself for not allowing the individual to arrange things according to his desires. The result, of course, is a child who is constantly angry because life and persons are not constantly adapting to his desires. Children who have acquired this viewpoint have been labeled "spoiled brats," and they do not necessarily lose these qualities as they grow into adulthood.

When we pamper and coddle our children in an attempt to protect them from life, we succeed only in programming them toward a fundamentally incorrect attitude toward life, which may later become an established part of their developing personalities. To avoid this mistake, parents must recognize their obligation to instruct their children in ways, means, attitudes, and values with which to cope with life. To do so effectively, children must first be taught to examine that with which they are confronted and then to seek to discover what they—not someone else—can do about it. Even very young children can learn to do this if they are carefully taught to do so.

For example, if two-year-old Peter tears one of six-year-old Sally's storybooks, she may become angry but must realize that the deed cannot be undone. By use of one or more directly placed questions concerning what she could do about it, mother may enable Sally to realize that she will not be able to force her brother to stop tearing her books but that she can keep them out of his reach. The basic question the child must learn to ask is, "What can I do about it?"

Because adults feel a sense of superiority, they are prone to simply assume that their children are too small and innocent to solve problems or to take frustration in their stride. Many if not most parents seem to underestimate their children in this regard. In reality, the child's cerebral cortex is, on the average, 90 percent developed by the age of five, and he has learned half of all he will ever know by then. Further, the child's potential for emotional self-control requires only training for the child to become reasonably self-directing by this age. For these reasons, parents must learn to acknowledge their child's strengths and replace skepticism with trust and confidence in the child's abilities. As parents learn to recognize their child's potential, they may also realize the necessity of proper guidance for the child as he or she develops.

Parents must also learn that just as overprotection is dangerous for the child, the abandonment of the child to his fate by allowing him to experience the full impact of life all at one time is also dangerous. Mothers and fathers must be constantly alert for opportunities to step into the background to allow the child to experience his strength and his success. But at the same time, they must stand ready to step in at points when problems become too much for the child. This process should begin at birth, with parents handing off their children's life and its problems, challenges, and satisfactions little by little with care and guidance. Rather than becoming the wall behind which their child basks in innocence, parents must become a sieve through which they can filter life experience in amounts that the child can meet with success.

Don't Spoil the Child

Children who desire and demand continued pampering are often called spoiled children. In "spoiling," we are faced with a particular and elusive problem that presents a very serious impediment to the child's adequate development. The parental attitudes and behaviors that we call spoiling are not easily defined because they include a wide variety of actions and enduring learned predispositions. The very word is expressive of false methods of adapting the child to life, suggesting that instead of training the child to meet the responsibilities of living, he has somehow been damaged so as to be unfit to perform them satisfactorily. At the root of this process, in most cases, will be found a well-intentional desire—exhibited by anxious parents who are strongly attached to or greatly concerned over their children—to spare a certain child from the experience of unpleasant realities of living.

Children who are most often exposed to this danger are usually (1) oldest or youngest children, (2) children involved in a difficult pregnancy or birth, (3) children involved in long periods of involuntary illness, (4) children whose next older brother or sister has died, or (5) children who for some other reason arouse pity or sympathy. The last listed of these five categories most often include children who are delicate or sickly, who are in some respect handicapped, or who have suffered some significant loss—such as one of their parents—at an early age. Strikingly good-looking children are also likely to be pampered as are those whose upbringing has been subject to considerable influence from grandparents. Although exceptions in any of these categories may of course occur, in general, anything that in any way heightens the solicitude of parents toward their children tends to increase the dangers of spoiling.

In their attempt to shield a child from unpleasant experiences, parents often allow a breach of the order and regularity that is so essential for harmonious living. This pattern of protectiveness may begin at any time but is often initiated soon after birth. Even newborn babies may be gotten off to a wrong start since they are just as easily stimulated to defiance of order and regularity as they are to conformity. For example, a definite feeding schedule is not only in line with the rhythm of a child's physiological functioning but is also an experience that is an essential aid to help that child to an early recognition of the benefits of regularity and order. The early resistance of an infant to such regulation, with crying being the most outstanding example, is often misunderstood by anxious parents who interpret it as an indication of hunger or pain. Although that interpretation may be a correct one, such resistance often means only that the child wants some attention. Ordinarily, it is best for parents to remain calm and to resist their temptation to break the well-considered regularity of feeding, unless, of course, the child is ill, in which case some deliberate change in his schedule may possibly be in order.

Pursuit of a planned and well-ordered schedule soon helps the child to recognize and accept order (see chapter 2). In the example cited above, he simply cannot hasten mealtime by crying. Usually, within six weeks to three months, a child can become accustomed to his specified and orderly feeding period. In cases of failure, however, overprotective parents who feel unable to discipline the situation in their desire to spare their "helpless" child his first annoyances are usually at fault. Such parents often argue that later, when their child is stronger, that child will "simply get used to order on his own."

As a baby grows older, however, it becomes progressively more difficult for parents to compensate or make up for past indulgence. The older the child gets, the more strongly he or she will object to any change in the irregularity, which has by now become habitual. Parents who for some reason believe that their child's health or well-being may suffer from this irregularity are then likely to allow their anxiety and concern to increase proportionately. If at this point the parent—usually the mother—makes a half-hearted try to enforce some sort of order, the child will then only redouble his struggle and outcry since he is by now sure of success. In the end, at least partly because the child's vocal powers are developing so well, most parents simply give up the struggle.

Unfortunately, the detrimental attitude concerning this point, which is currently held by many adults, has been reinforced by a tendency among some pediatricians to advise feeding the baby whenever he is hungry. This is appropriate during the first six weeks to three months. This trend grew out of certain concepts, which considered emotional frustration to be the prime source of human maladjustment. Within the context of this theory, there can be no doubt that some children do develop satisfactorily, regardless of the type of feeding regimen they experience as infants. And some children will develop a desire for regularity without a specific plan of parental help. We also agree that an overly rigid schedule has its dangers if it provokes anxiety in the mother since the anxious mother may become a slave to her schedule as she watches the clock with apprehension instead of allowing herself to relax and accept regularity.

So, know each baby's patterns and signals. Parents usually prefer to establish or create a "fairly predictable" routine, which is correct. But they should allow the baby to feed long enough to be satisfactorily fed because some babies are slower than others. Again, after from six weeks to three months, parents can start initiating a routine, which will evolve naturally. The key is to follow a regular pattern as the child grows older so they can get to know what to expect, especially when it comes to the evening routine of bath time, feeding time, and bedtime.

Still, some parents deliberately indulge their children, especially those who begin when the child is very young. This predictably will have at least some detrimental effect. This sort of deliberate irregularity and indulgence at the start of life coincides in our society with a general tendency for most overanxious parents to excessively spoil their children. While there is no doubt that the "demand schedule" concept may have some beneficial effects in removing a cause for struggle between parents and children at any level of their development, the same effect may be obtained if parents can refrain from pressure and demonstrated anxiety. This principle is equally true whether the issue is simply concern over the amount of food eaten, for example, or a more complex pattern of long-term struggle. Disturbed family relationship and the hostility, which is its result, do not begin with the baby who is frustrated but rather with his parents who become confused and anxious.

A child's happiness is based on acceptance of order without rebellion, not on the satisfaction of vague emotional needs. Experience clearly reveals that the baby or child of friendly, calm parents will not continue to fight any reasonable schedule, which he is allowed to experience during his early months and years of life.

All acts of spoiling may be expected to follow essentially the same general pattern, which involves a child succeeding in the evasion of a necessary duty followed by an increasing violation of the requirements of order necessary to redress this error. In such a pattern, one infringement leads to another and so on. A child exposed to such experience grows and develops in a pampering atmosphere in which the natural order that otherwise regulates human conduct is not in force. The pattern of pampering and spoiling may assume innumerable forms and shapes.

One example among many might involve a child who cries because he wants food between meals. In response to his crying, his mother picks him up and rocks him. He likes this response from mother. Soon, when he should be lying quietly or sleeping, he makes a practice of crying until someone again comes to rock him. When someone is not present to rock him, he will simply not get the undisturbed rest and sleep necessary for his growth and development.

Such a child in a very real sense is wrapped in a protective layer of tenderness and affection and is insulated against the necessity of justifying his existence for himself through his own accomplishments. In such a condition, he is beyond the jurisdiction, influence, or control of the rules of responsibility that obligate all other members of his family. Because his parents' sympathy and indulgence shield him from the unpleasant consequences of his actions, he is relieved of the exertion necessary to deal with the inconveniences of life. His parents' exaggerated anxiety prevents the child from encountering anything that might involve danger or require courage. As he is exempt from essential tasks, with his desires "catered to" and granted without justification, he will find it possible to get his own way, even in those cases where order may be seriously upset in the process.

Experiences such as these create a handicap to the basic social adjustment of the child from which he will suffer later in life as he faces the necessity of subordinating personal desires to those of others. For this reason, spoiled children are not especially happy. Since in real life, no one can have all of his or her wishes or desires fulfilled, spoiled children may come to regard the rebuffs of life as an unfair presumption or interference on the part of elements of their environment or even of destiny itself. As part of this process, lack of self-reliance then often becomes characteristic of such children and, in many cases, may cause them to break down under even the slightest hardship or responsibility.

Many may never feel that they are ever quite a match for life. For them, life is too hard, leaving them with a feeling of inability to cope. The impatience, discontent, and joylessness that characterize so many spoiled children reveal how very little the practice of parental indulgence has succeeded in making their lives easier or more pleasant. This may be seen in contrast to other young people who have learned to manage their lives, problems, and concerns much more as a matter of course.

As each child grows and matures, he or she will face increasing responsibility, which in turn makes increasingly difficult the practice of continual parental pampering. As a child finds difficulty in understanding why he must suddenly do without the amount of indulgence and help he has learned to expect, he is likely to balk or rebel at being denied the satisfaction of his whims while being forced to manage on his own resources. When his parents stop giving in to all of his demands as they must, the child often interprets this change in their behavior as a sign of either indifference or unkindness. For this reason, any kind of spoiling leads predictably to conflict with the child. During the process of this shift or change, parents may see little cause for satisfaction with their child's conduct and, feeling both irritated and annoyed, may add to the intensity of their child's dissention by punishing him for the consequences of their own inadequate training methods. The result, which may dominate this entire process of pseudo-training, may be an interplay of affection and desperation within a context of unplanned laxity and severity.

This degree of spoiling may seem extreme, but even in lesser degree, it is detrimental. In most families, it probably cannot be avoided entirely, particularly in the case of a youngest or only child. Many parents derive a very real enjoyment from what is, in reality, the spoiling of their children as they protect and mother them, do little favors for them, shower them with affection, and help them or do for them that which they could or should do for themselves.

In their emotional indulgence, parents become insensitive to the needs of orderly human relationships while their desire for personal superiority simultaneously stimulates them to take undue responsibility, and their anxiety induces them to be overprotective. At the same time—through impositions, slight infringements on requests and responsibilities, and numerous subtle and deceptive strategies— the child further induces his parents to spoil him. Unfortunately, these occasions usually seem so insignificant that parents either fail to realize how much such small indulgences disturb their relationship with the child or do not feel it is worthwhile to make an issue or special effort to stop the process.

For these reasons, the child is likely to continue his practice of demanding undue attention, putting others into his service, avoiding responsibilities, or disturbing the order of the household. While parents of such children may have our sympathy and understanding, they will not only pay a big price for their many small mistakes but will also find that they must expend much effort to correct their family relationships as the unfortunate consequences of their own actions become increasingly obvious and progressively more troublesome.

Display Love and Affection Wisely

Even though parents who consistently dislike their children now seem to be the exception, many unwanted children do exist in our society. In recent years, of course, the trend toward planned parenthood through birth control and abortion has significantly reduced the number of unwanted children. But when this condition does exist, a sense of being unloved may prevent the child from adjusting himself to the society in which he is developing. This occurs because it arouses in the child feelings of extreme defiance and hostility, while at the same time depriving him of certain rights as a family member. The child who feels unloved is not prepared to adapt himself to the code of conduct of the society in which he lives. Although he may learn to conform superficially, inwardly, he will become a bystander whose social sense will become atrophied.

In spite of the fact that most parents seem to like their children, at least most of the time, innumerable children feel rejected or unloved. The spoiled child, for example, may feel disliked or rejected if his parents fail to continue in their practice of indulgence. For such children, not receiving attention or expected gifts, not being fussed over or admired and, in general, not having their way are from their viewpoint sufficient reasons to believe that they are no longer loved. In a very real sense, such a child learns to believe that people who will not do as he asks or as he wants them to do simply do not like him. As intrafamily conflict involving such children grows in intensity, parents often reach a state where they feel they can no longer tolerate the child's demands. It is at this point that they respond with scolding, nagging, or punishing behavior, which only makes the situation even more unpleasant. Because children are easily impressed with such overt hostility, they quickly learn to feel that they can no longer trust their parents' demonstrations of affection.

The effect is the same whether the child is actually disliked or only believes that his parents no longer like him. Then, as the child's conflict with his parents continues to increase in intensity, that child may find that he can get attention best or perhaps only if he misbehaves. This is usually because his parents—especially his mother—may now take a well-deserved rest from him during periods when he is either agreeable or quiet. Such a child's mistaken attitudes often become especially well-defined in families where younger brothers or sisters simultaneously push ahead and succeed in getting increasingly more attention for themselves. A child who then competes for attention in negative ways through misbehavior will succeed only in provoking further expressions of parental criticism, dissatisfaction, and censure, which in turn further convinces him that he is not loved and that he has been and is being mistreated.

All children need love and close warm interpersonal relationships with others for adequate development. However, an *excess* of affection may also do harm since it may condition a child to a life-long quest for the love and tenderness that he or she once received from a parent. A pattern of overcharged and extravagant affection that binds a child too closely to its parents is likely to impair later capacity for love in other forms and may in some cases cause the individual to become bitterly disillusioned by his or her fellow human beings. In general, any exorbitant excess of affection provides a faulty preparation for the normal conditions of life. In some cases, immoderate affection on the part of parents may even cause premature sexual development in children. For this reason, it has been suggested that it may be harmful to kiss children too much, especially on the mouth, or to allow them to share their parents' bed, even for short periods in the morning or on weekends.

While it is true that excessive display of affection may promote close relationship between the generations, its value is questionable if intimacy and confidence are achieved exclusively by this means. Such behavior may cause the child to become increasingly dependent, and it does not prevent conflict. More often, it actually serves to both evoke and intensify conflict which, because of the course it takes, may assume certain well-defined forms. The child may display many indications of goodwill with no suggestion that open rebellion could occur while clearly revealing his inner opposition through apparent ineptitude and helplessness. Bad dreams, violent objection to school attendance, vain concern with impressing others, or lack of self-confidence may also occur. Nuisance behavior, fidgeting, giggling, clowning, and general loquaciousness used in an attempt to win personal recognition may often accompany this general situation.

Probably the most common general manifestation of over-affection is what parents often refer to as "nervousness." Unfortunately, many parents who undoubtedly cherish their deep feelings of love and attachment for their child and deeply enjoy the physical signs of his or her affection fail to recognize that their overemphasis may delude their offspring concerning his or her position in life. Rather than helping their child to acquire recognition through tangible achievement, such parents—mistakenly and without realizing the implications of their behavior—lead their child to the conclusion that his aim in life should be to win love and affection through his mere existence as a love object. Parents who center on their children all of their desire for affection, which has perhaps remained unsatisfied from other phases of their lives, should bear these facts in mind and may need professional counseling assistance to do so.

When a child gets into mischief, his or her parents may not want to be hardhearted but may at the same time give this impression by becoming cross or appearing irritated. Whether such parental behavior is a sincere response or only a bluff or deception, it is in line with a popular school of psychology, which goes so far as to recommend this type of withholding of affection to overcome the child's resistance (while simultaneously suggesting that it is the only truly effective method of child training).

While we definitely do not agree with this viewpoint, it must be conceded that certain objectives can be attained by this method. To a child, the sense of being rejected by the persons who care for him and of feeling he has lost or forfeited their love and concern may easily be sufficiently painful to cause him to suppress certain unruly tendencies. Because a child does not want to lose the love of his parents, he is very likely to attempt to modify or control those impulses which elicit their disapproval. However, under these conditions, it is a mistake to believe that such tendencies will have been eradicated since they will be only repressed and never eliminated. So, other very different methods must be used to accomplish this result.

In most cases, an attempt by parents to deprive a child of their love will be met with a counter-attempt to force them into a display of affection. Children may use many techniques with fear at bedtime being among the most common. This occurs because the child's courage is seriously impaired by each incident of apparent parental alienation, which serves to make the child increasingly conscious of his relative weakness and dependency. Even more serious consequences of being angry or cross with a youngster may involve an increasing lack of trust and an increasing degree of doubt in the absolute reliability of parents. Finally, the twin developmental tasks of (1) developing a social sense and (2) acquiring faith in human nature become increasingly difficult for the child whose "best friends"—or at least his earliest and strongest companions—frequently or even periodically reject or rebuke him.

As suggested earlier, parents have at their disposal much more suitable means for correcting their child's faults or mistaken ideas. These means involve either making or allowing each of their offspring to experience the natural or logical consequences of his or her improper behavior. Coercive methods should not be used since the mood or spirit of comradeship between the child and his parents may be damaged by incorrect attempts to alter its direction or content. Research with children has revealed that parents cannot alter their relationship of friendliness to their children without at least implanting in the child's mind the seeds of fear, conflict, and dissention. Fortunately, proper methods of child training never require an alteration of friendly parental relations with children, so these seeds need never germinate.

Children are much more prone to forgive a sharp word blurted out in an unguarded moment than a cold and deliberate withdrawal of affection, which to them is simply a way for parents to say, "I don't like you anymore." It is this sort of feeling of rejection that marks the beginning of a struggle for open display of parental love, esteem, and affection. More extreme forms of apparent rebuff—such as actual unkindness, harshness, aloofness or continued refusal to talk—are defensive punitive measures that can fail to force the child into a counter-defensive attitude.

Work with families has shown that most parents have affection for, positive regard for, or at least care about their children under virtually all circumstances, even when they are angry over improper or childish behavior. The child should and needs to know this, but many children do not. It is—or at least should be—the behavior of the child that the parent disapproves, not the child himself. It is because children feel rejected by their parents and think no one likes them that they come to believe they can get attention only when they are disturbing and not while they are well-behaved.

Since young children who experience an excess of scolding and punishment come to wrong conclusions which include the mistaken assumption that they are not liked, it seems logical to consider whether or not one should ever show disapproval. The answer, of course, is that absolutely impersonal, objective, and matter-of-fact behavior is not only impossible but is at the same time both unnatural and insulting. No parent can—nor should he or she—continuously avoid disapproval, and on some occasions, it is necessary that disapproval be clearly displayed. On these occasions, it becomes very important that the parent censure the child's behavior and not the child. People who fail to distinguish between the action and the person who acts confuse the value of the individual—including one's self—with the value of that individual's action or behavior.

Adults should feel free to express their dislike or disapproval of certain behaviors *if* they are careful to clearly indicate to the child that it is not he or she as a person who is disliked. Parents who fail to make this distinction cause the individual who becomes the focus of their criticism to doubt his or her value in society in cases where that person's actions do not measure up to the standards that they set for themselves or which others may attempt to set for them. What adults must understand in this context is that these are not bad children, only unhappy and discouraged ones who have not yet found the proper method for integrating themselves into the human society in which they live. Parents as well as teachers and other adults who make the mistake of classifying individual children or youth in terms of more or less incidental achievements or failures should realize that they risk damage to the child's concept of both himself and his world, often for the remainder of his life.

Control Display of Anxiety and Self-Doubt

Parents who experience fear and anxiety encounter powerful and conflicting emotions which cause them to see their environment as fraught with danger from which they feel compelled to shield their children. It is just such a parent who feels over-concerned that something might happen to his child who is most apt to fail to realize that the child must learn to take care of himself. A child who has already been hurt may strive for dependence, but he too must acquire the ability to recognize dangers and to cope with them adequately on his own initiative. We now know that children who do not acquire this capability are more rather than less liable to come to harm as they turn on the gas, climb on furniture, or play with matches, for example. Lack of courage on the part of parents of such children is likely to deprive them of valuable and highly necessary experience. Children without firsthand experience may continue to be unable— or more likely unwilling—to judge risks. Because they have been led to feel that others will take responsibility for their acts, they may use them to manage the behavior of others.

As the parents' anxiety level increases, it may only become necessary for them to relax their vigil of surveillance and supervision for a moment for the dreaded "accident" to occur. On the other hand, children who are more correctly reared show adequate caution in the face of hazards. Youngsters who grow up with any degree of self-reliance are not nearly as incautious as their parents are often prone to believe since in this respect, as in so many others, adults often greatly underrate the child's astuteness. It is only during the first two years of life while still gradually becoming acquainted with the nature and function of separate objects in the environment that the child is liable to unintentionally expose himself to danger in the home. During this learning period, it is much more advisable to simply point out the various dangers, and when necessary, to arrange harmless but unpleasant natural consequence experiences than to frighten the child with safety lectures and/or suggestions of imminent but poorly defined dangers.

If training during this period is carefully done, the child will quickly learn to correctly evaluate the risks to which he or she is exposed. While this training should be continued outside the home and beyond age two, parents who have done their work well will soon realize that most of what the child has learned will transfer to other new situations. For example, observation at a busy intersection will often reveal how much more careless and frivolous many parents are concerning safety than are their children, at least in a moment of actual danger.

Many adults are surprised to learn that pedestrian research reveals that more adults than children are struck by automobiles in spite of the fact that large numbers of children often play unsupervised along country roads as well as city streets. While it is true that some children who are eight or nine years of age—or even older—cannot be trusted to cross a street by themselves, the blame in such cases nearly always rests with their overanxious parents. Such parents have almost invariably failed to allow their children to learn proper self-protection so as to be able to look out for and take responsibility for themselves. All children must learn to take care of themselves, and the earlier they learn to do this, the easier will be the job of mothers and fathers in their role as parents.

Neither be Frightened nor be Impressed by Fears

Children who acquire timid or squeamish notions from their parents do not become better prepared for life. They only become more anxious. Parents need to realize that their child's level of anxiety is often a direct result of their own anxiety, which may have induced them to communicate to their children exaggerated ideas of the risks, dangers, and the hazards of living. Many parents sincerely believe that they are training their offspring to be cautious when they dwell upon such things as the dangers of disease and illness, the frequency of accidents on the streets, or the depravity of mankind in general.

Observation of families who have behaved in this way reveals that excessive caution may very often lead to the same kind of results as does thoughtlessness. This is true because anticipation of danger not only causes hesitancy but, for a variety of reasons, may also tend to direct people in a rather reckless fashion toward the very dangers they wish to avoid. The avoidance of such risks requires both a calm presence of mind and a clear, correct assessment of the situation.

In general, courage is superior to anxiety as a preventive against danger since individuals who become overanxious—and often awkward—in their actions are the ones who are most likely to have an "accident." Although a minimum of anxiety may sharpen one's attention, a maximum of anxiety is debilitating. Parents who intimidate their children by creation of unnecessary fears succeed only in putting their children in harm's way. Fortunately for children, but much to the annoyance of many of their would-be custodians, a healthy stubbornness usually prompts young people to ignore much parental agitation or nagging.

The closely related goal of some parents to frighten their children in an attempt to enforce compliant behavior yields results that are no better. Telling children that policemen put "bad" children in jail, for example, is an expedient measure that may seem to work for the moment, but time will always prove it is in error. Neither parents' nor family life in general will ever profit from intimidation. While such practice may initially force the child to display timid behavior, it is likely that the child will later use his fears as weapons against his tormentors in dozens of devious ways. In this case, the old maxim, "He who sows fear reaps worry," seems valid.

Children, of course, do learn fears which they display to others for various reasons. In general, parents must learn to be unimpressed by displays of fear while simultaneously displaying concern for the well-being of the child. Some parents who have failed to do so seem thoroughly trained by their children who use fear to control the adults who love them. Mother, for example, may feel compelled to rush home so as to arrive before four o'clock when her daughter usually returns from school. Mother feels that should she be late, her six-year-old daughter would feel terrified and cry. The fear of the child involved in this example may be devastatingly real to her. She may have learned it so well that her life can be made most uncomfortable because of it and, of course, her mother does not want to add to her child's misery.

How could such a situation have developed? And what can be done to deal with it effectively? What do we know about this phenomenon, which occurs in more families than many parents realize? First, we know that all persons of all ages have emotions that both prompt and control their actions. We need our emotions since without them, our behavior would be weak, indecisive, and often without meaningful direction. However, what many of us fail to realize is that both adults and children create those emotions needed to fortify their intentions and do so without realizing that they do so. Knowing this may help us to realize that no one is "possessed" by fear in the sense of being under an external control. Rather, we possess or contain fears that are often of our own creation. Children too possess fear, and the fact that they create it for themselves does not make that fear any less real. Such fear is not a pretense; it is very real indeed. But even in view of this fact, children often use their fears to control adults, especially their parents.

Most children discover the possibility of using fear as a control technique by accident. As they come to realize the benefits to be obtained by its use, they quickly capitalize on this perception while becoming entrapped in a web of their own making. Parents must also share in the responsibility for this pattern of childhood learning, however, because it is most often they who, by acting impressed by their child's fears, provide the child with success experiences in the use of fear to gain attention or demonstrate power.

Detailed study of fear has revealed that it is not experienced at the moment of danger to life but only before or after when the individual's perceptions and imagination are allowed time to create images of what will be or could be or what might have been. It is only after the crisis is over that the palpitations and trembling begin. This, then, contrary to popular opinion, indicates that human beings do not need fear to avoid dangers. In reality, fear often increases danger since it implies the assumption that we are unable to control the situation. By so doing, it fragments attention to the feared object as the individual casts about for escape. For example, when an individual is afraid he cannot do something, he begins a process of paralyzing himself so that he, in fact, cannot. In this sense, fear may prompt the occurrence of a so-called "self-fulfilling prophecy."

A distinction must also be made between a shock reaction and fear. A sudden fall or loud noise may upset a young child, but this will usually be only a short, temporary reaction. The emotion of fear as a continuation of an initial frightening experience develops only when parents also become frightened and therefore susceptible to their child's continuous fears, which are themselves rooted in parental display of fear. Thus, a cycle is begun which, without intervention, may tend to fuel itself. When a child is suddenly faced with a new and surprising situation, he may stop and wait to see what adults do or he may withdraw and escape. He has three choices since he can also try fear and will do what he has learned is successful in prompting desired parental action.

Tone of voice and the general behavior of adults in response to emotion-producing incidents may be particularly conducive to development of fear reactions in the child. When adults display hectic busyness in their behavior and strident overanxious tones in their voices, children take careful note of the context in which it occurs. Children learn rapidly that by simply being or acting afraid, they are able to produce much activity and excitement among adults. As one incident follows another, it becomes clearly evident to the child that intense fear reactions produce even further exaggeration in adult assurances as well as very specialized kinds of attention. As the child is picked up, soothed, and talked to, for example, his conditioning becomes complete. In this way, natural reluctance can be converted into fear as fear becomes increasingly useful as a means of motivating and creating adult activity, which is focused directly upon the child.

Children love to act or overact, and they constantly play to the gallery. Because very young people are still unaware of many of the consequences of their behavior, they display few if any inhibitions. Later, as they gradually experience the results of their behaviors, they begin to develop a "front" or mask of actions or behaviors to show to the world. This finally develops into the "sophistication" of adulthood. But because young children are as yet very little concerned with behaving in socially acceptable ways, they respond freely in a relatively uninhibited fashion. Their feelings are displayed on the surface of their behavior with very little reservation. When the child encounters a new or unexpected situation or circumstance, he will simply hold back, size up the situation, and look for clues as to how adults would or will respond to it. Within the context of our present consideration of fear, when parents or other adults indicate that they expect a child to be afraid, he is very likely to quickly meet their expectations, and in doing so, will work to put them into his service.

Parents can learn to express confidence in their children's abilities to meet and manage their own new experiences. To do so, however, requires that mothers and fathers refrain from assuming how their child will respond and from attempting to arrange his reactions for him. If the child has learned that he is expected to feel and display fear in certain situations, he will feel constrained and will oblige and do so. This is particularly true if the fear can be used for its dramatic shock value since parents respond especially well to dramatic screams or cries. Lucy, for example, screamed each time she saw an earthworm. Each time her brother presented one, her reaction yielded attention to both. This "game" continued until mother learned to stop playing.

Successful correction of any child's mistaken fear response always requires that the child be allowed to successfully meet and solve "the problem." But how can this be done? When the child displays fear, the parents may remain completely unimpressed. As long as parents continue to be afraid that their child will be afraid, they will continue to precipitate that which they wish to avoid. However, if the child cannot impress mother or father with his or her fear, the emotion will cease to be useful.

Probably the most useless response parents can make to their child's expression of fear is to tease or tell him he is silly. This sort of parental behavior serves only as a challenge to the child to maintain his position and role of terror-stricken helpless child. Only if parents can be unimpressed by Lucy's screams at seeing a worm will they succeed in elimination of the purpose of the fear. In taking such action, which is devoid of sermons on foolishness and of rebuke, parents "take their sails out of her wind." This same parental approach can be successfully used regardless of the focus of the fear, including fear of the dark at bedtime.

Children seem to many adults to be so small and helpless that we as parents may often feel compelled to respond to our offspring with protective sympathy. Our typical impression may be that "life probably does appear frightening to them." Children *can* be very persuasive, especially when they express terror. For this reason, only when we understand what is behind the child's behavior will we become capable of awareness that with our sympathetic response, we may not only fail to help the child but may also train him further in use of fear as a means of control.

It is, of course, very difficult, for example, for a mother to act as if her child is asleep when the child screams again as he has for several nights, claiming fear of the dark. In such a case, if mother has tucked her child in for the night and turned off the bedroom light, while possibly leaving a night light or partially opened door to the lighted hall beyond, she has done her duty. Having left her child with a word of encouragement, such as "You will learn not to be afraid," she may now fail to respond to unfounded fears. This will be impossible for a mother to do, however, until she can discard the commonly held assumption that parents are cruel when they ignore such "suffering" in a child. We as parents do feel impelled to respond to and comfort any "suffering" child who displays upset for any reason. However, when we realize that by doing so over time— night after night—we merely increase his suffering, we can see the sense in discontinuing our practice of providing attention and sympathy in this non-helpful way.

It is obviously necessary to teach our children to exercise caution in potentially dangerous situations, but fear and caution are not the same thing. Fear is a discouraged and paralyzing withdrawal, while caution is a reasonable and courageous recognition of real and possible danger. We as parents must, of course, teach our children to use caution in crossing streets, that swimming in deep or unknown waters is dangerous, never to accept special attention from strangers, and that guns are lethal weapons and not toys, for example. But this kind of information about environmental dangers can be taught without instilling or creating unnecessary fear in the child. The child must be helped to learn how to manage himself in situations that appear dangerous or difficult. It is a matter of each child learning his or her own strengths and limitations.

Fear, on the other hand, is not only potentially dangerous, it also saps the child's courage as it serves his mistaken purpose. Our children cannot resolve life's problems and difficulties when they are full of abstract fears. Fear does not increase but rather diminishes the child's ability to cope with problems. The more a child learns to be afraid, the more he or she courts danger. But of equal importance is the point we have been making that fears serve a child beautifully as a means to gain attention and to put others into his service. In general, if parents do not respond to fears, their children will not develop them. Only under these conditions can parents and children alike be free from the torture and suffering, which results from unnecessary fear.

Pain is a part of life, and since there is no way to escape its existence, we must prepare our children to face it and deal with it. Because most young children may have had very little experience with real pain, in some cases they may introject adults' experiences of fear and then build ideas in their imaginations that extend far beyond reality. No parent wants to see his or her child suffer, but there are times when real pain is inevitable. At these times, it is the child who is courageous who actually suffers less. Fear of pain magnifies perception of pain by causing the sufferer to become increasingly tense, which actually adds to the pain that is experienced. For these reasons, we must help our offspring to learn to accept inevitable pain and stress. Children become fearful and timid only when we act impressed with their learned fear.

Avoid Excessive Supervision and Mind Your Own Business

Anxious parents tend to over-supervise their children. Because they do not trust themselves or their children or the future, they may often exaggerate application of the child-rearing methods they use. As they resort to defensive and preventive activities, their behavior often tends to become ineffectual or even destructive. Such parents tend to prescribe even minute details of the child's behavior in ways that prohibit independent action. This most often happens when parents are unsure of themselves but are equally in doubt about their child's self-management abilities. In general, the less capable a parent feels concerning the management of his (or her) own affairs, the more that adult may try to manage his (or her) children through giving unsolicited advice or through other unnecessary interference in their affairs.

Through a seemingly inexhaustible repertory of commands, such parents may attempt to plan or dictate the child's life. Under such a pattern of comments, criticism, prohibition, instruction, and generally constant supervision and management, the child's every action may become subject to blame or praise with criticism usually being the most damaging. Surprisingly, many parents who are guilty of this failing seem not to be aware of the significance of their attitudes. Until shown this pattern in their behavior, perhaps through a tape recording, video recording, or telephone recording made in the home, they may tend to deny it completely.

The degree to which such parental supervision is at the very least unnecessary becomes clear only when one is able to realize that educational influences have lasting value only when they make a deep and lasting impression on the child. The true value of any adult-planned educational act is that it gives the child an occasion for thought and reflection. While no solitary experience is likely to significantly alter the character and temperament of a child, a single forceful experience can provide a stimulus to new attitudes and approaches to problems.

In cases where a child must take a definite stand and draw his own conclusions from the results, the development of his or her personality may be profoundly influenced by a few related strikingly impressive experiences. However, many incessant parental efforts to influence a child may make very little impression because they cease to compel evaluation of the situation while simultaneously provoking opposition. Only when adults exert their educational influence sparingly will they be likely to impress and effectively influence the child. When children become blunted to the effect of parental over-effort, they simply no longer pay attention. When elements of a multiplicity of parental responses either contradict one another or otherwise confuse or anger the child, he or she may become impudent, sullen, and unresponsive or may give up and abandon all efforts at independent action.

If one parent "disciplines" a child with a slap, for example, that child may run to the other parent for comfort. Too often, this general sequence of events can lead to a parental argument over methods of discipline and child-raising, which the child takes in from the sidelines. The principle to remember in such cases is *mind your own business*. As an adult, neither mother nor father can live the life of the other, nor do they have the right to attempt to manage or dictate the behavior of the other. Further, individual relationships between any two people belong only to those persons. A son's relationship with his mother, for example, belongs exclusively to them, and father has no business trying to control that relationship. But the same is true for all other combinations of family members.

When Johnny comes to "tell on" mother, daddy is entitled to his own feelings, but he need only reply by saying something like, "I'm sorry Johnny, but if you don't want mommy to slap you, perhaps you can find a way to prevent it."

Later, when the immediate conflict has subsided, the father may choose to initiate a discussion with his son to help his offspring see how a person might avoid provoking a slap. Parents cannot afford to take sides in family arguments if they wish to educate their children in meaningful ways.

When parents do take sides, they usually cooperate beautifully in making their "game" work according to a ritualistic formula that they are likely to repeat from time to time with variations. In such situations, one or more children will usually be found to be or to become most adept at keeping things stirred up between the parents. One parent who may or may not be the dominant parent will often unite with a child in attempting to subdue the spouse. As we examine such families, we discover that the child is usually quite clever in utilizing points of parental disagreement, to his or her own ends. When a child becomes skilled in manipulating his parents, it usually is done out of a felt need to find a champion and protector who will assist him in defeating demands made by the other parent. The personality development of a child who is able to do this may gradually become distorted as he or she seeks protection from adverse situations rather than personal skill in dealing with them or managing them alone.

In part, because parents fail to recognize their child's game or the harm being done to his developing self-concept, they fall into his trap. In the example cited above, the mother slapped her son out of a feeling of desperation, which she reported was rooted in the "excessive indulgence by the boy's weak father who never listens to me, and God knows we fight about it enough!" If this mother continues her determination to cancel out the father's indulgence, she may continue to slap her child whenever provoked by him. If, on the other hand, mother remains determined to control her son's life while forcing father to comply with her system, she will probably continue to berate her husband.

In such a game, the child may feel he wins on all fronts. Son and father cooperate to keep mother in disfavor while son and mother cooperate by getting father involved. Then father and mother cooperate in an attempt to show each other who is boss. These are games people play within the family unit. This is not harmonious living nor is the child being induced to respect others when subjected to such conflict.

The child, of course, does not enjoy being slapped, but he is willing to accept this temporary discomfort in order to compromise mother while winning father's cooperation and protection. Father, feeling as he does about physical punishment, doesn't like to have his son slapped, so he uses these occasions to impose controls on his "liberated" spouse. Father, too, should mind his own business and stop trying to manage and control the business and lives of other individuals. He has the right to follow his own convictions by not slapping his son, but he has no right to tell his wife how to treat him. It is not his business to attempt to control the relationship between his wife and his son since this relationship belongs only to the two people involved. (Here, the gender roles could easily be reversed. And, extreme behavior, of course, may alter the above perception.)

What is the proper treatment of a child within the family? To decide on a specific answer to this question requires "authority," and in the democratic family, no individual has such authority. Any acceptable answer will require agreement not only by both parents, but in most cases, by all of the persons involved. Within a democratic social system, we must recognize the child's input and his right to make decisions. Because each child in our society learns to feel free to demand his rights, we can see that each child in his own way feels free in a way which stimulates much of the treatment he or she receives. For this reason, it becomes our duty as adults and parents to work to understand the total situation in which we find ourselves with our children. But we must also understand the goals of the child and our interaction with that child within the existing situation. We must then use this understanding to stimulate the child to cooperate with the needs of the situation while at the same time training him or her toward acceptance of the order necessary to do so. Only in this way can we promote proper behavior.

All parents are individuals, however, and for this reason it is only natural that at times they may not agree on how the child should be raised. Although it is best if they can agree, such agreement is not necessary for parents to perform satisfactorily. And even if mother and father do agree on general principles of child-raising, each will in fact treat the child differently because of the child's own active part in each relationship. The child will decide what he will accept or reject from each individual in his environment. For this reason, the child is not confused by the differences in treatment that he may receive from the various adults in his environment.

Most children learn quite early to gain the greatest benefits for themselves from each relationship they experience, whether it be with parents or grandparents, other relatives, or family friends. Within this context, a high positive correlation has been found between the confidence of mothers in their ability to deal with each of their children and the level of the mothers' resentment of the treatment their children receive from others. The less a mother feels able to cope with the problems her child presents, the more sure she is likely to be concerning what others should do to manage him. Typically, we see a lessening of a mother's concern about what others do or at least what she feels or believes they should do, only when she herself becomes increasingly effective in stimulating proper behavior. As a mother's skill increases, the involvement of other adults becomes increasingly only a part of the reality of the total situation within which she finds she must deal with the child.

Children need experience with a wide range of persons to enable them to learn to both understand and correctly evaluate people. We must constantly remember that the child too is an individual who will need to develop his own uniquely personal relationships with those persons with whom he has contact. As parents, our primary obligation must be limited to watching for opportunities to support our children in correct evaluation of their experiences. Since every child lives in an environment that includes adults other than his parents, mothers and fathers need to learn and accept the fact that it will be quite impossible for them to control the influence that other persons will exert on their child.

Children do and will continue to encounter unfavorable influences during their developmental years. When this occurs, many parents often seem to feel compelled to confront or oppose all individuals involved in the apparent hope of either diminishing or totally eliminating the influence of that person or those persons on the life of their child. Such action by parents is not only futile but unnecessary. The child does not need to have his life arranged for him nor does he need to be protected from his environment. What he does need is guidance in his response. In cases that involve the "potential corruption of life," the stimulus to which the child is exposed is much less important than his response to it. We can never protect our children from the reality of life, but we can help them prepare to meet it.

As the child grows and develops, neighbors and relatives—including grandparents—are usually his or her first and closest contacts, to be followed by his parents' friends, teachers, and a continually widening circle of other persons in the community. The child's relationship with his or her grandparents is often a source of special concern, which in turn reflects a larger set of changes now coming about in our culture that are related, in general, to our break with tradition. Grandparents enjoy and take pride in their grandchildren. Their position is different from that of parents in that they may experience many of the privileges but few or none of the responsibilities of raising their grandchildren.

Modern parents often have entirely new or different ideas concerning child-raising, which may lead to resentment of interference from their own parents. However, when parents make the mistake of trying to force grandparents to accept these new ways, they usually succeed only in upsetting everyone concerned. What can be done? A mother or father can withdraw from such a conflict situation with a grandparent by merely saying, "You may be right. I'll have to think about it." The parent then need only proceed to do what he or she feels is right.

Of course, a doting grandparent may also "spoil" the child by giving him the impression that he can do and has the right to do whatever he wants. When this happens, the child may soon learn to view those who oppose his desire as enemies. In such cases, the most productive thing a parent can do is help the child to change his mind. Through aiding the child's response, a parent can stop the grandparent from giving the child a mistaken impression about his rights and about his life in general.

Parents who become upset over the "spoiling" behavior of grandparents succeed only in revealing their own doubt and pessimism concerning their own ability to influence the child. Energy spent in trying to "correct" a grandparent is misdirected and futile and will only add tension and strife to an already unfortunate situation. The relationship between the child and his grandparents is the business of the child and the grandparents only and not of the parents. Parents may choose to discuss their concern with the grandparents, but they have no right to attempt to force or control the thoughts, attitudes, or behaviors of other adult human beings. Even if they were sure they had this right, in all but very exceptional cases, they would fail. We, as parents, simply must not attempt to shield our children from reality, nor can we change reality. We must help our children in their response to reality; in this case, their grandparents' spoiling behavior.

Divorce and remarriage create similar problems for both children and adults. On visiting days, for example, as formerly married persons again encounter each other and their child or children, old hostilities may again become evident. When this occurs, the children may easily become involved. They are not merely innocent bystanders. When confusion occurs, children may take a stand and, in doing so, very often quickly learn to play one parent against the other. The next predictable step usually involves the child provoking further disturbances to gain additional sympathy, special consideration, or consolation.

When these sorts of incidents occur, it is essential that parents not fall for such behavior and that they exercise care so as not to exaggerate it. For example, if eight-year-old Tommy returns from a visit with his father and father's new wife to report that the woman became angry and slapped him, mother may feel a need to become involved to protect Tommy. If she does vent her anger on "the other woman," her son will soon learn that he can gain from this "game." However, if her son is unable to create a disturbance in this complex situation—that is, if mother refrains from responding to what happens when he visits the other home—Tommy may develop a better relationship with his father's new wife. Mother can most productively help her son in this situation by suggesting that perhaps he could behave so as not to get slapped or by discussing with him how he could avoid being slapped. If mother indicates that she believes he will find a way to keep out of trouble with his father's new wife, she will help to supply the encouragement he will need to manage this segment of his life.

The resourcefulness of children should never be underestimated. Tommy is not stupid. If things get too bad, he may refuse to go or demand to see his father alone or any one of a myriad of other possibilities. The choice is his. He will find a way to keep out of trouble with her and, in doing so, will have gained from the experience. Children must learn to live their own lives. No parent or anyone else can do it for them. It is part of the business of being a parent to help each child to develop proper attitudes and effective approaches to the realities of living. Contact with an interrelationship with other people is part of this reality. When parents attempt to control or modify this reality, they are not helping the child but rather are giving him the false impression that they or someone will always be there to take care of problems.

In the case of boys fighting, it is very easy for parents to become involved in an attempt to protect their loved one. However, a child who is continually shielded need not make any real effort toward developing the art of social participation. A parent may choose to discuss this problem with his son or parents of the other boy, but it is the son who must finally assume responsibility for his own relationships. Still, without preaching, a father can suggest that his son reevaluate his approach to others. "I just wonder if you and Stevie don't enjoy these fights. It seems to make his parents very angry. Perhaps you and Stevie can discover other ways of having fun. It is your choice. I wonder what you will decide to do about it."

The same can be said in situations when a child feels mistreated by a known but nonfamily adult, such as a teacher or neighbor. The child who reports that her teacher embarrasses her in class may serve as an example. Of course, children do not learn their lessons in school by being humiliated, but just as is true in the home, the child undoubtedly has a share in provoking the teacher's attitude and behavior. And to be realistic, mothers are usually not able to do much to retrain their children's teachers. They may try, but when they do try, they most often succeed only in making matters worse.

Assuming the relationship between the child—let's call her Susan—and her teacher is poor. It is not mother's business to change the teacher. But it is her business to help her daughter see how she contributes to the poor relationship and perhaps to suggest a course of action that the child might take to make herself more comfortable in the school situation. Since a direct attack on the problem will usually only add to the difficulty, Susan must be helped to see that her part in this drama must be done in an indirect manner. Mother, of course, may consult with the teacher to gain more information so she may play her role correctly.

Susan might be helped to imagine how a teacher would feel when a student disliked that teacher or what she would do if she were a teacher, and one of her students hated her. Then mother and Susan might try to decide what Sue could do to be more comfortable in such a situation. If mother were to challenge her daughter's evaluation of the situation, she would only increase the child's antagonism and induce her to defend her attitude and position. If mother were to side with Susan, she would be supporting her provocative behavior in school, which would also be a mistake. If she were to side with the teacher, she again would incur her daughter's antagonism. Mother's only practical solution will be to acknowledge Susan's discomfort, frankly discuss it with her, and then seek more cooperative forms of behavior, perhaps with the teacher involved to relieve her discomfort and unhappiness.

Children who experience difficulty in school are often "helped" by their parents. When parents—often mothers—resort to "discipline" or "force" to make their children do their homework or when they establish a habit of always "doing it together," they set the stage for failure. While mother learns the homework in such a situation, her child is learning and proving that no one is going to make her learn. It is the child's job to study and do the homework, not the parent's job. As long as the parent remains determined that the child will do well in school and continues to "help" and/or force the child, that child will continue to do poorly. If parents approach this problem head-on, they will only invite a power contest.

A much better approach would be to discuss the problem with the child or children and together establish a time when the studying will be done. By helping to maintain this sort of order, parents help to provide the required stimulus. If the child is experiencing unusual difficulties, a tutor should be provided. It is usually at least a questionable practice at best for parents to attempt this role themselves because of the various other pressures and problems of family living. Very often, the child's problem is related at least in part to his resistance of pressure from a parent or parents who are personally involved out of concern both for their responsibility for the child and for his future. Such parental pressure only adds to the power contest. To be of most help to such a child, parents should extricate themselves from the contest, provide a tutor, and then make it clear to the child that no one can make him study nor can anyone always do it for him. Whether or not he will study and learn or fail to do so must be his choice.

The same may be said regarding children who neglect to practice their music, if this is an interest which has begun to develop. Although a young person may want to play a musical instrument, he or she cannot hope to do so without the necessary self-discipline and work. Here again, parents must ultimately learn to mind their own business since continued interference and pressure will only turn anticipated enjoyment into a detested chore. It is the work of the music teacher to stimulate the child to work. Parents need only appreciate the progress being made. Of course, minding our own business does not mean that we must abandon the child to his instrument and teacher. By providing situations in which the learner can play alone or with others for a small audience of adults or peers, we can reinforce the progress being made. If encouragement can be offered without criticism or pressure, music can become both an enjoyable and a functional experience and not merely an unpleasant drudgery.

Parents need to be aware exactly of what it is that is the business of their child so they can leave those responsibilities to him or to her. Some parents feel a need to manage or control everything the child may do, even to the way the child may spend his allowance. What children do with their allotment of "the family's money" is one further example of something that is not the business of the parents. When parents give a child an allowance, that money belongs to that child. Parental interference in the use of this money is seen by the child in the same way that the mother or father would view a friend who tried to dictate their use of their own money. They would feel that the friend was intruding into something that was none of that friend's business.

In the same way, and out of the same feeling of respect or lack of it, parents should mind their own business and let their child spend or otherwise use his or her money as that child sees fit. Parents may choose to discuss the issue of spending and saving with their child, perhaps including a clear differentiation between necessities such as clothing to be purchased by the parents and other areas of possible desire or need that may be left to the discretion of their offspring. However, it is the parents' responsibility to remain firm as to the amount of allowance and when it will be given. They should not provide more for the child if he or she should be indiscreet in the use of the allowance money. Later, of course, he may try again.

When parents see their child developing mistaken values, they should initiate a friendly discussion. To open such a discussion without prompting the child to immediate rebellious reception, the parent might use phrases such as, "You might want to consider" or "I wonder if you have thought about" or "What do you think would happen if everyone thought this was best?" When such discussion is undertaken, it should be done without criticism, which would only cause the child to cling to and defend his own evaluation of the situation more vehemently.

Because objectivity is essential to any true evaluation of situations and choices, it is important that the parent present all possible angles and aspects of the problem, even though some may seem grossly in error. In this way, parents may assist their child to discover those values that will be of greatest benefit to that child, both now and in the future. Through use of adult consultation and logical consequences where appropriate, a child can learn to manage his own life satisfactorily and without additional outside help.

Don't Pity the Child

When parents feel sorry for their child in moments of distress or unhappiness, they display pity that they may define as compassion. Even when it may seem understandable and justifiable, such pity can be damaging to the child since children are extremely sensitive to adult attitudes, even if they are not openly expressed. For this reason, if we pity the child, he may quickly learn to believe that he has the right to pity himself. As he learns to feel sorry for himself, his misery becomes more intense. Some children seem to actually gather abuse. Such individuals have learned to rely on the pity of others who are willing to console them instead of facing the predicament and doing what can be done to alleviate it. As this process continues, the child may lose more and more of his courage and willingness to accept reality as it is. Children who become convinced that the world owes them something in repayment for what they have missed may maintain this attitude throughout their lives. Such persons feel abused when things don't go as they desire. They then seek out and count on what others will do for them rather than doing what they can do for themselves.

It is important that parents realize that pity and sympathy are not the same. Sympathy involves feeling sorry about the something that has happened, while pity is feeling sorry for the person to whom it has happened. Pity implies a subtle patronizing and superior—and perhaps somewhat contemptuous—attitude toward the person pitied. "I feel sorry for you, you poor little thing," it suggests, "but I'll do all I can to make up for all that you suffer."

Sympathy, on the other hand, implies understanding of how the other may feel, how much it hurts, and how difficult life may now be for that person. It suggests that one is sorry about what has happened and will help the other person to overcome the difficulties of the situation.

Parents who act on the assumption that disappointments will be extremely hard on a child because "he is so little" display both lack of confidence in and disrespect for that child. As suggested earlier, parents often underrate their children's strength and resilience. Disappointments are not more than the child can bear, although parents may consider their child to be too helpless and weak to meet the problems of life. This attitude displays pity, which stimulates the child to make false assumptions about himself or herself.

Parents can best help their children in distressing or unhappy situations by remaining casual. Children *will* learn to manage disappointments if parents avoid pity. Parents may also be helpful by discussing all possible outcomes—including failure—in advance of the event. If plans for outside play on a new "Jungle Gym" for all guests at six-year-old Jennie's birthday party are spoiled because of rain, for example, mother should maintain her equanimity. It is natural that Jennie will feel distressed when it rains on her birthday, but a casual acceptance in mother's own mind of the need to adjust to weather conditions should be quickly conveyed to her daughter. In doing so, she will reinforce her child's strength against deep disappointment. If possible, mother and daughter might have discussed alternative plans in advance, just in case bad weather did occur. Whether that was done or not, however, mother may feel she cannot help it if she feels sorry and displays pity for Jennie. But she can.

The principle of avoiding pity applies in all areas of the child's life. Consider, for example, the child who leaves the hospital on crutches. In such a situation, it would be easy for a doting parent to do things for him and to attempt to make up for the possibly savage or seemingly unfair blow dealt to the child by life. The child tries to walk and whimpers about the pain. Mother responds with statements like "Oh, my poor baby," etc. When daddy tries to intervene, mother scolds him for asking too much of their child. Arguing ensues in the presence of the child. The child withdraws from daddy and quickly learns to lean on his mother.

Soon the child is changing from the happy, courageous, self-helping child who had come home from the hospital to a demanding, petulant, semi-helpless invalid. In a case such as this, understanding, firmness, and concerted effort will be required to overcome the initial debilitating effects of this mother's pity, to put the child back on the road to self-help and progress. Mother must first acquire an understanding of her child's goal-directed behavior. Then, in view of this understanding, both parents must follow a course of self-discipline and restraint.

It is probably beyond human nature for most adult human beings to avoid feeling sorry for injured or physically handicapped children. A child who is held back from certain activities—as a result of an accident or a birth or hereditary injury such as crippled limbs, deafness, or blindness—may easily become the object of pity. Therapists are, of course, very much aware of the danger of pity in such cases. They realize that by pitying the child, parents only add to the child's handicap. In reality, handicapped children often display courage and cleverness with which they can either overcome or sidestep a handicap. Medical and psychological personnel often note, however, that children who had made progress under their direction seem to crumble under undue sympathy and loving pity showered on them at home by misguided parents, relatives, and friends. Then, as these professionals attempt to educate the parents, they find they are subjected to misguided abuse from mothers and fathers who misjudge their professional firmness of approach and see it as lack of sympathy, lack of caring, harshness, or even cruelty. While it is true that it may be easier for therapists to avoid pity since they are not as emotionally involved as some parents, they (too) often learn to love children who remain under their care for periods of time. Yet, these professionals have learned to refrain from reacting with pity to the child's predicament. Their more enlightened approach is often to stimulate the child to be proud of each accomplishment, which he may make under his own unique conditions of difficulty.

Children do absorb adult pity and, in doing so, learn to pity themselves. Unfortunately, we cannot protect our children from suffering. It is a part of life. At best, we can only meet the child's needs while he is ill, help him to tolerate suffering, and show him how to manage under difficulty. Even more than the healthy child, it is the child who is ill who needs our moral support, our understanding and sympathy, and our faith in his courage. Pity during periods of illness only adds to the child's feelings of demoralization and saps his courage as it implies a patronizing attitude. Display of pity does not encourage nor does it support courage. For this reason, in any distressing or unhappy situation, parents probably show the greatest kindness to their child when they firmly refuse to treat the child as more helpless than the conditions of the situation actually warrant. Even a difficult period of convalescence can be made easier for both parents and child if sympathy and courage replace pity and undue service.

Parents who ignore or fail to realize this reality during periods of extended disability may spoil their child so severely that he or she may later find it difficult, if not impossible, to make any really constructive contributions to either self or others. Without this conscious parental awareness, a child may be allowed to absorb the attitude that he or she is "unfortunate, so the world must make it up to me." When children learn to consider themselves as "special" in any way, they begin to acquire mistaken values and to develop false expectations. This may be especially true in the case of adopted children. Pity is an easy trap into which adoptive parents may fall. For the sake of the child's future—his or her adaptation to life—this developing human being should never be given a special position in the family. The adopted child needs and should be given exactly the same respect and care as a natural child. Adopted children make an issue of being adopted only if their parents do.

Tragedies occur in the lives of all human beings at one time or another. When a loved one dies, for example, we as adults are expected to manage our emotions and make the best of the situation. In tragic situations, our inclination is to feel sorry for any innocent child who may be involved. Well-meaning pity, however, can bring about even more damaging effects than the tragedy itself. No matter how legitimate the reason, when an adult expresses feelings of pity for a child, that child feels justified in pitying himself. For example, for a child, loss of a parent is often one of the most serious predicaments that he will have to face. If it is the mother who dies, the child's difficulty in the situation may be compounded. Following such a loss, the child's period of psychological reconstruction may influence the remainder of his life. Children in such a circumstance do need all the sympathetic support possible from everyone around them, but the thing they don't need is pity. Death is part of life and must be accepted as such.

Of course, we hate to see a child hurt by the passing of a parent or other loved one, but while death occurs, life goes on. Pity at such a time saps the courage that the child urgently needs. It is a negative emotion which not only weakens the individual's self-reliance but also damages and very often destroys his faith in life and the future. Our point here is that we cannot protect children from life. In fact, we must not since it is during childhood that persons build the courage and strength that they will need to meet the realities of their remaining years of living. It is during childhood that we all learn to adapt to hardship and then go on. It is for this reason that parents must discipline themselves to forego the indulgence of pity if they hope to strengthen their child's ability to go on to what comes next. If parents hope to do this, they must endeavor to teach their children the satisfactions that can come from overcoming handicaps.

Adults will be of most help and value to children when they can show their sympathy and understanding by supporting the child in his grief while simultaneously supporting his courageous search for a way forward. In doing so, they do not abandon the child to his trouble but instead rally to his support just as they would do in the case of an adult in trouble. However, as parents, we must always *exercise care* to express sentiments of understanding without implying doubt concerning the child's ability to face the ordeal courageously. Children look to adults in times of crisis for clues to guide them in dealing with unfamiliar situations. When they sense our attitude, they use it as a guide. Adult respect for children demands that parents and others support each child's sense of dignity without lowering it by stimulating self-pity.

To repeat our earlier point once again, for emphasis, parents and adults in our society far too often underestimate the strength and resilience of children whom they seem to consider "small and worthy of pity." Since most adults are also far too often inclined to doubt the child's ability to adapt, they respond to childhood hardship with thinly disguised pity. When we as parents do so, we succeed only in discouraging our children and in helping them to diminish their resourcefulness. The end result is a retreat by each child who is influenced into a sad passivity, which can quickly degenerate into complaints and demands as it very often does.

Use Action, Not Words

In any relationship, words may be used as a means of communication or they can be used as instruments of conflict. Unfortunately, while engaged in the process of rearing their children, most parents simply talk instead of acting or even thinking. No matter what some children do, their parents have something to say. When parents don't know what else to do, they talk, but their words do not help because they nearly always fail to present a constructive plan. This is not to say that words are unnecessary because, of course, they are important. It is possible to make deep and lasting impressions through use of words, and children do sometimes need explanations or instruction—but too often, words are used without either meaning or direction.

Since words that have no direct effect in child-rearing are superfluous and may even be injurious, such words are not an expression of personal cooperative contact but are instead a disturbance in human relationship. For this reason, it is important that parents decide, whenever they talk with a child, whether they wish to do so for release of their own anger, annoyance, and tension or whether they wish to influence the child. If the goal is to truly modify the child's perspective, it is important that parents not begin to talk until the child is ready to listen.

Because words may seem offensive and may arouse hostility, opposition, or other intense responses, they may have the effect of producing violent discord. For this reason, it is important that parents carefully monitor their own emotions since only when they are completely calm will they be in a position to communicate constructively. But of equal importance, adults must carefully observe the effect of their words, which means that they must stop talking if they note that the child is not susceptible at a particular moment. When the child or his parent becomes agitated or excited during a conversation, the time to stop has arrived. Of particular importance in this context is the suggestion that a parent never tell the child what he already knows nor should he repeat what he has just said. It is much better to stop and think than to add another remark or comment that will probably meet with no greater response than that which has already been said.

The common parental response of showing a child his mistakes also falls into this category of useless words because in most cases, the child already clearly realizes that he has made a mistake. Because irritation is an annoyance that simply acts as an introduction to unpleasant bickering and because repetition tends to exasperate the child, whenever possible, words should be replaced with actions. If the parent's comment was useless the first time, it will be harmful the second, even if it seems to serve its immediate purpose. In some cases, complete silence may make a deeper impression on the child who has done wrong than the most forceful of words since it too may be a very forceful expression of disapproval.

In general, parents will be most effective when they think much, talk little, and act according to a plan that will allow the natural consequences of the child's action to take effect. Phrases such as, "I told you so," "That was just beginner's luck," "I just don't think you've got it in you," "Don't start something you can finish," or "Just looking at you is enough to make a person ill" among hundreds of others are far too often used by parents or other adults. Such statements, as they are thoughtlessly used in one's daily life, not only discourage the child but also either weaken or damage his performance in those areas of his life that are usually most in need of improvement. Parents who are careful about what they say to children and how they say it will refrain from annoying, inhibiting language. Instead, they will use words in the helpful, stimulating ways for which they should be intended.

When information related to a child's misbehavior is to be communicated in words, one "telling" will indicate to the child that his action has met with disapproval. From that moment forward, he knows that his continuation of this behavior is unacceptable to others. For example, a mother may ask as she does each day, "How many times must I tell you to wash your hands before coming to the table?"

Still, her child continues to "forget." Why? For what purpose or result is this behavior continued? The child does it because his mother makes a fuss, and in doing so, he gets her attention, perhaps by distracting it from baby brother. Mother has defined the "game," but her son has defied her game rules and, in doing so, has gained his desired response. In this case, mother has played into the hands of her son and now serves his purpose. It would be foolish to wash his hands. If he did, his mother would not react to him. For this reason, her words are futile.

If this mother really intends to change her son's behavior, she must refrain from talking and act. Mother cannot decide what her child will do; she must respect his decisions regarding his own behavior. But she can decide what *she* will do. She may tell her family that she will not serve a meal when everyone's hands are not clean or when some members of the family have dirty hands. She may decide to remove the plates and serve no food to people with dirty hands. After having made her point *once*, she will not have to tell her family again why she does not serve food when she sees dirty hands. By defining what she will do, mother has changed the situation. Since her child (or children) no longer has mother busily trying to manage them, what purpose can dirty hands now serve? The influence of other hungry family members, including brothers and sisters will, of course, also have an important influence on the child.

Many parents pile up words in an almost unending way as they attempt to reason with their offspring without punishing. But because the child has a purpose behind his behavior, he will have no intention of changing it. The child will merely find all the talk to be a bore and quickly develop an immunity to it. The boy or girl will become "mother deaf" or "adult deaf" to his or her parents who are then likely to complain that their child "never hears a word I say." In conflict situations such as this, words become weapons rather than serving as a means of communication. At this point, either humorous misbehavior or deliberate defiance are the child's most common means of response to the adult.

Nothing meaningful can be conveyed to a child using words at the moment of conflict. Whatever is said will only be gathered as ammunition for the child's own verbal retorts. At this point, a verbal war has begun. If the child is forced into silence, he will only wait to carry his rebellion into action. Toleration of the tirade seems a small price to pay to get his own way. If he appears to listen, he does so only to serve his own purpose. Close attention to the child's facial expressions in such a situation often clearly reveals not only that he is not listening and has no intention of carrying out the instructions he is receiving but also that he may be tacitly mocking his tormentor.

Most mothers—as well as fathers when they are playing a "mothering" role—simply talk too much, often using words to generate fear to threaten their children. In many cases, parental action need consist of nothing more than keeping the mouth closed. Parents who try to do this for the first time may find the effort to be very great because they have learned to feel an uncomfortable pressure to do something in each and every conflict situation. Work with parents has revealed that mothers and fathers who can manage their response often quickly discover that their silence is in itself their most helpful tool for use in reduction of tension and restoration of family harmony. Parents' body language can, of course, sometimes speak even louder than words, allowing some mothers or fathers to literally shout with their mouths closed.

What happens when the child cries during a conflict situation? Often, he is merely using another mode of power—"water power." When faced with a screaming, rebellious child, many mothers feel helpless and, as a result, compelled to resort to attempts to pressure the child into submission, again with words. Then, when pleading and cajoling words fail, she turns to threats that she rarely if ever really intends to carry out. Again, we see a mother attempting to force her child in this case to stop crying instead of extricating herself from his pressure as she should do to get results. In such cases, nothing is accomplished toward training the child toward cooperation.

Uninformed parents often seem to feel that words have a punitive, hence, helpful effect; but they are wrong. After a tirade, most parents simply retreat, leaving the child as the unrestrained, uninhibited, and uneducated victor. In such cases, the correct action has been taken at the wrong time and after its effect has already been neutralized. The uninformed parent may be vaguely aware of this error, but on the next occasion is likely to redouble her efforts to teach the child by reasoning with him, again with the same progression of results. To extricate themselves from this dilemma, parents must learn to replace words with action. The rule to remember in times of intergenerational conflict is keep your mouth closed and act. Until parents learn these simple facts, we will continue to see children who have their parents better trained to take care of what the children want than the parents have the children trained in proper behavior.

As an example of the above points, consider again the frequent misbehavior of children in supermarkets to which we alluded in an earlier section. This pattern has become so common in some communities that it is accepted by many adults as "normal." The supermarket, of course, is not a playground, and our children can be trained to understand this difference and to behave accordingly. Before entering the store, the mother should clearly point out that the store is not a play area and that the child may walk down the aisle with her to help her collect the groceries that she has listed for purchase. If and when her child begins to misbehave, she need not shout or lecture. Rather, she should immediately lead him by the hand out of the store and into the car or back home, as the case may be. Only words such as "I'm sorry you don't feel like behaving in the store, Bobby. You may wait for me with your father in the car" are necessary. Mother must resist the temptation to use words as threats. If she threatens to leave him in the car if he doesn't behave before entering the store, perhaps extracting his promise before entering, she will be disappointed. He will not do it, regardless of the vows mother may have required from him. It is only through her own firm but fair behavior that mother can show that she means business.

Bobby is a misguided boy who feels that unless he has his own way, he has no place; but more than this, he is a tyrant. He does as he pleases, and no one can stop him, at least not with words. In the store, just as at home, he stops his annoying activity only when he is ready to stop after having sufficiently annoyed his mother. In the past, his mother's continuous admonitions were barely heard, let alone acknowledged. Since his mother has done nothing but talk, Bobby has continued to do as he pleased. If he now refuses to remain in the car, his parents should drive home without their needed groceries. The consequences of this decision may be obvious to the entire family at the next meal, which would suggest that the issue be examined by the entire family at the next family council.

Mother/father may also follow through by not taking him on the next shopping trip, but on a subsequent one, she may allow him the choice of accompanying her if he thinks he can manage his behavior properly. Only two forms of parental action do not express hostility, and by so doing, decrease the child's hostility. They are the use of natural consequences when possible, or if this is not possible, removal from the situation.

Bobby also enjoys having his own way at home. He especially enjoys walking into a neighbor's flower bed because the neighbor gets so very angry. Then he bursts into sobs in response to the neighbor's anger, which elicits the defense and comfort of his mother who angrily states her opinion that the neighbor cares more for flowers than for children. When mother feels her child is under attack, she instantly offers her sympathy, which is (maybe) unwarranted. If a child such as Bobby acts in such a way as to provoke this sort of anger and hostility, however, he should be allowed to experience rejection of his behavior. He should not be shielded against the natural consequences of his acts with ill-advised sympathy.

By feeling sorry for him, his mother has succeeded in further encouraging Bobby in his role of tyrant. He now knows that not only can he do as he pleases at home but that his mother will protect him from the unpleasant results of his behavior away from home as well. Since tyrants have no social function, Bobby is learning behavior, which will not find acceptance anywhere in the society in which he must learn to live.

Bobby, of course, like other children, wants to belong. And his parents love him and want to express their love. He is so beloved that his parents have indulged his every whim. In doing so, however, they have undermined his natural inclination to belong through usefulness and have prompted him in his mistaken assumption that he can belong only if he can overpower the powerful adults in his environment. If Bobby's parents are to help him out of this mistaken approach to life, they must first realize their own mistaken concept of how to express their love for him.

Again, they must learn to replace words with action. Although the action this mother took at the supermarket would furnish a good beginning, she could probably have done so at home with much less expenditure of time. Bobby badly needs to learn respect for order. He already knows very well what he should and should not do, so he need not be told again.

Since Bobby is already functioning as a tyrant, his new treatment will very likely be met with tempered resistance. Mother will effectively counter his resistance as long as she remains cool and quietly establishes her right to maintain order. If she does what is necessary, no power contest will develop. Her firmness will be understood, and eventually, her action will bring respect. But if Bobby again begins to march through the garden, for example, mother should simply remove him to the house, saying, "You may play outside again when you want to behave as you should."

Bobby should always be given another chance to try again but should always be returned to the house when he shows unwillingness to comply with the requirements of the situation. As Bobby's parents deal with one situation at a time, gradually involving all of the areas of his misbehavior, they may effectively guide him to more successful and socially acceptable behavior. But it will be their *actions*, not their words, which will bring this about.

Neither Urge, Neglect, nor Extract Promises

Since all children will periodically need some urging or prodding, it is important that encouragement be provided as the child's parents call his attention in a friendly way to the need for his cooperation. When the child offers resistance, however, any attempt to persuade him will usually be useless and may be especially harmful when the compliance requested requires prior preparation and skill or an inner psychological readiness that he may not yet have developed. For example, it is never wise to try to persuade a child to silence an expression of emotion such as crying or to eat or to fall asleep or, in fact, to perform any function that proceeds only from an internally initiated motive.

A child's emotions cannot be influenced by pressure. Crying, pouting, or sulking will not stop until the child is inwardly prepared to stop it. For this reason, parental pressure will only increase a child's emotional resistance. This means that in such instances, words are useless and may become harmful in cases where they produce the opposite of the desired effect. Purely external duties, on the other hand, may often require a little friendly encouragement or direction. For example, a mother's suggestion or request that her child dress himself more warmly before going out to play is certainly both proper and appropriate parental behavior.

The degree to which it is possible to influence any child in specific situations depends on whether or not one can prepare the child to behave as he should by winning him over to the proper or at least a *more* proper attitude. The objective here is to help the child to feel within himself the necessary incentive to do what appears necessary. Even in cases where the child may at first feel a solid inner resistance or opposition, an appropriate shift may often be effected with relative ease through use of natural consequences. Crying may seem to pose a special case, but once the child's attention and interest have been diverted to other matters, the crying will usually end almost at once. Even those children who are especially defiant will usually compose themselves if they are left to themselves and are not cajoled or coaxed.

Parents who urge their children or otherwise express either worry, annoyance, or discontent over the behavior of their offspring simply do not achieve the objective of their oversolicitous concern. To be maximally effective, parents must learn to allow the child to accumulate his own experiences by interfering as little as possible with his learning. Extension of this principle beyond reasonable limits, however, can involve harm since very obviously, children do need physical concern and care as well as understanding, stimulation, and appropriate human sympathy. Children who do not receive at least an essential minimum of sincere attention and concern may be seriously damaged by this neglect. The results of such neglect are often linked directly to the child's developing ability to work cooperatively with others as that child learns to adapt himself to the requirements of social living.

It is from adult interest in him or her as a person that each child draws the stimulation needed for continued development, provided that this interest is not allowed to take an offensive or an oppressive form. Parents who take too little interest in their child's physical growth, intellectual and moral development, and appearance are likely to do as much harm through their neglect as might be done through a display of excessive interest in ways that might arouse the child's antagonism or hostility. Still, in terms of cooperation and purely human relations with the child, there should be no arbitrary limits imposed on the parents' interest in and activity with the child.

All children possess an increasing need for warm interpersonal feeling and activity as they grow and develop. On the other hand, at least some self-limitation will probably always have to be imposed by parents, primarily in regard to the application of methods of training the child since a limited number of such "methods" will suffice to produce order if they are correctly employed at the correct times.

It has often been noted by those who observe family behavior that many parents who may neither urge nor neglect their children do make a closely related error. They attempt to induce compliance to certain of their desires by requiring their children to make promises for better conduct. Such parental behavior is not only entirely futile but may be harmful in its further consequences. Adult requests that a child "promise me that you'll never lie again," "that you will never say that word again," or "that you will never do it again," for example, may prompt a promised commitment. It will usually be given rather absentmindedly, however, with no real intent other than appeasement of the child's tormentor or to avoid punishment.

Usually, the child's behavior remains unchanged because his attitude remains unchanged. Very little is likely to be gained, even in cases where the child consciously intends to keep his promise.

Later, when the child—apparently thoughtlessly—repeats the condemned offense, his parents are likely to add more items to their list of his faults, perhaps now using labels such as untrustworthy or unreliable. Forced again to justify himself, the child is likely to attempt to evade these charges, often through distortion of facts and rationalization so that he will appear at the very worst to be forgetful, unthinking, or careless. Because of these typical dynamics, extraction of a promise from a child not only fails to correct the original fault but may also add the additional failing of unreliability to the original offense. Perhaps most important, it discourages the child by promoting his tendency to accept, behave in terms of, and hide behind his new found weakness.

A vastly superior method to prevent repetition of the mistake involves convincing the child—or more correctly, allowing the child to convince himself—of the unpleasant consequences of his unacceptable acts. The practice of eliciting promises is a mistake for various reasons but primarily because it becomes a ritualized response through which the child will escape the actual consequences of his actions. In those cases, where a misdeed results only in the extraction—or extortion—of a promise, experience has shown that the child will gladly accept this superficial or false consequence. Then, when the next occasion occurs, he will promise again with a serenity and composure that reflect the comfort he has found in his new parent-handling device.

Parents who "feel sorry for" their children when they get into trouble often very much desire to spare their beloved offspring from the uncomfortable results of their improper conduct. Some go so far as to display anger or tell lies to do so. Then, to justify their deviation from the logical course of events, they require the child to promise that he will change or improve his conduct. Such parents should not be surprised when in the future, this same child—who earlier, if briefly, had seemed contrite—again and again and again tries to evade the unpleasant results of his actions by gladly if not eagerly promising anything and everything that may be suggested. Here, of course, the parents are effectively teaching their child to distort facts, if not to lie, and to refuse responsibility for his actions.

Some children go even beyond this point by using promises as a means of acquiring specific personal advantages. For example, a child may make promises or commitments to obtain a special treat or favor of some kind or a demonstration of affection. In such a case, the child is simply using the promise as negotiable currency to purchase what he wants. Or he may use it as a bribe. Knowing something may be required of him which he finds to be unpleasant—or minimally unpleasant or even pleasant—he may indicate his commitment not to cooperate, "unless…"

Whatever is done to please a child should be done with no strings attached. It is all too easy to become confined by the empty words of a promise, which very often leads only to additional attempts by the child to use promises to his own advantage. On the other side of the coin, parents who permit themselves to be bribed by promises that are a substitute for actions succeed only in developing the child's facility for development of wordy rationalization coupled with increasing undependability. While it may seem gratifying to a parent when he hears his own child make a friendly promise on his own accord, one can never be too careful in handling such promises.

Although the pattern outlined above may not occur in all cases, it is important that the parent take care that the child does not use the promise as a means for gaining some sort of advantage or for buying himself out of some form of unpleasantness. The major point to be made here, of course, is that no one should—or at least need to—ever in any way elicit a promise from a child since to do so only invites trouble. There are other much more productive methods to influence a child's behavior.

Relax and Think

Some parents make statements to their child such as "shape up" or "pull yourself together." This approach to bringing about the compliance of a child is also detrimental because it in no way encourages the child nor does it allow that child to feel that we believe he or she will be able to do so. The suggestion implicit in such a demand is that the child should stop acting as if he is weak, should be strong, and should use his "willpower" to manage his behavior and his life. Because the floundering child will understand this meaning in such a command, he or she will usually draw conclusions that are quite different from those that we as his parents may desire. Instead of realizing and acting on his strengths, he learns to feel weaker and even more impotent and powerless than before.

Such a child may seem to try to act differently, but because his efforts leave his intentions unchanged, he is very likely to merely go through the motions of attempting to manage or control himself. Because the results of his efforts lead only to increasing feelings of helplessness, the child becomes increasingly convinced of his lack of ability and willpower which, of course, does nothing to improve his behavior.

When parents tell their child to "get control" of himself, they force the child into an attitude that can have far-reaching unfortunate implications for his later life. The psychological mechanism which often develops as a result of such parental action may form an important basis for the development of what are called psychoneurotic disorders. This type of appeal to the child's willpower proceeds from a false psychological premise that emphasizes discouragement rather than encouragement. Even when the child is misbehaving, his behavior has a definite purpose, although his conscious will may not always be in harmony with the actual deep-seated intentions which produce his behavior.

As the child expresses his conflict through his pattern of behavior, his intentions are, of course, not friendly. However, while trained adults may clearly recognize this antagonistic tendency in his behavior, the child's true intentions remain unavailable to his own conscious perception, which means he is completely unaware of the true purpose of his acts.

Observation of family interaction reveals that even in cases where the child seems able to follow a parental order to "pull himself together," his fundamental attitude does not change. As his compulsive efforts to evade responsibility, protest, defy others, and strive for recognition continue, his attitude remains virtually untouched by his parents' authoritarian appeal. Under such circumstances, it is simply not possible for the child to genuinely meet his parents' demands for modified performance.

Within this context, we see that failure to recognize the roots of the antagonism leads to an inability to work toward resolution of the basic interpersonal conflict that is feeding it. As the child learns to attend less to his stressful environment, he may appear to become increasingly forgetful as he progressively enters into sham conflict with himself, which leads nowhere. Although he may point apologetically to his fruitless endeavors and may try not to be dull, lazy, untidy, or aggressive—as the remarks of others may have labeled him—this experience will tend to aggravate his sense of weakness and deficient willpower. And because there has been no real modification of his inner system of purpose, neither his highly uncomfortable position nor any conscious effort he may make to improve or correct his faults will be to any avail.

When parents intervene in this struggle with criticism and fault-finding and reproach the child for his lack of willpower to change, they succeed only in further damaging the child in his struggle to become an adequately self-managing human being. When such a child gives in to his impulses and gives the impression of being unable to manage or control himself, he often forces his parents, relatives, or friends to make decisions for him or, in some cases, to assume almost complete responsibility for his actions. At the same time, however, the child's actions may be designed to prevent parental protest through his obvious "effort" to fulfill his obligations.

Our point, of course, is that parents who do not want to set their children on this road to serious neurosis must avoid exhortations such as "pull yourself together," which not only discourage but simultaneously distress and depress the child. Parents who note either apparent or assumed ineptitude in their children should seek to recognize the purposes of each child's behavior as a prelude to providing assistance in the solution of specific "difficulties." Efforts made to shape the child's behavior can only be effective when the origins of the problem are well enough understood to allow the adult to help the child to alter the premises upon which his inadequate behavior is based. Flaws—such as lack of control, lack of initiative, or thoughtlessness—are never based on a lack of strength or energy, only on their misdirection. For this reason, parents should never give the child reason or opportunity to learn to believe in his or her own assumed weakness.

A related difficulty involves parents who seem to strain to the utmost in their efforts to be "fair," perhaps as a result of having assumed responsibility for one child while having "pushed" another. When one child gets a piece of candy, a toy, or a new article of clothing, for example, parents may begin to feel that each child should be given exactly the same. This sort of overconcern contradicts good intentions and is damaging. Parents who do this succeed only in creating tenseness and intensified competition among their children.

Children who find themselves in such situations usually very quickly form an unspoken alliance to keep mother or daddy involved in anxiety over what is and what is not fair. Parents who come to believe they must be completely "fair" to their children and show no favoritism are likely to work to display this mistaken conviction. But in reality, no parent can arrange everything so that it is completely fair. When they attempt to do so, parents develop an overconcern that puts the emphasis on getting rather than on contribution. Neither parents nor children can feel happy and satisfied as long as the family unit operates on the basis of this false premise.

A parent caught in this dilemma needs to relax, take it easy, and give up his or her concern over fairness. If, for example, mother decides that each of her children may have two pieces of candy, she should give each two and let it go at that. Then, if they whimper or cry that one got more than the other, mother may simply withdraw—to the bathroom, if necessary—to allow her children to solve this artificial and unnecessary "problem." As long as parents assume such responsibilities, they will remain issues or problems that the children will never learn to assume and solve for themselves. As mother learns to manage her behavior, however, most such problems will simply cease to exist.

Parents need to learn to relax and take it easy as they confront all of the problems of child-rearing. Let us again refer to the common problem of shopping with children, which causes so many mothers so much tension. Suppose in this case the mother is shopping in a department store with her child—let's call him Tommy. In such a situation, most children like to run, play hide and seek, lag behind, or wander away. These patterns of behavior keep mother's attention divided between shopping and keeping track of her child.

When Tommy finally disappears, mother feels frantic. Then, when he is found, she feels compelled to tell him how frightened she was to have lost him in a big store. Having done that, she now forces from him a promise to stay near her for the remainder of the shopping trip. Soon Tommy is again out of sight. Why? Because he likes this "game" of hide and seek that he enjoys whenever he goes out with his mother.

It is fun to see mother get upset and act frantic. Tommy does not feel lost since he knows exactly where he is. From his point of view, it is up to his mother to stay with him and keep track of him. But, two can play this game. Mother can take time for training her child by refraining from displaying her fear that he will get lost. When mother notices that Tommy is no longer with her, she can choose to quietly remain out of sight. When Tommy becomes aware that mother isn't looking for him, he will return to where he left her, but now mother is gone. Now Tommy begins to feel anxious, so he starts his own search, but mother continues to remain out of his sight until his level of concern has reached a high level. At this point, she may step quietly back into sight while at the same time continuing her shopping as before.

Tommy's mother refuses to act worried about her son getting lost, and in so doing, she steps out of his game of hide and seek. If she can relax and refuse to become upset, she can train her child so that soon, he will be sure that he keeps track of mother. When her child runs up to her, frightened and perhaps crying, she can fail to be impressed by his display of fear and agitation. A quietly spoken statement, such as "I'm sorry we lost each other," will suffice. By acting in this restrained manner, mother shifts responsibility to her son.

A similar approach is useful when children do not arrive at home from school or elsewhere at a prearranged agreed upon time. When mother's response to such situations is predictably frantic and/or angry, the child quickly learns that all such situations are under his control, hence subject to his whims. He may think very little at all about the excited lecture he will probably receive upon his late return home. He knows he has not had an accident or been run over by a car or been kidnapped or whatever else mother may include in her repertoire of excited lecture. If he even gives mother's lectures a second thought before deciding to have a bit more fun before heading home, he is likely to decide his fun is worth her anger.

Mothers faced with this problem, again, should learn to take it easy. They may explain their feelings, desires, and concerns to the child but remain under control when the child returns home. But sometime, when he is late, she might be "gone."

Much of the worry and concern displayed by parents over the behaviors of their children is needless. We can and, of course, should prepare both ourselves and our children to prevent and to deal with dangerous situations as well as unexpected danger. But worrying about possible disaster will never prevent it since we can deal effectively with such trouble only after it happens or after we become aware of a real unexpectedly dangerous situation. Why is this so important in raising a child? It is important because we know that as children become aware of unnecessary parental worry and over-concern, they quickly learn to use it as a tool to get our attention, to promote a power contest, or to get even. In other words, they learn mistaken goals for their behavior.

As parents, our best refuge is to develop and display confidence in our well-prepared children. In doing so, we help each other to build a sense of mutual respect and trust. In this way, we help each child to learn to accept his or her share of responsibility for family order. Perhaps no less important, we remove some unnecessary stress from ourselves until such time as our talents and strength for coping with disaster are genuinely required. For these reasons, we must train our children for self-discipline within a context of healthy and mutual trust and respect for persons, places, and things. Then, if and when we are needed, we can be of real value to our children without damaging their personal development and without alienating ourselves from them in time of real need.

A closely related factor that requires some special attention in this context is the element of guilt. Once the child has for any reason experienced parental—usually maternal—overreaction to a specific guilt-related statement, such as "You just don't love me anymore," that child will begin to respond to this parental attitude in ways designed to use it for his own private purposes. Although the child is not consciously aware of it, he knows mother's (or father's) vulnerable spot and can use it as a tool to keep her continually and deeply concerned with his feelings and behaviors. Such a mother will bend over backward trying to prove her love for her child as long as he expresses his doubts about it. Without either individual consciously realizing it, mother has provided her child with an endless source of control. Mother needs to realize that she is a good mother as long as she fulfills her child's present necessities, and for this reason, she can stop falling for his expressions of doubt. She knows she loves her child, and he knows it just as well as she. By becoming aware of the purpose of his behavior, mother can render it ineffective. She can learn to be unafraid of the expressions of her own child.

The child who displays jealousy of another individual presents a similar problem. Unknowingly, we often teach our children to be jealous or perhaps we should say to display jealousy. The first sign of childhood envy for a new baby is an excellent example. As long as parents or other adults are impressed by the child's display of jealousy, he or she will find it to be useful. Here again, our best defense against this harsh emotion is to remain casual and to avoid pity. The child can learn—and must learn—to deal with these sorts of unpleasant situations and emotions since they are a part of life. As such, he must eventually learn to take them in stride without undue fuss.

Experience has revealed that a child will learn to adjust himself to his new role if his parents refrain from feeling sorry for him and do not try to compensate for what he has "lost." If they display their love for him and continue to give him individual time and attention as before, he will learn from and not be damaged by the experience.

Any child will feel jealousy and will display such feelings in a protracted fashion, only if it pays off for him to do so.

When parents strive to make life perfect for their children, their effort is futile; they will never succeed. But it is possible to be of real value to children as they develop. Much of our concern as our children grow is based upon our own latent feelings of inadequacy. Often, we feel we just don't know what to do or which of several alternatives might be best. However, it is not necessary for parents to deal with or attempt to manage every little problem that may occur. In fact, to do so is often counterproductive.

Many, if not most, of the day-to-day problems experienced in families will simply disappear if parents will just relax and refuse to become overexcited or overinvolved. We must all learn to take it easy since it is our children themselves who promote many of these problems just to keep us concerned. It often seems amazing to note how many things some parents can find to be concerned about in the lives of their children. Some press them to do well in school while also pushing them into "self-development" activities. Some of us are suspicious and want to be aware of their every activity. We may fret about their moral attitudes, worry about their health, watch for signs of bad habits or unacceptable thoughts, and superimpose our own interpretations onto whatever may happen to them. We assume we know how our children feel or will feel about a given situation instead of finding out how it appears to them.

Many of us as parents expend tremendous amounts of time and energy trying to live our children's lives for them. We often behave as if we really believe that children are born bad and have to be forced to be good to be saved from tragedy in life. How much better it would be for us—as well as for our offspring—if we would relax and have confidence in our children as we offer them support and give them the opportunity they need to live for themselves. Within an environment of mutual trust and respect, our children will be free to let us know if and when they need our consultation or help. And, if we guide without pushing, they *will* let us know.

Avoid Excessive Pressure and Criticism

Many situations do require immediate response from children, particularly in the case of impending danger or when, for some other reason, the child must be held to the observance of necessary order. The demand for submission in every case is a mistake, however, since emergencies do not occur often, and demands for immediate response in these few cases will usually require no more than firmness. Those parents who feel compelled to use force in situations where they feel the child's objection to requests is an unacceptable abridgement of their authority and prestige should ask themselves sincerely the following question: "Is such an attitude—which is usually rooted in a domestic power contest defeat—justified?"

A child will always have his own thoughts or ideas on an issue and must be allowed to develop them if he or she is to be fully equipped for success in later life. Persons as well as situations which restrain the freedom and flexibility of the child's developing personality may constrict the growth of his will and may restrict the power of his judgment. This in no way suggests that parents should give in at every turn, but it does require a complete and sincere consideration to determine when the child may make his own decisions without detriment to others and when he or she should subordinate his will in the interest of social order.

Even in situations where a child must subordinate his will by relinquishing one of his desires, it is not always necessary that he do so immediately. Although parents who consider every act of resistance as a threat to their personal prestige may find it hard to wait, their failure to do so—which usually involves application of force, irritation, and anger reactions—often marks the onset of conflict that both can and should be avoided. If parents' desire for prestige permitted them only a little more patience, they might come to the realization that a little thought and restraint can go much further than a great deal of anger or force.

Parents who are willing and able to stop and consider the content of the situation will find they are in a position to devise means for influencing the child in the right direction. They may also learn that other means are much more suitable and appropriate than forced or even violent insistence on blind obedience. In most cases, they will find they are able to use natural consequences to steer the child toward voluntary surrender of undesirable wishes and intent. Finally, parents also need to realize that children who lie within the context of parental insistence on blind obedience do so only as a result of their desire to evade painful arguments and altercations.

Especially at those times when the child is in some stage of revolt, as a result of an increase in his responsibilities or problems or as a result of previous family friction, it becomes increasingly important for parents to realize that it will be impossible for them to accomplish everything immediately. For example, when the child is ill, when a younger sister or brother is born, or when he begins school, the child may easily tend toward rebelliousness. In most cases, this is most likely to occur between the ages of three and four and again near the time of puberty. At these and other sensitive periods in the child's development, parents who lack self-assurance often experience increasing fear of leaving anything undone as they face increasingly upsetting manifestations of family struggle. As parents face critical situations during these periods, their own personal struggle for prestige and control can be especially damaging in its effect. Our point then is that the commonly held assumption of many parents that disastrous consequences will result if they fail to immediately achieve whatever at that moment seems most important is very definitely in error.

If we as parents were to make it a practice to listen to ourselves, particularly our tone of voice, we would soon discover the amount of disrespect we show our children. Study of family interaction reveals that parents seldom talk to children in the normal tone of voice they use when talking with each other. When we speak to our children, they frequently hear more in our tone of voice than in the many words we use. In fact, many adults often actually provoke their children to certain behaviors through the tone of voice they use. Consider the "Oh no you won't, young man!" tone of voice. Such words are often spoken with dictatorial firmness intended to express determination.

But they very predictably initiate a power contest and reflect a latent fear on the part of the adult speaker of a loss of control over a child.

Many statements made to children by parents or other adults simply add to the child's discouragement. Parents communicate both discouragement and scorn when they use statements like, "Oh, Jim, what are we going to do with you?" or "Surely you can do at least that much." In making such statements, mother or father clearly indicate that they have very little faith in their child. The same is true of condescending simple speech, sometimes called "baby talk," which parents too often use with their children. We would never use this manner or tone in speaking to a friend, and our children know it. In using this mode of speech, we succeed only in communicating our feeling that children are inferior. When we talk down to children, speak with saccharine sweetness to win cooperation, or exude excitement and splash false gaiety to stimulate interest, we underestimate our children's understanding of us as we display our lack of respect for them.

Listen to your own tone of voice as you speak to your child. What do you express with it? And what does your child hear? Once we become aware of errors in our tone of voice, we are in a position to change for the better. Only if we can learn to speak to our children as friends and equals will we be able to keep the doors of communication open between parent and child.

The press of parental impatience can quickly evolve into a pattern of constant nagging with its monotonous repetition of trite phrases. Probably no other single parental attitude so irritates, annoys, and antagonizes the child. Because of its increasing poverty of flexibility and inventive imagination—with everything becoming subject to criticism and nothing ever good enough—even trivial slip-ups may be represented as terrible offenses. The practice of nagging only strengthens the child's resistance as it promotes disobedience and hastens failure. For this reason, it is of absolutely no value or benefit in a child's education or training. Because parents who nag act from an inner necessity, (1) their attitudes are based on their own needs rather than those of the child, and (2) they too often simply do not stop and think of what they are doing.

It is likely that most parents would be immediately startled into changing their tactics if they would only stop to observe the immediate effects that are produced by their over-supervisory behavior. Fault-finding and nagging are usually focused directly toward belittling and deprecating children in ways that simply reassure adults of their own superiority. While parents who frequently do this may also frequently rationalize their behavior as well as their dissatisfaction in dozens of ways, most rarely realize the true root of their discontent that nearly always turns out to be their own feelings of frustration and disappointment in life.

Parents often tell themselves that they find fault with their children to show the children that they have not acted properly. But the child usually knows before he is corrected that he has made a mistake. Study of children's reactions to adult behavior clearly reveals that adults stimulate the child's ability to discriminate between right and wrong most productively by emphasizing that which is right. Parents who are willing to make the effort and experiment with their own actions can easily see how tractable children can be when given encouragement and friendly instruction. If they will then compare these results with the effects of fault-finding, they will soon realize how very little can be achieved by the latter means.

Because fault-finding involves disparaging comments and actions presented in a characteristic reproachful tone of voice, it is not the same as giving instruction. When a parent says to a child, "No, that's not correct. This is the way it should be done," he or she is giving instruction and is not fault-finding. There is a marked exception, however, that involves a small minority of children who react favorably when they are harshly criticized. Encouragement and friendly persuasion that produces the best results in most children may seem entirely futile with these children who respond to no technique or procedure other than fault-finding or criticism. Children who react in this fashion are tenaciously obstinate individuals who have been hardened by conflict to a point where they will bend only to force. The personality characteristics displayed by these children will be outlined in more detail later in this chapter since the peculiar attitude that they seem to display in common is more clearly distinguishable within that context.

Fault-finding also occasionally produces favorable results when used with very ambitious children, but in these cases, it is equally possible that the net effect will be detrimental. Although it may act as a spur to the ambition of such children when used sparingly and with discretion, frequent and intense fault-finding may so discourage the ambitious child that he will immediately abandon his efforts. In this situation, as with others reported in this volume, we see how an identical attitude on the part of parents may produce different results in children having different personal backgrounds and goals.

In general, the practice of finding fault with the behavior of children has a fairly uniform effect on their future behavior, with the exception of those special cases reviewed above. Since it discourages most children and impedes both their achievement and their conduct, it might seem almost preferable if they could become so habituated to their parents' criticism that they would no longer pay attention to it. We now know that in many cases, domestic tragedies have had their origin in this sort of faulty relationship. In such cases, an unhappy cycle is usually created where the parents find fault, but the child fails to improve, followed by increased fault-finding as the child becomes increasingly obstinate, and so on. As this vicious cycle continues, the relationship between frustrated parents and their discontented children continues to deteriorate, becoming increasingly uncomfortable or even dangerous.

Parents who continually censure a child for his shortcomings run great risks and should consider the effects of their behavior. In their desire for the child's improvement—if not perfection—mothers and fathers need to realize that their severe words of criticism, blame, or disapproval will have at least one sure result. They will, at the very least, clearly give vent to the adults' feelings of disappointment and irritation. Suppose the child is awkward. Will telling him that he is like a bull in a china shop or that he is clumsy or that he seems to have two left feet stimulate him to have greater dexterity? Of course not. Since it is certain that his clumsiness is at least in part due to discouragement, the opposite effect is more likely. By their actions and statements, such parents will only confirm their child's low opinion of himself; they tell him nothing new.

Under such circumstances, and because he will now be likely to thoroughly believe that he is awkward, the child is sure to behave accordingly. "What's the use of making an effort? I just can't help being awkward. That's just the way I am." At this point, a child's parents can be quite sure he will not undermine their apparent opinion of him or their clearly articulated expectations for his future behavior. As such, a child learns to take his "weakness" for granted, and he will also have the satisfaction of seeing others fret about it.

An analogous effect is often produced by repeatedly scolding, chiding, or berating a child about his untidiness, "stupidity," laziness, or other faults. As the parents' comments completely rob the child of the courage necessary to improve himself, the defect takes firm root. If he did not already believe he had these failings, the remarks of his adult models will certainly convince him. For this reason, discouraging attitudes displayed by parents may be the direct cause of a child's development of bad habits.

A good example of this phenomenon can be clearly observed in many cases of untruthfulness in children. Adults who misunderstand the lively imagination of a child and his tendency to confuse reality and fantasy may accuse him of lying. If this occurs on successive occasions, he may learn to believe that he is, by nature, untruthful. At this point, he may really begin to lie. Adults who in their irritation are pushed by feelings of harassment into expressing their poor opinion of such a child may tend to exaggerate his faults. Of course, this may all seem unintentional since parental statements may sound stronger than they were meant to be, but the result is the same. Parents who vent their feelings in this way for the sake of relieving an irritation or annoyance may succeed in the creation of several more.

Parents who belittle the child or deprecate his efforts to adequately deal with his environment either discourage the child or arouse his defiance. When they nag or find fault in much of what they see the child do, they not only generate conflict through their disparagement but also very often produce precisely the opposite of the effect they intended. When a bad habit such as untidiness, nail-biting, or nose-picking occurs, the attitude of most parents toward it is displayed in a miscellaneous mixture of reproach, promises, admonishments, and threats. However, extensive observation of the growth and development of children reveals that these are exactly the forces that would need to be brought to bear if one wished to create or implant such habits in the behavior of the child.

If someone were to search for the best method of teaching a child to pick his nose, persuasion would prove inadequate, and merely setting an example would not always work. However, one method would almost unfailingly provide the desired result. If an adult "teacher" were to wait until the child put his finger in his nose and would then immediately slap him, the adult would find that in a short while the finger would again be in the nose. If the adult were then to shout at the child and forbid him to touch his nose, then repeat the ritual, augmenting the vehement impatient tone of his voice with threats and slaps, the likelihood of that adult being successful in his training would be very great. In short, within a rather limited span of time, the child would, under these conditions, have acquired the habit of nose picking.

That is, of course, the very same method that many parents may employ with their children in the mistaken belief that it will serve to remove the child's fault. Most parents seem entirely unaware that the method they use will inevitably lead to exactly the opposite result. As in so many other cases because their own parents may have subjected them to this treatment, they too uncritically use the same— at the very least ineffective and often harmful—method in training their own children.* Although in most cases, the child's defiance is aroused and he offers resistance, most parents seem unable to read this clue and modify their approach without outside help. The explanation for this apparent parental blindness or insensitivity probably lies in their lack of insight into the varying positive and negative effects of various training or educational measures in the life of the child with only the superficial results seemingly obvious from their

---

* This example was adapted from thought-provoking remarks made by Dr. Rudolph Dreikurs to a class of parents and graduate students at the University of Wisconsin-Platteville during the Summer of 1970.

parental viewpoint. Unfortunately, large numbers of parents seem ignorant of the fact that childhood disobedience, failure in specified tasks, "naughtiness," and a wide variety of other faults are often due to psychic wounds which must be handled with discretion if they are not to be made worse.

Difficulties may, of course, stand in the way of maintenance of an objective attitude toward one's own offspring. As suggested in earlier sections, selfish personal interest is characteristic of many parents concerning various training methods that are of no real benefit to their children. Most parents—if they can for a moment be objective with themselves—will discover how often they feel compelled to slight their child, whether it be as a result of anger, boredom, weariness, or for some other "reason." Realistically, even the clearest understanding of the mistaken goals of children will be of no value to parents if they are unwilling to view the situation objectively or if they defend against such objectivity either out of a personal inability to cope or as a result of some other unmet personal need.

A great many adults, for example, seem afraid to sincerely and enthusiastically acknowledge the accomplishments of their children. As a result of this apparent fear, many are reluctant to praise or express approval of the child's action or, if they do, they add some discouraging or disparaging afterthought. "You were very good this morning, Jamie. Why can't you be this good every day?"

Because many adults refuse to recognize—or are unable to recognize—the selfish interest behind their own attitude, they continue to point out only the mistakes and errors of their children while taking good conduct for granted. Some parents then add insult to injury through the rationalization that to do otherwise might make the child conceited. In reality, however, neither acknowledgment of success nor encouragement will lead to conceit if applied with discretion.

Parents who feel confident and self-assured in their relations with their children will guide each through difficulty, quietly and calmly. This is not true of the parent who feels unequal to the situation, however, since the selfish interest of this parent will become clearly evident whenever his child gets into mischief. Such a parent may feel he has no time for the child at that moment or, even more likely, he may not know how to meet the problem properly. It is at this moment when the parent may be filled with apprehension and dread of unpleasant consequences of the child's subsequent behavior that the disparaging or deprecating attitude usually begins, often yielding an intensely critical response.

This impulsive, emotional, and disparaging type of response has become habitual with many parents. Many very quickly resort to scolding, nagging, reprimands, persistent irritability, and sharpness in all its variations, plus excessive supervision, belittling, and of course spanking. Because these parents are not well in control of their response to the child, they may feel guilt for which they may again try to compensate later. This may lead to swings in the parents' behavior, which may become extreme and confusing to the child.

Other parents systematically apply the technique of disparagement as a deliberate mode of child training. These adults who believe they will succeed only through premeditated punishment—such as spanking or other severity, including planned humiliations—fail to realize that this policy clearly reveals their desire not to help but rather to defeat the child. Such parents have, for some reason, developed a need to preserve their own sense of superiority and control through use of these extreme but unnecessary coercive measures.

Although such treatment may serve to temporarily uphold parental authority, it will inevitably lead to revolt. All authority that requires force for its maintenance is intrinsically frail and will one day fail. From the viewpoint of the child, regardless of how much he may appear to submit, within himself, he will continue the conflict as he waits for his opportunity to escape. Parental authority must be designed to teach the child to observe order. In all cases where random or arbitrary abuse of excessive parental authority occurs, it will invite the child to resist.

Some parents treat the disobedient child as if he did not "deserve" kindness. Such children, although they may rarely hear a pleasant, friendly word, may apparently remain obedient in their behavior. However, such children give their parents very little satisfaction nor are they likely to be happy or satisfied since they are not real participants in the life of a family. In such cases, the child may be uncommunicative, may allow obstinacy to surface only periodically, may only occasionally refuse to do an assigned task, or may obey only with obvious reluctance. In other words, the child may appear to be well-trained and controlled.

Although by means of certain methods, it may be possible to "tame" a child superficially, the clear-cut severity that will be required to do so will impede the growth of the child's feeling of belonging, and more generally, the development of his social interest. The experience of such a situation further aggravates the child's sense of helplessness as it makes him increasingly and more painfully aware of his weakness and dependence. The child feels anger toward his parents, and as he inwardly rebels against the severity of their behavior, he misses no opportunity to demonstrate to them his feelings of ill will or indifference. Although a systematically pursued policy of parental severity may not allow any sign of open opposition in families where it exists, both generations clearly recognize the thinly concealed acts of hostility that do occur for exactly what they are.

Avoid Insult and Brutality

Some parents require their children to "atone" for misbehavior through experiences such as standing in a corner, being shut in a room, kneeling on a hardwood floor, or parental insistence on self-accusation followed by a request from the child for punishment. In some cases, when devices such as these do not satisfy the creative imagination of the adult, which is sometimes stimulated by a sadistic urge, other even more extreme measures which usually include shouts, threats, or blows may be employed.

Parents who believe they can wear down a child's opposition or resistance by shaming, embarrassing, or humiliating him, and in this way break him of certain faults or bad habits, produce effects that are easy to predict. The mental processes which occur in children who are treated in this fashion are nearly always far different from what they may at first seem to be, based on the child's overt behavior. This is because the child will nearly always automatically and mechanically but involuntarily do what is expected of him under conditions of extreme stress. Such a child is reared into a pattern of habitual pretense of virtue, pretended piety, and hypocrisy. Behind this mask, however, silent contempt, jeers, and sneers and curses will accompany his modest, unpretentious, polite actions and mild, submissive words, making the value of his externally controlled "good" conduct doubtful at best.

The child's psychic constitution may be seriously affected as part of this process since experiences of the sort outlined above often induce emotional disturbance that can develop into neurosis with tendencies toward masochism being a possible early symptom. In such cases, parents may believe they are causing the child discomfort when in reality, they are providing him with an increased sensuous pleasure that results as the child finds it possible to transform the supposed punishment into a source of enjoyment. In this way, the child may triumph at the very moment when to all appearances, he is most objectively humbled.

Other adults may strike or even beat their children in an attempt to force the recognition of parental superiority and authority. During recent decades, however, the use of corporal punishment as a systematically applied method of child training has fallen more and more into disuse. Legal action has helped in this regard. Those who use this method often argue that since the young child is impervious to reasoning, striking or spanking him is the only means of persuading conformity which will consistently produce a result. And as their children grow older, and as certain difficult situations are encountered, some parents go so far as to report that all other methods seem futile. When these kinds of arguments are presented by parents, they usually refer to a practice of systematic spanking or beatings. Still other adults, who deal out blows only when they feel extremely nervous or emotionally upset, may be aware of the general undesirability of physical punishment but still resort to it under certain adverse conditions.

There is a much more effective method of training, however. It was mentioned in the preceding chapter as the practice of letting the developing individual experience the logic and consequences of his or her actions. This technique may be applied effectively in early infancy as well as during later stages of the developmental process. Physical blows are clearly not indispensable in training a child nor are harsh words. The latter, however, *may* be superfluous while the former *can* be damaging.

When little Billy wants to handle some object that might do him harm, the object can simply be removed and put out of his reach whether he cries or not. His parent need not slap his hand nor spank him nor shout nor lecture. It is unnecessary. Just say no. Matters can be arranged on other occasions without actual danger so that Billy's baby brother, Jimmy, may also experience the painful potentialities of certain objects. Or suppose Jimmy insists on standing up in his stroller while it is being pushed by his father. With all due precautions, the parent might gently tip it backward, arousing a sense of danger that would cause Jimmy to sit down of his own accord. If one such experience is not enough, the parent can expose the child to several of a similar nature with the end result that the child may soon lose his desire to unnecessarily provoke these unpleasant sensations of falling.

The same is true for older children with many approaches available for using this principle in difficult training situations. If, for example, one of two brothers repeatedly turns on the gas on a kitchen stove each time he passes it. Mother may apply natural consequences by announcing to both children that only the one who knows that the gas should not be turned on will be permitted to go into the kitchen as often as he chooses to do so. The other brother will have to stay out until he demonstrates that he is capable of passing the stove without touching it. If carried out consistently, and under certain existing conditions, procedures such as this can be helpful in allaying further disturbance.* However, individual circumstances must be carefully evaluated in each case as rigorous discussion of this example has suggested. Removing knobs was suggested as an option for example. What would you do?

---

* Anecdote adapted from a controversial story told for thought and discussion of the limits of this technique by Dr. Rudolph Dreikurs during the Summer of 1970.

If parents could know what their children think and feel when they strike them, most might be so greatly shocked as to never do so again. At the moment of such corporal punishment, children who are frequently beaten often develop intense thoughts and feelings of hate and rage, which may include momentary desire for the death of their tormentor. For this reason, we should not expect any impulse toward good conduct to emerge from such an experience. While it is true that from earliest infancy the child must learn to respect and observe order and must learn to accommodate his desires to this necessary condition, physical punishment is never essential to attain this, even in those cases where the child himself considers it to be deserved. Even the most savage blows can have no beneficial effect on a child's attitude. The exact reverse is true since inner resistance will probably not be broken but instead is likely to be strengthened in ways that will prompt the child's further determination as it continues to alienate him from the encouragement and positive experience he needs.

A clear distinction must be made between children who are spanked frequently or regularly and those who are spanked only on rare occasions. Although children who have never before been struck in anger may be so shocked by the experience that the impression it makes on their thinking and emotions may in turn prompt their careful avoidance of a repetition, this situation is probably the exception. In most families, children learn to fear and yield to force and, in the case of purely physical force, a bit of their courage, self-reliance, and dignity is very likely to be destroyed with each stroke.

An apparent exception involves the child who seems to obey only when spanked very hard. These children often exasperate their parents with willful, capricious, and impertinent behavior and sometimes appear to deliberately invite punishment as they almost systematically provoke adult anger. Because persuasion, warnings, and threats are usually completely ineffectual in such cases, the distraught parents may finally give vent to their emotions through blows or other physically punishing responses. Because such a child may often act compliant, affectionate, and well-behaved, i.e., he acts like a changed person, immediately afterward, such obvious results are considered to be evidence of the efficiency of corporal punishment.

When we carefully examine the reasons why this child responds so favorably to bad treatment, however, we see that the results are not as positive as they may at first seem. Although some psychologists have suggested that such children can acquire their apparent desire for punishment through a sense of guilt, which supposedly craves chastisement, the root cause in many cases may be much less complex. Many such children begin their patterns of unusually troublesome behavior soon after the birth of a younger sister or brother. In virtually all such cases, parents are dealing with a child who now feels ignored or rejected and for this reason has resorted to disobedience or mischief to divert the attention of his parents from this new rival to himself. As long as this attitude prevails, the child will not be content until his parents become so disturbed that they disregard all other matters to focus their attention on him.

After an outburst of their temper, the parents may then attempt to modify the situation or to make amends by petting, caressing, fondling, or kissing the child. When they do so, they should not really be surprised when their child then begins to provoke their anger, spanking, or blows in a more preconceived way in order to attract attention or perhaps even to become a favored target of their notice or concern. Although some children seem to especially enjoy the feeling of power derived from exciting their parents to the high emotional pitch required to elicit an angry response, the fact is that beatings more often signal an intensive concentration of attention on their recipient, which is the primary factor that drives many children into this particular attitude. The good behavior displayed by such a child after physical punishment or abuse is the price the child is willing to pay for the fulfillment of his or her craving for attention.

This sort of provocative misbehavior is a direct manifestation of the child's unconscious plan, either to get attention or to excite and punish his parent. However, this is not the purpose parents have in mind when they physically punish their child. Although they *think* they are training him, they are deliberately—but without realizing it—making themselves the instrument of his desires. A second related response seemingly in opposition to such childhood rebellion against parents may also occasionally be observed, however. Although brutality will usually induce emotions, which range from fear or hate, it may sometimes produce a pronounced attachment or even devotion. Here, as in the situation cited at the beginning of this section, the child may often try to provoke blows and then nullify such parental violence by making it a source of pleasure.

All persons who were beaten as children reveal the results of these blows in their later personality development. Some individuals assert that they are actually grateful for the physical discipline, including spankings, blows, and beatings, which they received during childhood. In cases where stern parents are especially loved, admired, and respected in later years, the adult may no longer clearly remember the unpleasant emotions he felt as a child whenever he was abused. This can occur, and when it does, it is usually encountered in an individual who has learned to feel and show respect for anyone who is either willing or able to exercise power. For example, the father who chose to deal openly with children using physical abuse as a controlling measure may be seen in retrospect as a symbol of power to be loved and revered, but only when time has tempered the individual's wounds and the father is no longer a threat.

Often, the second generation will imitate the first with children of brutal parents maturing to approve, justify, recommend, and use many of the same methods with their own children that they themselves experienced. Having experienced no other methods of child-rearing, they adapt and use those which they have seen used on themselves during their own developmental years. They believe that because they were physically punished as children and "turned out well enough," the same methods should be good for their own children. Such parents simply perpetuate a system of inadequate child-rearing practice. It is just as true in these cases as in any other that physical brutality in the guise of a child-training technique has had a profound influence, but these persons simply fail to recognize it.

Probably the most typical results of beating or otherwise physically punishing a child during his early developmental years are (1) arrogant and offensively self-assured behavior as he grows older or (2) a combination of timid, deferent, and submissive characteristics in one who is at the same time sly, cunning, and subtly deceitful. However, such a person may become very efficient and competent in his transactions with others and will often display a firmness, hardness, or harshness that may make him particularly well-fitted for success in some business or professional pursuits.

Such a person may strive to build his prestige and power through material superiority. To the degree that his lack of consideration for others reaches the point of tactlessness and tyrannical actions, one can clearly recognize that behind his seeming superiority or noticeable need for authority is fear. Because such a person is likely to continue to harbor a latent fear of recurrence of the degradations and humiliation that he experienced as a child, he is also likely to display a lack of genuine gentleness, warmth, and the capacity for intimate human relationship.

Almost everyone who was beaten in childhood and does display these callous, unfeeling characteristics will also display a tendency toward brutality. It is not that such a person is incapable of deeper, more gentle feelings, but rather that he cannot rid himself of the anger, fear, and distrust that he learned during this very impressionable period of his life. This pattern may occur in families where the parents truly love their child and are indulgent toward him or her in many respects but resort to spanking, hitting, or beating whenever they encounter an interpersonal conflict for which they have no more adequate child management technique. It is when parents feel frustration and a need to act in response to childhood misbehavior but are at a loss as to what to do that they most frequently make this type of child-rearing mistake.

The use of brutal force clearly betrays a fundamental weakness in the user, which is that he has no other resource at his disposal. For this reason—along with fear, an inner urge based upon anger, and habits learned from the previous generation—the method of corporal punishment continues to be used, although the fact that it is not only useless but harmful is now well-known. Parents who use it feel a need to give their children a vivid and drastic demonstration of their own superiority. They feel afraid that without such a display, they will be unable to subdue their child's resistance. Adults who use this method do not recognize or admit to themselves the degree to which their own cowardice is implicit in the procedures they use. The difference between an adult striking a weak, defenseless child and some boy who strikes a child who is smaller and weaker than he is not great. Both the boy and the adult assume the role of bully in doing so, and in neither case is their behavior necessary, nor will it produce the desired effects.

Parents who come to the realization that they (1) enjoy or have a strong need to demonstrate their power and superiority, (2) have a certain tendency toward violence, or (3) feel unable to tolerate limitations in their authority should seek the roots of these compulsions in their own character. However, the impulse to strike out at children is often sufficiently complex to require professional help to do so efficiently. Those adults who do examine their own motivations almost invariably discover that the moment they raise a hand to strike is also the moment they feel most weak and helpless—hence, frustrated and upset—in relation to the child. Because of the intensity of this feeling, the adult may not stop to think whether what he is doing is beneficial or even fair.

From this intense sense of adult helplessness and failure comes the source and the motivational root for his (or her) desire to show by any available means that he is the stronger one, even to the extent of doing so through physical superiority, brute strength, or unthinking cruelty. The feelings of guilt that often follow such an emotional display do very little to neutralize the effects of the parents' behavior, however, and may only compound the problem. Most parents know they should not beat their children but in a trying moment may feel sufficiently helpless to resort to violence in spite of this sense of wrongdoing. Then, later, as the parent attempts to rationalize his behavior and to salve his conscience, he may again suggest to himself that the child "needs" whippings or that his "nerves just couldn't take it" or that he simply "lost control of himself."

This sort of self-justification does nothing at all to help the child since his sense of social solidarity (community interest and fellowship), which is of such immense importance to his satisfactory development, is inseparably interconnected with his acceptance of the social order in which he lives. Since this sense of social solidarity is never advanced by punishment but is retarded by disparagement, physical punishment can only be counterproductive. Any method designed to train the child to become an active member of society must avoid all expedients which tend to suppress or humiliate him if he is ever to become a socialized and adaptable contributing member of society.

Respond to the Individual as Part of the Group

When children misbehave or do well, their behavior may often seem to be an individual matter. Upon this assumption has grown a popular concept that parents should deal with each child as an individual, awarding condemnation or praise as indicated by each child's behavior. Because most parents accept this assumption, it seems difficult for many to realize how often all children in a family do act in concert against adult family members. They may team up to keep a parent busy, but they may also do so to defeat that parent.

Consider the example of a hall wall being decorated with crayons; it has happened several times before. Mother calls her three children, but no one will confess to the deed. The three act in alliance, following an unwritten peer group code which forbids "telling" or "tattling" or "squealing." What is to be done? This mother decided since none would confess and since at least one was obviously lying that she would punish all three. She would, as we say, "put them all in the same boat." After spanking each in turn, she again asked for a confession.

Soon, Tom, the child responsible, confessed and was given a cloth and pan of warm soapy water to clean the wall. Was this mother right or wrong in her action? As we pointed out earlier, spanking can be replaced by more productive methods, but this mother's decision to apply the principle of "group management of behavior" was a wise decision. She did what had to be done, but why?

Parents who deal with each child individually after some misbehavior such as the one cited in the preceding example tend to promote competition among the children in which one child will seek parental approval and elevation at the expense of the others. Under such circumstances, it is easy for parents to fall into the trap of playing one child against another, which stimulates each child to seek satisfaction from approval rather than from contribution. Because an individual child can be helped to contribute under almost any set of circumstances, mutual contribution is a realistic and obtainable goal, which may lead to increased family unity. The seeking of approval, on the other hand, must be recognized as a false goal since it is impossible for anyone to win constant approval. For this reason, when parents stimulate unnecessary competition among their children, they succeed only in reinforcing each child's mistaken goal.

In situations such as the ones cited above, a "good" child is not good because he wants to be good, but only because he desires to be better than and to keep ahead of the child who gets less approval than he. The interest of such a child is not centered upon the needs of the common welfare but rather upon himself in a truly selfish sense. The "bad" child—or more correctly, the deficient child—remains so because he gets his recognition in the same way but on "the useless side" of life.

In the example cited above, the parent could have asked all of her children to clean the marks from the wall with no further effort to find out who made those marks. In doing so, the parent would (1) prevent the "bad" child from seeking revenge or from promoting a power contest while (2) eliminating the opportunity for the "good" child to prove his "goodness" to the others' disadvantage. These principles apply whether there are a large number of children in the family or only two.

When we treat children as a group, putting them all in the same boat, we overcome existing intense competition as well as its damaging effects. Although this may seem to some to be a revolutionary step to take, treating all children as a unit eliminates personal preferences, moral judgments, and the spirit of competitiveness from the parents' action. It helps us all to realize that man is his brother's keeper and not necessarily his competitor or enemy.

Children can easily work together as a team against their parents. One may be aggressive while a second acts helpless, and a third is "good" or almost totally obedient. When this occurs, we must realize that their cooperation and competition is for our—their parents—benefit.

In the example of the decorated wall, which we used to illustrate this principle, once the competition for parental recognition was eliminated, the children acquired an opportunity to develop respect for each other as well as an incentive to assist each other in behavior management. In that example case, however, the children might have voiced the objection that it is unfair to make the innocent clean up a mess they did not create. Our children do acquire ideas of what is fair and unfair—from us—and then use these concepts to our disadvantage.

Let us consider for a moment some broader aspects of what is fair and unfair. From what we have thus far pointed out, it would seem unfair to each child to reinforce his or her false goal or mistaken concepts of value and role since to do so would disrupt harmony and cooperation. What we do as parents depends, of course, on what we want for our children as they grow and develop. If we want to teach responsibility in group misbehavior, we must begin by overcoming our own narrow assumption or conviction that the procedure of treating children alike and holding the group responsible is unfair as a childhood training device. If we as adults can decide to accept the concept of group training, and if we can act consistently on that decision, our children may also discover its justification.

We are simply "taking our sails out of their wind" when we put all members of a group in the same boat. We do so by making our children responsible as a group for what each member of the group chooses to do. Under such conditions, they will no longer have a desire to impress each other. Under such conditions, motivation for misbehavior loses its value while the reasons for cooperation become clear and of increasing value. The same general principle applies to jealousy among children. Jealousy, too, becomes useless if parents fail to be impressed by it. Jealousy, like competition, grows by what it feeds on.

It is interesting to note in work with parents that the tool of treating misbehavior within a group by making the group members responsible as a group for what each member does usually works better than is at first expected by those who try it. The act of treating all of the children as a unit results in a mutually valued sense of mutual responsibility. Referring one final time to our example of crayon drawings on walls, Tom, who committed the act, seemed reluctant to participate in the clean-up job assigned to all three children by his mother. However, he has never again written on the walls of his home. Why? Because after his mother's informed response to the act, there was no longer any "sense" in or reason for this behavior. This is true in the case of any "bad" behavior. If it no longer provokes a fight to engage mother in the long negotiations, which the child has learned to enjoy for the attention they give to him, the behavior is no longer of value.

It is always difficult to establish who is guilty in a fight since fighting is rarely, if ever, the sole result of misbehavior of one child. Usually, all participants contribute—often almost equally—to the disturbance, which is the result of their combined effort. The "good" child may push or dare or otherwise provoke or "egg on" the "bad" child toward the desired result of involving a parent—usually mother—in the situation. Because children do coordinate their efforts, whether for the furtherance of family antagonisms and tensions or, more ideally, for the welfare of the family, they must be helped to recognize and accept their responsibility for each other.

All children in a family unit are so closely coordinated in their behavior in a united front for dealing with their parents that when the behavior of the "bad" one gets better, that of the "good" one will predictably become worse. Parents who can be helped to see this and to treat all of their children as a group often experience rather dramatic results as their children learn to utilize their interdependence to display concern for and to take care of or manage each other.

Bibliography

Background Materials on Human Development/Children—Adlerian Viewpoint

Adler, Alexandria, *Guiding Human Misfits*. Revised edition. (Reprint of 1948 edition). New York: Kraus Reprints.

Adler, Alfred. *The Case of Mrs. A.* 2nd ed revised. Edited by Bernard Shulman. (Individual Psychology Pamphlets. Medical Pamphlet No. 1) Chicago: Alfred Adler Institute, 1969.

Adler, Alfred. *The Education of Children*. Chicago: Regency, 1970.

Adler, Alfred. *Education of the Individual*. New York: Greenwood, 1958.

Adler, Alfred. *Practice and Theory of Individual Psychology*. New York: Humanities Press, 1929. (Reprinted 1971.)

Adler, Alfred. *The Problem Child*. New York: Putnam, 1963.

Adler, Alfred. *Problems of Neurosis*. New York: Harper-Row, 1964.

Adler, Alfred. *The Science of Living*. Edited by Heinz I. Ansbacher. New York: Doubleday, 1969.

Adler, Alfred. *Social Interest*. New York: Putnam, 1964,

Adler, Alfred. *Understanding Human Nature*. New York: Humanities Press, 1962. (Reprint of 1926 edition.)

Adler, Alfred. *The Neurotic Constitution*. New York: Books for Libraries, 1972. (Reprint of 1926 edition.)

Adler, Alfred. *What Life Should Mean to You*. New York: Putnam, 1959.

Allred, G. Hugh. *On the Level with Self, Family, Society*. Provo, Utah: Brigham Young University Press, 1974.

Ansbacher, Heinz L. and Ansbacher, Rowena R. (eds). *The Individual Psychology of Alfred Adler: A Systematic Presentation in Selections from His Writings*. New York: Basic Books, 1956.

Ansbacher, Heinz L. and Ansbacher, Rowena R. (eds). *Superiority and Social Interest: A Collection of Later Writings*. 2nd ed revised. Evanston: Northwestern University Press, 1970.

Ansbacher, M. "Adler's Place Today in the Psychology of Memory." *Journal of Personality* 15 (1947): 197–207.

Asselin, C., Nelson, T., and Platt J. *Teacher Study Group Leaders Manual*. Chicago: Alfred Adler Institute, 1975.

Aston, Athina. *How to Play with Your Baby*. New York: The Learning Child, 1971.

Baruch, Dorothy W. *New Ways in Discipline*. New York: McGraw-Hill, 1949.

Beecher, Marguerite and Beecher, Willard. *Parents on the Run*. New York: Julian Press, 1955.

Beecher, Marguerite and Beecher, Willard. *Mark of Cain: Anatomy of Jealousy*. New York: Harper-Row, 1971.

Beecher, Marguerite and Beecher, Willard. *Beyond Success and Failure*. New York: Julian Press, 1966.

Bermosk, Loretta S. and Corsini, Raymond J., (eds.). *Critical Incidents in Nursing*. Philadelphia: Saunders, 1973.

Bettelheim, Bruno. *A Good Enough Parent*. New York: Amazon, 1958.

Brodsky, P. "The Diagnostic Importance of Early Recollections." *American Journal of Psychotherapy* 6 (1952): 484–493.

Burne, Eric. *Games People Play*. New York: Grove Press, 1967.

Camp, William L. *Understanding and Managing the Difficult Child*. Meadville, Pennsylvania: Christian Faith Publishing, 2021.

Camp, William L. *Understanding the Adult-Child Relationship (Adlerian Teaching-Parenting)*. Meadville, Pennsylvania: Christian Faith Publishing, 2021.

Camp, William L. *Adlerian Counseling Theory and Practice*. Meadville, Pennsylvania: Christian Faith Publishing, 2021.

Corsini, Raymond J. and Cardone, Samuel. *Role-Playing in Psychotherapy*. New York: Aldine, 1966.

Corsini, Raymond. *Critical Incidence in School Counseling*. Englewood Cliffs, N.J.: Prentice-Hall, 1973.

Corsini, Raymond. *Current Psychotherapies*. Itasca, IL.: Peacock Publications, 1973.

Cox, Allan J. *Work, Love and Friendships: Reflections on Executive Style*. New York: Simon and Shuster, 1974.

Day, John. *Facts About Sex for Today's Youth*. Lansing: University of Michigan Press, John Day Company, Inc., 1973.

Deschweinitz, Karl. *Growing Up*. New York: Macmillan, 1952.

Dinkmeyer, Don C. *Child Development: The Emerging Self*. Englewood Cliffs, N.J.: Prentice-Hall, 1965.

Dinkmeyer, Don C. and Caldwell, E. *Developmental Counseling and Guidance in the Elementary School*. New York: McGraw-Hill, 1970.

Dinkmeyer, Don C. and Maro, James J. *Group Counseling: Theory and Practice*. Itasca, IL: Peacock Publications, 1971.

Dinkmeyer, Don C. and McKay, Gary D. *Raising a Responsible Child*. New York: Simon and Shuster, 1973.

Dinkmeyer, Don C. and Carlson, Jon. *Consulting: Facilitating Human Potential and Change Processes*. Columbus, Ohio: Charles R. Merrill Publishing Co., 1973.

Dinkmeyer, Don C. and Dreikurs, R. *Encouraging Children to Learn*. Englewood Cliffs, N.J.: Prentice-Hall, 1963.

Dobson, James. *Hide or Seek*. Old Tappan, New Jersey: Fleming H. Revell Company, 1974.

Dreikurs, Rudolf. *Adult-Child Relations*. Chicago: Alfred Adler Institute, 1972.

Dreikurs, Rudolf. *The Challenge of Child Training*. New York: Hawthorn Books, 1972.

Dreikurs, Rudolf. *The Challenge of Marriage*. New York: Hawthorn Books, 1946.

Dreikurs, Rudolf. *The Challenge of Parenthood*. New York: Hawthorn Books, 1948. (Translation of earlier edition written in German.)

Dreikurs, Rudolf. *Character Education and Spiritual Values in an Anxious Age*. (AAI Monograph Series No. 1 Reprint of 1952 edition.) Chicago: Alfred Adler Institute, 1971.

Dreikurs, Rudolf. *Child Guidance and Education*. Eugene: University of Oregon Press, 1957.

Dreikurs, Rudolf. *Counseling the Adolescent*. Winooke, VT: Vermont Education Television Network, 1971.

Dreikurs, Rudolf. *Dynamics of Classroom Behavior*. Burlington, VT: Education Television, 1969.

Dreikurs, Rudolf. *Psychodynamics, Psychotherapy and Counseling: Collected Papers*. Chicago: Alfred Adler Institute, 1967.

Dreikurs, Rudolf. *Psychology in the Classroom*. Second edition. New York: Harper-Row, 1968.

Dreikurs, Rudolf. *Social Equality: The Challenge of Today*. Chicago: Regency, l971

Dreikurs, Rudolf. *Understanding Your Children*. Burlington, VT: University of Vermont, 1969.

Dreikurs, Rudolf and Cassel, Pearl. *Discipline Without Tears*. New York: Hawthorn Books, 1973.

Dreikurs, Rudolf and Grey, Loren. *Logical Consequences: A New Approach to Discipline*. New York: Hawthorn Books, 1968.

Dreikus, Rudolf and Grey, Loren. *A Parent's Guide to Child Discipline*. New York: Hawthorn Books, 1970.

Dreikurs, Rudolf and Grunwald, Bernice S. *Maintaining Sanity in the Classroom*. New York: Harper-Row, 1971.

Dreikus, Rudolf and Grunwald, Bernice S. *Motivating Children to Learn*. Winooski, VT: University of Vermont, 1970.

Dreikurs, Rudolf and Soltz, Vicki. *Children: The Challenge*. New York: Hawthorn Books, 1964.

Dreikurs, Rudolf. *Encouraging Children to Learn: The Encouraging Process*. New York: Hawthorn Books, 1970.

Dreikurs, Rudolf and Gould, S., and Corsini, R. *Family Council*. New edition. Chicago: Regency, 1974.

Dreikurs, Rudolf. *Coping with Children's Misbehaviors*. New York: Hawthorn Books, 1972.

Dreikus, Rudolf. *Fundamentals of Adlerian Psychology*. New York: Greenberg. 1950.

Dreikurs, Rudolf and Others. *Adlerian Family Counseling: A Manual for Counseling Centers*. Eugene, OR: University of Oregon Press, 1959.

Dreikurs, Rudolf. "The Psychological Interview in Medicine." *Journal of Individual Psychology* 10 (1952): 99–122.

Ellis, Albert and Harper, Robert A. *Guide to Rational Living*. Englewood Cliffs, N.J.: Prentice Hall, 1951.

Ferguson, E. D. "The Use of Early Recollections for Assessing Lifestyle and Diagnosing Psychopathology." *American Psychologist* 18 (1963): 353.

Frankl, Viktor E. *Man's Search for Meaning*. Revised edition. Boston: Beacon Press, 1963.

Freud, S. "Screen Memories." In *Collected Papers*, vol. 5. London: Hogarth, 1950.

Freud, S. *Psychopathology of Everyday Life*. Translated by A. A. Brill. New York: The New American Library, 1956.

Friedman, A. "Early Childhood Memories of Mental Patients." *Individual Psychology Bulletin* 8 (1950): 111-116.

Friedman J. and H Schiffman. "Early Recollections of Schizophrenic and Depressed Patients." *Journal of Individual Psychology* 18 (1962): 57–61.

Gazda, George M. *Group Counseling*. New York: Allyn, 1971.

Ginott, Hirom G. *Between Parent and Child*. New York: Avon Books, 1965.

Glasser, William. *Schools Without Failure*. New York: Harper-Row, 1969.

Gordon, Thomas, *Parent Effectiveness Training*, New York: Peter H. Wyden, Inc., 1970.

Grey, Loren. *Discipline Without Fear*. New York: Hawthorn Books, 1974.

Grey, Loren. *Discipline Without Tyranny*. New York: Hawthorn Books, 1972.

Harper Perennial. *Individual Psychology of Alfred Adler*. New York: Harper Perennial Press, 1964.

Harris, Thomas R. *I'm OK—You're OK.* New York: Harper-Row, 1969.

Hazelton. *Understanding Life.* New York: Hazelton Press, 1998.

Hedvig, E. B. "Children's Early Recollections as Diagnostic Technique." *Journal of Individual Psychology* 21 (1955): 187–188.

Hedvig, E. B. "Stability of Early Recollections and Thematic Apperception Stories." *Journal of Individual Psychology* 19 (1963): 49–54.

Hoome, Lloyd. *How to Use Contingency Contracting in the Classroom.* New York: Lippincott, 1959.

Jackson, M. and Sechrest, L. "Early Recollections in Four Neurotic Diagnostic Categories." *Journal of Individual Psychology* 18, (1962): 52–56.

Johansen, Thor. *Religion and Spirituality in Psychotherapy: An Individual Psychology Perspective.* New York: Springer Publishing Company, 2009.

Kadis, A. L. "Early Childhood Recollections as Aids in Group Psychotherapy." *Journal of Individual Psychology.* 14 (1958): 182–187.

Laskowitz, D. "The Adolescent Drug Addict: An Adlerian View." *Journal of Individual Psychology* 17 (1961): 68–79.

Lippitt, Ronald and Ralph K. White. "An Experimental Study of Leadership and Group Life." In *Reading in Social Psychology,* edited by E. Maccobby, T. Newcomb, and E. Hartley. New York: Holt, Rinehart & Winston, 1958.

McCarter, R. E., H. M. Schiffman, and S. S. Tomkins. "Early Recollections as Predictors of Tomkins-Horn Picture Arrangement Test Performance." *Journal of Individual Psychology* 17 (1961): 177–180.

Maltz, Maxwell. *Psycho-Cybernetics.* Englewood Cliffs, N.J.: Wilshire Book Company, 1960.

Mead, Margaret. *Coming of Age in Samoa.* New York: Morrow, 1928.

Mead, Margaret. *From the South Seas: Studies of Adolescence and Sex in Primitive Societies.* New York: Morrow, 1939.

Mead, Margaret. *Growing Up in New Guinea.* New York: Morrow, 1930.

Mikelly, Arthur G. (ed). *Techniques for Behavior Change*. Springfield, IL: C. C. Thomas, 1971.

Mosak, Harold H. *Early Recollections as a Projective Technique*. (AAT Monograph No. 33) Chicago: Alfred Adler Institute, 1972.

Mosak, H. H. "Early Recollections: Evaluation of some recent research." *Journal of Individual Psychology* 25 (1969): 56–63.

Mosak, H. H. "Predicting the Relationship to the Psychotherapist from Early Recollection." *Journal of Individual Psychology* 21 (1965): 77–81.

Mosak B. and Mosak, Harold. *Adlerian Bibliography*. New York: John Wiley, 1975.

Mosak, Harold (ed.). *Alfred Adler: His Influence on Psychology Today*. Park Ridge, N.J.: Noyes Press, 1973.

Mosak, Harold and Shulman, Bernard H. *Introductory IP: A Syllabus*. Chicago: Alfred Adler Institute, 1961.

Mosak, Harold and Shulman, Bernard H. *Individual Psychotherapy. A Syllabus*. 2nd ed. Chicago: Alfred Adler Institute, 1974.

Mosak, Harold and Shulman, Bernard H. *The Neuroses: A Syllabus*. Chicago: Alfred Adler Institute, 1966.

Newman, Mildred and Berkowitz, Bernard. *How to be Your Own Best Friend*. New York: Ballantine Books, 1974.

One World Publications. *Social Interest: Adler's Key to the Meaning of Life*. New York: One World Publications, 2009.

One World Publications. *What Life Could Mean to You*. New York: One World Publications, 1998.

Ohlsen, Merle M. *Counseling Children in Groups*. New York: Holt, Rinehert and Winston, 1973.

Orgler, H. "Comparative Study of Two First Recollections." *Journal of Individual Psychology* 10 (1952): 27–30.

Orgler, Martha. *Alfred Adler: The Man and His Work*. New York: Liveright 1963.

Painter, Genevieve. *Teach Your Baby*. New York: Simon and Shuster, 1971.

Parent and Child Institute. *The Lifestyle Library for Young People* (4 Volume Set). Pennsylvania State University: Parent and Child Books, 1987 (Second Edition).

Patterson, G. and Gullison, B. *Living with Children*. New York: Amazon, 1960.

Plottke, P. "First Memories of 'Normal' and of 'Delinquent' Girls." *Individual Psychology Bulletin* 7 (1949): 15–20.

Putney, Shell and Putney, Gail. *The Adjusted American*. New York: Harper, 1964.

Rasmussen, Paul. *The Quest to Feel Good*. New York: Routledge Press, 2010.

Rom, P. "Goethe's Earliest Recollection." *Journal of Individual Psychology* 21 (1965): 189–193.

Salk, Lee. *What Every Child Would Like His Parents to Know*. New York: David McKay, Inc., 1972.

Salz, V. *Communication: Parent and Child*. Louisville, KY: Passionist Press, 1970.

Satir, Virginia M. *Conjoint Family Therapy, Revised Edition*. Palo Alto, CA: Science and Behavior Books, 1967.

Shay, Arthur. *How a Family Grows*. New York: Reilly & Lee, 1968.

Schoenaker, Theo. *Encouragement Makes Good Things Happen*. New York: Routledge Press, 2010.

Showers, Paul, *Before You Were a Baby*. New York: T. Y. Crowell, 1988.

Shulman, Bernard H. *Essays in Schizophrenia*. Baltimore: Williams and Williams, 1968.

Shulman, Bernard H. *Contributions to Individual Psychology*. Chicago: Alfred Adler Institute, 1973.

Skinner, Burrhus Frederic. *Beyond Freedom and Dignity*. New York: Harvard University Press, 1959.

Smith, C. E. and Mink, Oscar G. (eds.) *Foundations of Guidance and Counseling*. Philadelphia: Lippincott, 1969.

Sperber, Manes. *Masks of Loneliness: Alfred Adler in Perspective*. New York: Macmillan, 1974.

Spiel, G. *Discipline Without Punishment*. London: Faber and Faber, 1962.

Spock, Benjamin. *The Common Sense Book of Baby and Child Care*. New York: Duell, Sloan & Pearce, Inc., 1957.

Strain, Frances. *Being Born: A Book of Facts for Boys and Girls*. New York: Arthur Baron, 1947.

Sutton-Smith, Brian. *How to Play With Your Children: And When Not To*. New York: Hawthorn/Dutton, 1976.

Sutton-Smith, Brian and Sutton-Vane, Sybil, *Victoria*. New York: Hawthorn/Dutton, 1974.

Toffler, Alvin. *Future Shock*. New York: Lippett & Wiley, 1958.

Verger, D. M. and W. L. Camp. "Early Recollections: Reflections of the Present." *Journal of Counseling Psychology 17* (1970): 510-515.

Walton, R. and Powers, R. *Winning Children Over*. Chicago: Practical Psychological Association, 1974.

Watson, John B. *Behaviorism*. New York: Simon & Shuster, 1959.

Wender, Paul H. *Minimal Brian Dysfunction in Children*. New York: Wiley-Interscan (John Wiley & Son, Inc.), 1971.

Wexberg, Irwin. *Individual Psychological Treatment*. Bernard Shulman, ed. Chicago: Alfred Adler Institute, 1929. Reprinted in paperback, 1960. Translated by: Eiolart, Arnold. 1st volume of Psychic Methods of Cure. England.

Wilmshurst, Linda. *Child and Adolescent Psychopathology: A Casebook*. New York, Sage Publications, Inc., 2010, Second Edition.

Wolfe, W. Beran. *Woman's Best Years: The Art of Staying Young*. New York: Emerson Books, 1949.

Wolpe, Joseph. *Reciprocal Inhibition*. New York: Amazon, 1968.

Yang, Julia and Milliren, Alan. *The Psychology of Courage: An Adlerian Handbook for Healthy Social Living*. New York: Routledge Press, 2009.

About the Author

Dr. William Lyman Camp earned his PhD from the University of Wisconsin, Madison, in 1968 and did additional postdoctoral study at the University of Chicago and at Mendota Mental Health Institute in Madison, Wisconsin. He was licensed to practice psychology in 1970. His formal academic training included study with such outstanding persons in the field of psychology and psychiatry as Carl Rogers, Rudolph Dreikurs, Richard Lee, Joseph Wolpe, William Sewell, John Rothney, and others. He spent many years teaching undergraduate and graduate courses at several universities and has supervised or helped to supervise doctoral and masters-level training and internships for counselors and psychologists. During those years, he maintained a private practice in clinical psychology while also consulting with and supervising treatment at a number of regional mental health clinics.

Dr. Camp has also published many articles and books and served on the Editorial Board of *Forum on Public Affairs*, a journal dealing with domestic and international topics.

Dr. Camp has been elected as a fellow of the American College of Advanced Practice Psychologists and the American Board of Medical Psychotherapists among many other professional organizations. He has also been the recipient of numerous honors throughout his career. Featured in *American Men of Science*, his biography has also appeared in the *International Scholars Directory*. In 2013, he was recognized by the Wisconsin Psychological Association with a citation that begins and ends as follows:

> For outstanding contributions to the Wisconsin
> Psychological Association... We thank you for

being a model of thoughtful professionalism, dedication, and vitality to your colleagues and for the next generation of psychologists in our state.

Dr. Camp was also featured in the seventy-second edition of *Who's Who in America* with a lifetime achievement award, and in *Marquis Who's Who in the World.*

Dr. Camp was married to Mildred Cavanaugh Camp on August 14, 1965. They have a son, Jonathan, and a daughter, Christine, and one grandson and four granddaughters.